International Businesses and the Challenges of Poverty in the Developing World

Also by Frederick Bird

THE MUTED CONSCIENCE: Moral Silence and the Practice of Ethics in Business

GOOD MANAGEMENT: Business Ethics in Practice

Also by Stewart W. Herman

SPIRITUAL GOODS: Faith Traditions and the Practices of Business

DURABLE GOODS: A covenantal Ethic for Managements and Employees

International Businesses and the Challenges of Poverty in the Developing World

Case Studies on Global Responsibilities and Practices

Edited by

Frederick Bird and Stewart W. Herman

Contents

Preface

The Global Responsibilities Project

This book is the first in a series of three volumes examining the global responsibilities of international businesses in developing areas. The complete set of more than 34 detailed case studies and essays in three volumes will provide a richly detailed freeze-frame of what international businesses are doing – or could do – to add value to the developing world.

The word 'global' applies for two reasons. The first is that the Global Responsibilities Project will cover international businesses' operations in most corners of the developing world. This volume includes firms in Southeast Asia, Sub-Saharan Africa, South America and the northernmost part of Quebec, as well as The Body Shop's partnerships with a number of developing areas in the world. Subsequent volumes will examine international business practices in East and South Asia, the Pacific, Mexico and Central America, as well as other countries in Africa and South America. The second reason is that the environment in which international businesses act with respect to natural and human resources is truly a global environment that is everywhere characterized by a wealth of assets, which we will consider in terms of financial, productive, human, social and natural capital. Already, in the light of these considerations, it is clear that there is a need for some comprehensive measure of business responsibility and performance. As a possible step towards eventually establishing such a measure, our case studies will explore ways in which businesses can make a significant impact by enabling their host countries to develop their overall capital resources in the broadest possible manner.

We use the word 'responsibility' because these case studies focus on the role that international businesses can play in fostering economic development and reducing poverty. We describe the performance of these businesses not by a single, one-size-fits-all yardstick, but by the 'global' measure proposed above. From this wider perspective, international businesses in developing areas need to work to strengthen local economies, augment local productive capabilities, transfer skills and technology and accumulate financial resources, as well as act responsibly relative to various social standards. In this volume we examine examples of both instructive contributions and missed opportunities. We ask whether the businesses reviewed in the following case studies have adopted policies and practices that effectively augment or diminish the capital made available to them. We explore how specific companies in specific settings apply – or miss the opportunity to apply – smart business practices that add value to low-income areas. Our aim is to highlight how firms have effectively and imaginatively responded to the specific sets of opportunities, challenges and contingencies of particular developing areas in terms of their own histories and prospects – or how they might have done so.

In the next volume, case studies set in Colombia, Mexico, South Africa, Pakistan, South Korea and Madagascar will focus on a set of generic challenges and dilemmas faced by international businesses in developing areas. How shall security risks be managed? What are the appropriate responses to cultural differences? How can productivity and quality be fostered in the workplace? What sorts of collaborative solutions are possible when working with indigenous populations? These and other questions are serious concerns for all international businesses.

A third volume will feature reflective essays on a number of topics which have emerged from the case studies: the quest for common ethical standards in a world of moral diversity; models of corporate social responsibility from the perspective of the developing world; causes and remedies for global poverty; and reflections on business–government relations in the developing world.

The case studies and essays in these volumes are being authored by a team of researchers from universities and research centres in the developing and the developed world. In the past three years our authors have attended periodic research workshops and seminars, commenting on each other's work and developing their own work in the light of what their colleagues were also writing. As befits a free and open inquiry, their perspectives differ: some, like Dr Bill Buenar Puplampu in this volume, are quite supportive of practices of the international businesses they study; others, like Dr Gail Whiteman (also in this volume), are quite critical. In some instances authors have separated their historical background studies of local or national economies from their case studies. In other instances they have integrated them in to single essays. This process of researching, writing and consultation has been an instructive process for all involved. I would like to thank all those who have participated in this research process.

I would first like to thank all those who have undertaken research, prepared research reports or assisted in drafting the essays that will be published in this series. These include Sylvie Babarik, Concordia University, Montreal (Canada); Dr Thomas Beschorner, Centre de recherche en éthique de l'Université de Montréal (Canada) and Carl von Ossietzky Universität Oldenburg (Germany); Dr Ding Bocheng, Beijing Administrative College (China); Dr Hevina Dashwood, Brock University, St. Catharines, Ontario (Canada); Dr Russell Daye, Pacific Theological College (Fiji); Dr Margaret Griesse (Brazil); Rifai Hasan, Concordia University; Dr Stewart Herman, Concordia College, Moorhead, Minnesota (United States); Dr William

Holder (United States); Dr Jan Jorgensen, McGill University, Montreal (Canada); Kathrine Jorgensen, Roskilde University (Denmark); Farzad Khan, McGill University; Dr Elise Kotze, University of Stellenbosch (South Africa); Dr Kobus Kotze, University of Stellenbosch; Dr David Krueger, Baldwin-Wallace College, Berea, Ohio (United States); Dr Terri Lituchy, Concordia University; Dr Alhaji Marong, Institute of Comparative Law, McGill University; Marco Mingarelli, Concordia University; Dr Titus Fossgard-Moser, Shell International (United Kingdom); Ander Riel Muller, Roskilde University (Denmark); Ida Mutoigo, Christian Reform World Relief Committee (Uganda); Rabia Naguib, Université de Montréal; Dr Robert Nixon, Universalia Management Group, Montreal (Canada); Dr Nelson Phillips, Cambridge University (United Kingdom); Dr Bill Buenar Puplampu, University of Ghana (Ghana); Dr Emmanuel Raufflet, Université de Montréal; Samuel Sejjaaka, Makerere University (Uganda); Dr Joseph Smucker, Concordia University; Dr Manuel Velasquez, Santa Clara University, California (United States); Dr William Westley, McGill University; Dr Gail Whiteman, Erasmus University, Rotterdam (Netherlands).

I would like as well to thank a number of people who participated in our research workshops and seminars, commented on our research and shared their own research with us. These include: Kathrin Bohr of Canadian Businesses for Social Responsibility; Michael Cole, a student in the Royal Military College of Canada; Dr Jay Drydyk, Carleton University, Ottawa (Canada); Diane Girard of The Ethics Practioners Association of Canada; Dr Taieb Hafsi, Université de Montréal; Stefanie Hiss, Bamberg University (Germany); Dr Bakr Ibrahim, Concordia University; the late Dr Bassem Khalifa, of the Canadian Institute of Technology and Concordia University; Dr Peter Koslowski, Hannover Institute of Philosophical Research (Germany); Jacqui MacDonald, Associate Director, Prince of Wales International Business Leaders Forum (United Kingdom); Nancy Palardy of the Task Force on the Churches and Corporate Responsibility (Canada); Brenda Plante, graduate student, Université de Montréal; Dr Kernaghan Webb, Carleton University; and Dr John Williams, World Medical Association (France).

I would like to thank the people who have helped prepare this manuscript for publication: Audrey Bean, Fred Louder and Johanne Rabbatt, for copyreading and editing; Munit Merid and Martine Montadon, secretaries for the Department of Religion at Concordia University, for their help with budgets, correspondence, logistics, data gathering and facilitating comfortable and pleasant working conditions. I would especially like to thank Stewart Herman for the considerable amount of time and thought he invested in helping to create this first volume of our projected series.

The research on which the essays in this book is based was made possible by research grants from the Social Sciences and Humanities Research Council of Canada, augmented by additional research grants from Concordia University, Santa Clara University, Concordia College (Minnesota), McGill University, Université de Montréal and the Resource Centre for the Social Dimensions of Business in London.

FREDERICK BIRD
Concordia University, Montreal

Foreword

Discussions about foreign investments in poor countries often resemble religious battles in the past. One side argues dogmatically that integration in the world economy and foreign investments are the only effective path for overcoming poverty. The other side see multinational businesses with diametrically opposite reflexes. Multinational corporations are associated with dependencies and the concentration of wealth and power. One side estimates that the creation of jobs will result at least in modest reduction of poverty. The other side thinks this view is simplistic. International investments, they argue, often aggravate inequalities, deplete resources, give rise to indebtedness, and foster corruption.

Frederick Bird introduces the collection of case examples in this book with a theory which could be attractive for both the schools. As long as alternatives to the commitment of private capital in poor countries are not demonstrated convincingly, it is difficult to argue against it. Governments and workers usually do support new investments in their countries, including investments caused by the widespread strategie policy to minimize costs in the short run.

Bird argues that companies can do more and develops an alternative to policies of short-term cost minimization. His alternative emphasizes the development of assets as a realistic business and societal-political objective. His approach views international investments not only in relation to productive and financial capital but also in relations to physical working conditions, the development of human and social capital as well as the strengthening of institutions which are essentially for production processes.

According to Bird this approach may be economically feasible for companies if a broader view of capital is applied, a view that includes human and social capital as well. The development of a deeper understanding of human and social capital is important for anyone interested in the success of businesses in developing countries, whether they are consumers, investing enterprises or representatives of development organizations.

In the early part of the volume edited by Bird and Herman, Bird describes the way to such an understanding in a theory. One expects that the following collection of case studies would try to exemplify this theory. This approach is usually called 'presenting best practices'. Fortunately, this is not the intention of this publication. The case studies in this book stay clear from the temptation to overemphasize positive accomplishments of businesses with respect to social performance. They could have done so with more justification than in many other books. Almost all described firms provide relatively exemplary working conditions for their immediate employees. Many of them are also good corporate citizens. Readers who search for best practices examples for conventional standards might well be satisfied. However, the authors of the case studies in this book do not settle for these standards and are not yet satisfied.

The authors acknowledge that most of the examined businesses have sought with good will to improve the situation in developing countries. However, the cases also examine the unrealized potentials and missed opportunities which these firms have overlooked. These potentials, the book shows, could have been realized through the formation of assets in and for the developing country. Such a development of assets is not seen as incompatible with the cost calculation and benefits expected from the businesses. Shell, for example, has already paid a high price due to the fact that it failed to fully develop its own assets, broadly understood, and those of its stakeholders in Nigeria. In the meantime, Shell has sought to alter its course.

The analyses in this book reflect the situation of businesses in a clearly determined time-span, 2000 to 2002. The concentration on this period of time helps the readers to put the findings into perspective. This concentration also enables the investigated firms and other firms operating in developing countries during the same period of time to profit from the feedback given by the study. This collection of case studies is of interest for business people operating in developing countries as well as for government official, academics and other observers of these operations. The conflict between creation of assets and short-term cost minimization is fundamental in the industrialized world as well. Many older enterprisers and managers have learned and practiced in the past what Bird recommends for the future. Formerly, securing the company´s sustainability, its success in the long run, was the prime objective given to a manager. Nowadays often the interests of anonymous shareholders of the company have become the central purpose of management. The book does not engage in the dispute on shareholder values. It offers, at least in a limited area of entrepreneurial engagement, an alternative.

Many developing countries face completely different structures of costs and internal and external risks. Investing in local managers, for instance, reduces cost when they replace expatriates. Working short term with local personnel and firms, unadjusted to the performance standards of the multinational company, may pose serious risks for this company here and elsewhere. Aggressive pricing and costs competitions that result in destroying existing local business structures seem dubious because the real bottlenecks in these countries are functioning institutions, equally in the private as in the public sector. Therefore, under such circumstances investing in sustainable assets may not merely satisfy the instincts of managers who did not entirely forget what they are actually there for. It could be well be the most intelligent business strategy.

The case studies will also be interesting for readers who deal profession-ally with Corporate Social Responsibility or the development chances of poor countries. The case study on Vietnam, for example, allows an under-standing of different forms of social capital in small and smallest firms. This focus on small and medium firms is widely neglected in current academic discussions as it probably is in many investment-decisions. A study on an US investment in the appliance business in Vietnam maintains that this investment in the modern sector could have become even more efficient and sustainable if it had included elements of traditional social capital. On the other hand it is mentioned that the entire traditional soft drink indus-try was ruined by investments of Coca Cola and Pepsi in Vietnam – a point made in many places when taking the balance of newly created and destroyed job as consequence of FDI.

As said above, the case studies are not dominated by the theory in the first chapter of this book. The theory and ensuing theoretical considerations, nevertheless, often deliver complementary perspectives which enrich the empirical analysis. The founder of The Body Shop attempted an integration of her social commitment with economic success. The case on The Body Shop in this book demonstrates that the success of both was a result of learn-ing from the experiences of the established fair trade organizations. These organizations have become interesting for the private sector after they were built up with the commitment of northern NGOs and the support by devel-opment organizations. The successful experience of the Body Shop with a sequenced partnership between NGOs, development assistance, and busi-ness could provide for a new pattern of Public–Private Partnership.

It should be emphasized that the articles are exciting to read and that the authors are very precise and sensitive to foreign cultures. Most studies of inter-national businesses in developing countries are neither as stimulating not as sensitive to other cultures. Equally unusual is the relevance of a level of analy-sis that is essential for activities in developing countries: the political and macroeconomical level. Bird mentions in the introduction the effects of over-indebtedness and thereby repression of developing countries under current economic theory. It is mentioned that standard economics does not adequately take assets and institutions into account. As a consequence apply-ing this economic approach has often destroyed these resources. While taking a stand Bird and the other authors do not bore the reader with well-known theoretical controversies. In the case studies, reality speaks for itself.

Each section of the case study begin with a short historical analysis of the country which provides a fruitful overview (also for managers who are work-ing in these countries). These introductions already focus on the different core relevancies of the countries in terms of their historical, economical, and especially political conditions. This perspective enables the authors to develop an understanding of the difficulties and potentials in the countries and it is the basis for the analyses of certain investments in developing countries.

In a globalized world it is increasingly risky to make decisions on economic and political commitments, without having a sufficient understanding of the world economy and, related to single countries, without knowing the historical-political conditions in these countries. If we read studies on specific countries, we notice that these studies are often written from only one perspective – mostly the perspective of a national economy. It is characteristic that the term 'good governance' just came up a couple of years ago and that we do not have a precise understanding of what it exactly means. The analyses of 'bad governance', such as corruption, are already much more differentiated. Nevertheless, the recent insights are not sufficiently applied to many countries to render them helpful in decision making processes.

Reading the multidisciplinary analyses in this book we are looking forward to the widening of this approach to other countries in the following volumes. And, after reading this book, we already know what we are missing with respect to the countries left out and will be at least a little bit more careful when passing judgments and making decisions.

Dr. Hansjorg Elshorst Potsdam

Notes on the Contributors

Frederick Bird holds the Research Chair in Comparative Ethics at Concordia University in Montreal. He is author of *The Muted Conscience: Moral Silence and the Practice of Ethics in Business* (1996) and co-author of *Good Management: Business Ethics in Practice* (1990). He is the author of many articles, including 'How Do Religions Affect Moralities?' (1989), 'Empowerment and Justice' (1999), 'Good Governance' (2001) and 'Early Christianity as an Ecumenical Movement' (2002). He is a graduate of Harvard College, Harvard Divinity School and the Graduate Theological Union.

Hansjorg Elshorst is a founding member of Transparency International, and was managing director from 1998 to 2002. In 1996 and 1997 he was a senior advisor to the vice-presidents for East Asia and for Strategy and Resource Management of the World Bank, where he concentrated on fostering partnerships in the area of institutional development and change. From 1974 to 1995 Dr Elshorst was managing director of the German Agency for Technical Cooperation (GTZ), a government-owned corporation for international cooperation.

Stewart W. Herman teaches in the Religion department at Concordia College, Moorhead, Minnesota and holds a PhD from the University of Chicago Divinity School. His recent books include *Spiritual Goods: Faith Traditions and the Practice of Business* (2001), *Durable Goods: A Covenantal Ethic for Managements and Employees* (1997). He also has published articles in the *Business Ethics Quarterly*, the *Journal of Business Ethics* and the *Journal of Religious Ethics*. In 1970–72 he managed relief and development programmes in Quang Ngai, Vietnam, for Vietnam Christian Service.

Ida Mutoigo is team leader for East and Southern Africa for the Christian Reformed World Relief Committee (CRWRC). With a Master of Management degree from McGill University, Montreal, she teaches courses in leadership and community development at the Uganda Christian University and Kampala Evangelical School of Theology.

Robert Nixon is a partner in the Montreal-based international development consulting firm Universalia Management Group. He works throughout Canada and internationally providing services in strategic planning, strategic human resource development and organizational development to international aid agencies, governments, businesses, non-government agencies and aboriginal organizations over an eight-year period. Dr Nixon provided consulting services to Falconbridge Limited on human resource development, training and organizational strategies at the Raglan Mine in the Nunavik Territory of Northern Quebec.

Bill Buenar Puplampu is a Senior Lecturer at the School of Administration, University of Ghana, Legon, where he teaches courses in Organizational Behaviour, Project Management, Strategic Human Resource Management and Change and Organizational Development. With a degree in Psychology from the University of Ghana, he obtained his PhD in organizational psychology from the University of East London (UK) in 1993. As a Chartered Psychologist (British Psychological Society), Dr Puplampu directs the consulting firm *P*syconH.R in Ghana and has published in African and European academic journals.

Samuel Sejjaaka is a certified chartered accountant and Senior Lecturer at Makerere University Business School in Uganda. He has worked in both the public and private sectors as a consultant on financial management systems, fiscal policy and economic monitoring. His research interests include privatization, corporate financial disclosure and private sector competitiveness in emerging markets.

Gail Whiteman is an Assistant Professor of Business-Society Management at the Rotterdam School of Management, Erasmus University, the Netherlands. She has published in the *Academy of Management Journal, Journal of Business Management* and *Conservation Ecology*. Her research interests include the impact of multinational corporations on indigenous peoples (in Canada and South America), ecologically embedded management and corporate social responsibility in developing countries.

Introduction

Frederick Bird and Stewart W. Herman

As key players in globalization, international businesses have interconnected the wealthy and impoverished areas of the world. An increasing number of firms from industrialized areas are engaged in the two-thirds world, to extract valued minerals and petroleum, to manufacture goods, to purchase products and produce from local suppliers, and to sell consumer products and services. The results have been ambiguous; in many cases, low-income people in the two-thirds world now live somewhat less impoverished lives. A positive outcome, however, is not automatic. In other settings, international businesses operations have aggravated the poverty of the poor. Either way, business operations merit close examination. Industrialized countries invest far more wealth in developing areas through business connections than through aid programmes. It therefore matters a great deal what kinds of practices international businesses follow.

While other studies have explored these problems from a macroeconomic perspective (Stiglitz, 2002; Chua, 2003; Legrain, 2003), this volume is unique in presenting a series of case studies focusing upon specific international firms in specific countries, examined in relation to the history of these countries. These case studies are written with the aim of showing how international businesses can further economic development and poverty reduction in the low-income areas in which they operate. We argue that international businesses can realize these objectives not primarily through philanthropy or social investments but through their regular business practices, understood as those activities by which they conserve and augment their basic assets, viewed in turn pragmatically to include human and natural resources as well as financial resources. The key question is how broadly they envision their business strategies: whether they focus narrowly on profit margins, or whether they stretch in the direction of building the assets and capacities of their host countries – not as a matter of charity, but in order to expand their own resource base. We look for evidence of their impact not in company pronouncements or publications, but in outcomes as viewed by directors, managers, employees and other stakeholders in the field. As a result, the case studies radiate the freshness of immediate contact. All the interviews were conducted within the same time horizon (2000–02). We examine both favourable and unfavourable outcomes, seeking to learn from both kinds of cases.

This volume is the first in an anticipated series of three volumes, containing some 34 in-depth case studies and essays covering more than 15 countries. The case studies and essays were researched and written by scholars from many different universities, research centres and countries in both the developing and developed world. The unprecedented scope of this study is intended to generate a wealth of detail about the involvement of business in globalization. By 'international businesses' we mean any firms within a developing area that are connected with firms in industrialized countries either as subsidiaries, partners, sub-divisions or as sources of goods, services or raw materials – ranging from multinational enterprises to small firms and community cooperatives. We have chosen this broader view of international business so as to examine the variety of ways in which businesses operating in developing areas may effectively foster economic development. Further, the study encompasses countries ranging in size from China to Guyana. We assume that each country provides a unique challenge because its opportunities for development are shaped both by its own culture, economic resources, and political history, and by the ways international firms and agencies have operated in its area. What works in Taiwan may not work in Korea. What fosters development in Ghana may have a quite different impact in Uganda. Hence the need for country-based case studies. However, we also know that developing areas share many common features. Businesses located in these areas face similar challenges. Hence, by studying the practices of firms in one area, assessing both their accomplishments and difficulties, we can educate ourselves about unanticipated problems and opportunities as we engage in internationally linked businesses in other areas.

Over the past half century, industrialization and commerce have increased the overall wealth of humans and reduced the rates of poverty in many areas; half the world's populations now live more comfortable lives. Still, more than one billion people out of a total of six billion live in abject poverty on less than US$1 per day and 2.8 billion live on less than US$2 per day (Forstater *et al.*, 2002, p. 26). As the world's population has continued to grow, the overall number of impoverished households has not been appreciably reduced. In many areas like Nigeria and Guyana (which are examined in this volume), the average household incomes in 2000 are much lower than they were 20 years earlier.

International businesses are in a position to make a difference. On the one hand, their practices can aggravate poverty, exploit human and natural resources, and exacerbate social conflicts. For example, a number of retailing firms have purchased apparel supplies from third-world factories where employees work in forced and unhygienic conditions and are paid unconscionably low wages (Klein, 2000). A number of international mining companies have extracted much wealth from low-income areas without measurable, sustainable benefits to those areas (Auty, 1993). They have often polluted streams and ground water, and heightened local inequalities. International businesses have sometimes aggravated social conflicts in low-income areas ranging from the Philippines to Colombia, from Angola to the Democratic Republic of the Congo, from Guyana to Sudan. Through short-sightedness, inadvertence or sheer ignorance, international businesses can effectively diminish the resources of their host countries (Ross, 2001).

On the other hand, international businesses can create job opportunities, provide settings for technology transfers, foster skills development, develop markets for local producers, help construct physical and commercial infrastructure and pay taxes. A number of studies have recently called attention to the beneficial role that international business can play in reducing poverty. In the most general terms, developing countries that are linked to industrialized countries through trade and investments – countries like India, Brazil and Mexico – are much better off than those that are not so closely linked, such as the poorest countries in Africa (The Group of Lisbon, 1995; Legrain, 2003, p. 50). Some studies have examined the ways in which individual businesses can make a difference. Forstater *et al.* (2002) draw upon a large number of cases to describe how international businesses can reduce poverty by developing relationships with poor people as value-adding consumers, employees, entrepreneurs and suppliers. Prahalad and Hart also make a bottom-line business case for expanding operations in low-income areas, focusing especially on the poor as consumers. They contend that businesses generally have overlooked the vast opportunities for expanding their operations among the poor. They review the successful operations of firms such as the Grameen Bank, which offer micro-credit in Bangladesh; Solar Electric Light Fund, which sells household-scale solar photovoltaic units to the rural poor in a dozen countries; and Standard Bank, which developed a low cost banking service for the poor in South Africa (Prahalad and Hart, 2002). A recent report prepared by AccountAbility and Business for Social Responsibility examines the multiple ways international businesses can leave a positive economic footprint on developing areas by gauging their impact on factors other than job-creation and social philanthropy. This report calls on international businesses to locate operations more strategically, to source more of their goods and services locally, and to offer more opportunities for investments from these areas (AccountAbilty/BWB, 2003).

These studies demonstrate through arguments and examples that international businesses can profitably foster development and reduce poverty as part of their regular business operations. What we call for in this book is not for more corporate 'social responsibility' as this term is often understood in terms of charity or philanthropy, but business strategies and practices that promote sustainable economic development.

International businesses are faced with three basic choices of strategy, in the face of challenging conditions in their host countries. (For a more extended discussion, see Chapter 1, 'Ethical Reflections on the Challenges Facing International Businesses in Developing Areas'.) First, they might decide to divest and withdraw, to conserve and redirect their resources. Interestingly enough, none of the managers, employees, suppliers, customers, governmental officials or community people we interviewed expressed support for disinvestment. Even where the extraction of wealth had been, or continued to be, exploitative, these stakeholders wanted international business to stay. A second strategy is cost minimization, in which a company makes most effective use of its capital by minimizing expenses, maximizing shareholder value and cultivating mutually beneficial links with host governments. Cost minimization had often proved viable in the short term; but as the cases from Guyana and Nigeria in this volume clearly demonstrate, this strategy may involve eroding or destroying the capital resources of host countries, and so is hardly sustainable. The third strategy is asset development, in which businesses protect their investments and seek to render them as productive as possible over time by investing in ways that add to long-term value for themselves and their host countries. The cases from Nunavik (Canada), Ghana, Vietnam and Uganda, as well as the example of The Body Shop, point towards ways in which international businesses can seek to sustain and even increase the capital resources they draw upon in their host countries.

We search out elements of asset development in the strategies of our interviewed companies. Of course, cost minimization must be part of every business strategy; but to avoid degrading or destroying the resources of their host countries, international businesses must pursue asset development as well. In this first volume we report both on opportunities that are being realized and opportunities that are being missed. We highlight instructive examples of how international businesses add value, and also explore how those companies that have consumed or degraded the capital resources of their host countries might have pursued more sustainable strategies. The basic question is: are these firms sustaining or adding to the stock of capital in their host countries, or are they consuming and degrading that capital?

Human Capital – do their employees have the opportunities to learn and enhance useable skills?
Natural Capital – do they make effective, sustainable use of the local endowments of land, timber, minerals, water and air?
Productive Capital – have they added to the capacity of low-income communities to use human and natural resources more effectively?
Financial Capital – have they paid the taxes, royalties and other financial obligations? Do they offer workers, suppliers and customers reasonable wages and prices?

Social Capital – have they worked to strengthen local webs of trust, social good will and communication and regulatory networks?

The case studies: an overview

The first case study examines the history of Royal Dutch/Shell in Nigeria from 1960 to the present. Dr Frederick Bird of Concordia University (Montreal, Canada) explains that for more than 35 years in the turbulent political environment of Nigeria, Shell attempted to run a responsible business in keeping with existing economic and social standards and expectations. The company operated in a partnership with a government-established firm, paid extensive taxes and royalties to the Nigerian government, developed a range of social programmes, offered employment and skills training to thousands of local citizens and loosely followed current environmental guidelines – a relatively enlightened cost-minimization strategy, leavened with corporate benevolence. However, by the mid-1990s, conflicts between the Nigerian government and the Ogoni, an important group where Shell has its operations, became exacerbated. This struggle gave Shell International what it called a 'wake-up call'. The company realized that it needed to take a hard look at how it was doing business, which is what this case study does. To see what Shell should be doing, it is important to look closely at what it did. After 40 years in which Shell extracted more than US$200 billion worth of oil from the Niger Delta, the people of that region were no better off. Indeed, they were arguably worse off, given the loss of natural resources underground, and the pollution that their extraction caused on the surface. For 40 years Shell burned off almost all the associated natural gas produced by extracting oil; this enormous resource, which might have been used to generate electricity for millions of Nigerians, was simply wasted because its extraction did not seem to make economic sense at the time. In effect, Shell followed cost-minimization practices guided by the then current economic and social assumptions – practices that in the long run left both the company and the people of Nigeria worse off. Shell invested to some extent in developing the human capital of its employees, and fostered some degree of goodwill and cooperation through its philanthropic programmes. Yet the people of the Niger Delta would have benefited more had Shell more imaginatively explored ways to utilize these natural and productive resources in conjunction with local businesses.

A second set of essays examines the role of international businesses in Ghana. Dr William Puplampu, who teaches in the School of Administration at the University of Ghana in the capital city of Accra, begins with political and economic history of Ghana since independence. Compared to countries like Korea, Ghana's economic development has been slow and uneven. After some promising developments in the 1950s and 1960s, economic development stalled in large part because the political situation of the country alternated between political instability and autocratic rule. Nonetheless, compared to other African countries, Ghana continued to move slowly towards democracy. It developed a diversified economy of mineral production, exportation of agricultural goods, manufacturing and local commerce. It remained a pluralistic society without being scarred by major and intractable regional differences. In his second essay, Puplampu examines the history and impacts of three international firms in Ghana: Valco, an aluminium processor; Unilever Ghana, a retail marketing company; and British American Tobacco, a manufacturer of tobacco products. Puplampu argues that the practices followed by the local divisions of each of these firms have been measurably affected by the commitment of their international headquarters to become socially responsible businesses. Still, the companies differ according to how well they have integrated backwards into the Ghanaian economy and so developed productive capital locally. Valco was established in tandem with a hydroelectric dam. The company shared more financial capital as it acceded to governmental demands to pay more for the power it used, but it continues to process only foreign aluminium ore rather than developing Ghanaian deposits. Unilever Ghana has supported the local economy not only by producing low-cost consumer goods but also by attempting to purchase as wide a range of locally generated products and services as possible. All three companies pay their employees well and to a large extent have replaced expatriates with Ghanaians, fostering a climate of increasing trust with their employees. The Ghanaian subsidiary of British American Tobacco has developed an especially favourable relation with the many farmers whose tobacco they purchase. They provide these farmers with various technical services, allow them to grow other crops as well and treat them with respect. All three companies have contributed to the formation of financial, productive, human and social capital in Ghana.

The third set of essays, on Uganda, offers a strong contrast at certain points. Professor Samuel Sejjaaka, who teaches at the business school of Makere University in the capital city Kampala, begins by reviewing Uganda's political and economic history since independence. Unlike Ghana, Uganda experienced long years of civil war and repressive dictatorship. The commercial class was decimated, as South Asians were exiled in the early 1970s. While it has enjoyed political stability since the late 1980s, Uganda continues to be affected by conflicts of neighbouring Rwanda, Congo and Sudan. During the 1990s, its economy slowly recovered, particularly in urban areas and near Lake Victoria. Still, the depression of international coffee and cotton prices has reduced its income from two potentially valuable export markets, and Uganda still faces huge external debts. Sejjaaka also examines the role of British American Tobacco, whose impact has been more ambiguous in Uganda than in Ghana. At the manufacturing end, the company follows the international guidelines, creates a reasonable number of jobs and works with a number of local suppliers. Its relationship with the 65 000 farmers growing tobacco seems much more problematic. Many own their own farms in isolated areas and produce only tobacco, which they sell at prices set by the company; these farmers make very little income above expenses. Transient farmers are in an even worse situation. They suffer broken family lives, and barely make ends meet. They move from plot to plot, destroying forest to grow tobacco, which they then process in the most polluting way. A missed opportunity is evident; currently, the company works with farmers in ways that inadvertently degrade Uganda's natural endowment of land and forest, restrict the development of productive capital, maintain farmers in their poverty and perpetuate social problems. Instead, it could help both groups of farmers reduce their dependence upon tobacco. In the next essay, Ida Mutoigo of the Christian Reformed World Relief Committee and Prof. Sejjaaka explain the remarkable impact of MTN, a newly developed cell phone company, on Uganda's economy. The authors are struck by the way cell phones serve to empower their users, especially women. Cell phones offer a powerful economic boost, and the large and growing network of franchisers illustrates asset development in a remarkable way. Still, MTN could increase its impact further by reducing prices, and so making its products and services available to a much broader market of Ugandan women. Regrettably, such empowerment does not extend within the company. Headquartered in South Africa, MTN retains power and wealth within the hands of the handful of expatriates who manage it, to the resentment of its Ugandan staff and extensive network of franchisers. Such inequities undermine the social capital which the firm otherwise might generate internally. As a result, it is through the product itself, more than through the jobs its has created, that the firm adds to the social economy of Uganda.

In the fourth case study Dr Stewart Herman, who teaches at Concordia College (Moorhead, Minnesota), examines two kinds of international business in Vietnam and focuses on human- and social-capital formation. He begins by reviewing how Vietnam's economy has been underdeveloped due to its turbulent political history. Vietnam suffered both from long stretches of war, fought both against colonizing powers and among political factions internally. Its 10-year experiment with a Soviet-style command economy further stifled economic growth. The situation changed in the late 1980s, when the Vietnamese government began to tap the resilient underground private sector, in the process of implementing liberal economic reforms presented by the World Bank. Since then, the economy and the well-being of the Vietnamese have improved greatly. The primary engine of growth has been the tiny household enterprise, and Vietnam thus faces the challenge of nurturing the social capital that enables larger organizations to operate effectively. While some large international firms, such as Nike, have invested in Vietnam, the primary engine of growth is likely to be small- and medium-sized enterprises. The question, then, is how international businesses might contribute to such growth. Prof. Herman first looks at three small international businesses started by Vietnamese who learned business skills in either Japan or Europe and then returned after the civil war to apply these skills back home. These entrepreneurs have chosen to develop the human capital of their employees by borrowing western technical and managerial skills. Yet they integrate their enterprises around distinctive Vietnamese patterns of authority and leadership. Prof. Herman next considers how a multinational corporation might benefit from such a blend. 'US Goodproducts' (a pseudonym) has built a remarkably efficient, market-driven joint-venture ('Vietsani'), run almost entirely by Vietnamese. While Vietsani employees, therefore, do not feel the resentment towards expatriates that is evident against (for example) British American Tobacco in Uganda, they nevertheless regret that Vietsani does not generate social capital as well as it might. The differences appear minor at this stage, but may become significant as foreign-invested enterprises are 'Vietnamized' over the next few decades.

In the fifth case study, Dr Gail Whiteman, who teaches at the business school of Erasmus University (Rotterdam, the Netherlands), examines the practices of the Barama Company Ltd, an international forest-products company, in Guyana. This firm, a foreign joint-venture controlled by the Samling Group of Malaysia, harvested lumber in the north-western part of Guyana for most of the 1990s. The impact of its operations has been devastating upon the natural and social capital of the Amerindian peoples, while generating very little financial, productive or human capital for Guyana as a whole. The rainforest was populated largely by indigenous Amerindians, with their own traditional subsistence economy. These people suffered from forced removals, increased poverty, social disruption and a severely disturbed environment. From the beginning, Barama had been warned of these impacts, but ignored these warnings and exacerbated the situation by carving roads through the rainforest. Guyanese from the coast and foreigners used these roads as means of entering otherwise inaccessible lands. These motley groups of miners occupied the lands, polluted the streams, sexually assaulted Amerindian women and girls and ravaged local villages. The traditional claims of the Amerindians to their homelands were ignored. In essence, the Amerindians lost their natural and social capital, with very little return in the form of financial or human capital development. Barama, for its part, might have explored feasible alternatives that would have yielded less damaging results. For example, Barama could have controlled access along its roads. It might have utilized its own contacts with legal experts to strengthen the indigenous peoples' land claims. It might have lobbied other international mineral firms to boycott gold not mined at established, less destructive mine sites in this area. It might have pursued the extraction of lumber in a more deliberate way over a longer time frame so as to provide more opportunities for indigenous people to develop viable defences of their own lands and ways of life. Unfortunately, these opportunities have been lost; after less than a decade of extraction, Barama has closed its operation. With the help of environmental groups, it is seeking certification for sustainable forestry as it develops a new rainforest region of Guyana. The remaining question, then, is whether Barama will establish its new operation in a way that avoids the mistakes of the first.

The sixth study, by Frederick Bird and Robert Mixon examine a copper and nickel mine that recently began operations in the Nunavik Inuit region of far northern Quebec in Canada. This region is populated by 8500 indigenous people, chiefly Inuit, who traditionally have lived by hunting, fishing and trapping. In contrast to Barama in Guyana, the Falconbridge international mining company sought to develop this mine collaboratively with the indigenous people most affected by its operation. As far as possible, it has intentionally protected the natural resources of the region, while carefully cultivating the other capital resources of the indigenous people. In 1995 the company adopted a set of guidelines, developed in consultation with the Inuit, and known as the 'Raglan Agreement'. This agreement guarantees that the mining operation will protect the environment, respect the local culture, provide reasonable royalties to designated Inuit institutions, allocate about one-fifth of all jobs to Inuit and provide them with adequate training. Since 1998, when the mine began operation, Falconbridge's performance has been monitored by a joint Inuit-corporate committee. The Raglan Agreement effectively has expanded in scope with the implementation of work schedules that permit the Inuit to spend more time at home and in their traditional occupations. The committee has established special language classes so that French-, English- and Inuktitut-speaking workers can gain elementary competence using each other's languages. Although these arrangements have received generally favourable reviews from both corporate and Inuit observers, they are not without their problems. For example, the turnover rates for Inuit workers remain much higher than expected. The new wealth and occupational patterns have contributed in part to increased social problems. Many Inuit workers feel they are treated unfairly or with condescension. Much of the new wealth is being consumed rather than invested in ways to strengthen social, physical and commercial infrastructures. This essay concludes by exploring possible ways to address the challenges of this collaboration.

The final chapter, by Frederick Bird, examines how The Body Shop developed a community trade programme with small producer groups in developing countries. By 2002 The Body Shop was purchasing over US$8 million worth of goods, accessories and materials from more than three dozen producer groups in 18 countries. Fifteen years ago, The Body Shop already had franchisee stores in many parts of the world, but it was not purchasing any of its raw materials or finished products from small local suppliers. It began such 'community trade' as a kind of crusade, to demonstrate that for-profit companies could reduce poverty in the developing world more effectively by establishing mutually beneficial trading relationships than by campaigning for corporate social philanthropy. Its initial projects in Brazil and India, Nepal and Ghana were accompanied by much publicity – and criticism. Some observers thought these projects involved more hype than substance; these were, in any case, special projects, to which Body Shop executives, franchise owners and staff variously contributed extra time, funds and concern. Rather than terminate the programmes, The Body Shop responded to criticism by seeking to learn from its experiences. By the mid-1990s, the company had greatly expanded its sourcing from low-income producer groups, while making these trading relationships more professionally businesslike. The Body Shop established ethical guidelines, and worked very hard to ensure that the producer groups developed business skills to produce quality goods in keeping with these standards. In this way, The Body Shop has helped develop the productive, financial, human and social capital of low-income areas. Producer groups have augmented their incomes and business skills. Yet the relationship has been mutually beneficial, in that The Body Shop has gained reliable suppliers at reasonable costs; improved its capacity to manage relations with a new kind of supplier and gained a considerable boost in reputation.

Towards a value-added (asset-development) approach

Before reviewing what we can learn generally from these diverse studies, it is important to acknowledge that the poverty and wealth of developing areas have been and are affected in major ways by factors that international businesses cannot measurably change for the better. Four factors have been especially influential: armed conflicts, widespread disease, international trade regimes and aggravated public debt. As we will see, international businesses can and have at times acted to aggravate these problems.

For example, we can see from the accounts in this book that civil wars, corruption and weak or autocratic governance have depressed the economies of Vietnam, Uganda, Guyana, and Nigeria over long periods at both local and national levels. Apart from efforts they might have made to reduce their own involvement with corrupt practices, international businesses have not been in a position to alter the political misfortunes of these countries in any major ways. Nonetheless, we are forced to recognize that in other settings, such as Guatemala, Iran or Manchuria (Litvin, 2003), international businesses have played major roles in aggravating or initiating such armed conflicts.

The economies of many countries have been affected badly as sizeable portions of their population have suffered from disease and chronic ill health. Just as the Black Death permanently altered the economy of mediaeval Europe, just as European diseases had a disastrous effect among indigenous populations of the Americas in the sixteenth and seventeenth centuries, so the spread of the HIV virus has gravely affected the health and economic well-being of a number of African countries, including Uganda. While international businesses in Uganda and the other countries examined in this book cannot affect the spread and cure of diseases in major ways, they can make a difference. Firms like British American Tobacco might act to provide health services and resources for the farmers from whom it buys its tobacco. Several large mining companies in South Africa, for example, have decided to provide free access for their employees to HIV/AIDS medications.

The economies of a number of developing countries have been adversely affected by international trade regimes. Their agricultural economies suffer from the high tariffs imposed on their primary agricultural goods and products by the North Atlantic countries. Because agricultural production plays such a large role in developing countries, these tariffs exert a major depressing impact on their economies (Oxfam International, 2002). It is not clear that internationally linked businesses in the countries examined in this book are in position to change public trade policies in Europe and North America. Having championed liberalized trading relations with respect to the developing world, it could be argued that these international businesses should, in the name of integrity and consistency, support liberalized agricultural tariffs in the developed world as well.

A number of the countries examined in this book, like Uganda, Guyana and Ghana, have been depressed economically by excessively large foreign debts. These debts were initially incurred in the 1970s and 1980s, when first-world lenders encouraged third-world governments to borrow in the expectations that their expanding economies, strengthened by investments paid for by these loans, would provide easy means for regular courses of repayment over time. These expectations were not met: their economies did not expand; their indebtedness grew. They were then persuaded to take on additional debts in order to augment depleted government revenues and meet the interest payments of their initial debts. Accordingly, a number of countries agreed to 'structural adjustment' policies, which called for them to further reduce public spending on social infrastructures and to liberalize their domestic trade policies. For a large number of highly indebted countries, the growth of their foreign debts, and the policies adopted to secure new loans, have further depressed their economies, weakened their governments and reduced consumer spending (Chossodovsky, 1997). It is not clear that international businesses operating in these countries can measurably act to reduce this debt problem, aside from supporting various initiatives to provide genuine debt relief.

Recognizing the economically depressing impact of wars, disease, trade policies and debt problems, what can we conclude from the case studies examined in this book about the ways internationally linked business might act to foster economic development and reduce poverty? Within their ordinary mandates, international businesses can act to make a difference in a number of important ways. Individual examples are found through out the essays that follow.

The first chapter, 'Ethical Reflections on the Challenges Facing International Businesses in Developing Areas', suggests in a general way that international businesses can act so as to augment their own assets and those of the countries in which they operate. Frederick Bird argues that international businesses, rather than retrenching in cost-minimization strategies, should give priority to asset development – a value-added ethical perspective that is a useful and morally compelling frame for evaluating their overall business practices. Business practices should be gauged in relation to their capacity to augment or deplete both their own assets as well as those of the communities in which they are operating. These assets should be understood broadly to include not only productive powers and financial resources but also human skills and commitments, social goodwill and reciprocating networks of communication, as well as accessible and useable natural resources.

From this value-added perspective, international businesses add to or reduce the assets of their communities not only through the wages and taxes they pay but also by the ways they strengthen or deplete social and commercial infrastructures. Unilever, British American Tobacco and Valco to some extent have helped strengthen the commercial infrastructure of Ghana by policies that favoured backward integration. In a similar way, small- and medium-sized Vietnamese firms strengthened the economies of their communities through the social linkages they fostered. In contrast, Shell might well have experienced more favourable relations with local Niger Delta communities in the 1990s if it had made more attempts in earlier periods to develop business partnerships with local groups – for example, to build and maintain roads, to drill for and distribute fresh water and to produce and distribute electrical power from natural-gas generators.

From a value-added perspective, these case studies also point to a number of future opportunities that should not be missed. For example, it could be argued that MTN's major contribution to Uganda's economy lies ahead – in the possibility that commerce and social life in general might benefit from the widespread availability of cell phones. From a value-added perspective, we would encourage this firm to seek increased revenues by markedly reducing the price of its cell phones (and by lowering expat salaries, thereby also reducing tensions within the firm).

From a value-added perspective we can also point, finally, to a number of practices that especially strengthen the institutions and resources of developing areas. The Body Shop's community trade programme is noteworthy not only because the company took the initiative to develop contacts with third-world producers, but also because it augmented the technological and business capacity of these producer groups. Likewise, as it developed its mine at Raglan, Falconbridge effectively collaborated in such a way as to strengthen Inuit organizations and their positions in their communities. Finally, since the late 1990s Shell has been actively engaged in a number of diverse community development projects in collaboration with local groups in the Niger delta. It continues in the present, as it has in the past, to offer thousands of jobs and skills-training opportunities for Nigerians.

This reference to Shell's contributions here is especially apt. The impact of international businesses on developing economies has often been mixed. Some assets have been developed while others have been depleted. The experiences of these businesses include both instructive examples and missed opportunities. We have written this book in the hope that others can learn from these cases and more frequently pursue value-added business practices that will help, in greater or lesser ways, to reduce the poverty in the developing world.

References

AccountAbility/BWB (2003): AccountAbility and Business for Social Responsibility with Brody Weiser Burns *Business and Economic Development: The Impact of Corporate Responsibility Standards and Practices.* http://www.economicfootprint.org

Auty, R. M. (1993) *Sustaining Development in Mineral Economies: The Resource Curse Thesis* (London: Routledge).

Chossodovsky, M. (1997) *The Globalization of Poverty: Impacts of the IMF and World Bank Reforms* (London: Zed Books).

Chua, A. (2003) *World on Fire: How the Exportation of Free Market Democracy Breeds Ethnic and Global Instability* (New York: Doubleday).

Forstater, M., MacDonald, J. and Raynard, P. (2002) *Business and Poverty: Bridging the Gap* (London: Prince of Wales International Business Leaders Forum).

The Group of Lisbon (1995) *Limits to Competition* (Cambridge, MA: MIT Press).

Klein, N. (2000) *No Logo* (London: Flamingo).

Legrain, P. (2003) *Open World: The Truth About Globalization* (London: Abacus).

Litvin, D. (2003) *Empires of Profit: Commerce, Conquest, and Corporate Responsibility* (New York: Texere).

Oxfam International (2002) *Rigged Rules and Double Standards: Trade, Globalization, and the Fight Against Poverty* (Washington, DC: Oxfam).

Prahalad, C. K. and Hart, S. L. (2002) 'The Future at the Bottom of The Pyramid', *Strategy + Business Magazine*, First Quarter.

Ross, M. (2001) *Extractive Sectors and the Poor: An Oxfam America Report* (Washington: Oxfam America). http://www.oxfamamerica.org/pds/eireport.pdf

Stiglitz, J. E. (2002) *Globalization and its Discontents* (New York: W. W. Norton).

1
Ethical Reflections on the Challenges Facing International Businesses in Developing Areas

Frederick Bird

Introduction

We now live in a world where the lives of all peoples are inextricably inter-connected. We have been brought closer to each other through modern systems of transportation and telecommunication. Commercially the links between people grow in number and complexity. Elements in the products we use, the clothes we wear and the food we eat may come from quite diverse places all over the earth. The volume of trade between countries has greatly increased. We are interconnected in other ways as well. A disease like AIDS begins in one part of the world and within a short span of years it has spread throughout the globe. How humans utilize natural resources in one part of the world may well affect those in other parts. Particles from insecticides used in the tropics eventually appear in rain and snow of arctic areas. Pollution caused by industry and vehicles in urbanized areas ends up disturbing the earth's atmosphere in ways that affect all humans. We have become interconnected in still other ways. Humans have migrated all over the earth. Vast numbers of people have moved from rural to urban areas, from continent to continent, in the process bringing with them parts of their varied cultures and traditions. Religiously humans are now more inter-mixed then ever. Christians and Muslims, especially, as well as Hindus, Buddhists, Sikhs and Jews are now found all over the world.[1]

Although humans enter the twenty-first century more interconnected than ever, we remain different in many ways. We remain deeply influenced by different cultural traditions. Even though there may well be common features among them, we follow different ethics. Although some languages have become more widely used, we speak in diverse languages. We have different tastes in clothes, food and recreation even though certain styles have gained greatly in popularity.

Most decisively, humans differ, often markedly, in their *basic life chances*. In some parts of the world people can expect to live much shorter lives than in other parts. In the economically developing areas of the world, humans are much more likely to face illness and hunger, to experience poverty and material deprivation, to receive less education and fewer opportunities. As humans have become more interconnected, the differences in wealth and income levels have remained. In many areas they have increased. Worldwide we have enough resources so that all humans could live well-nourished, well-clothed and housed and well-educated lives. Yet billions of humans suffer from poverty (Forstater, 2002, ch. 2).

What are the responsibilities of internationally interconnected businesses in a world like this? International businesses serve to transfer more resources and greater wealth between the economically developed and the economically developing areas of the world than do either charitable associations or formal government aid programmes. What are the responsibilities of international businesses in a world that has become more globally interconnected and yet remains culturally diverse and deeply divided between affluent and impoverished areas?[2]

These are not questions that can be ignored or avoided. While fairer trading relations offer the opportunities to foster economic development and reduce poverty in the developing world, the current patterns of trade have aggravated these conditions in many impoverished areas (Oxfam International, 2002). The situation of the developing areas directly and indirectly impinges on the economically more developed world. Economic and political instability of these areas affects all humans. As in the Asian crisis of the late 1990s, economic downturns in particular countries may spread to other countries. Economic instability in particular areas has occasioned protests, uprisings and insurgencies that in turn have affected or draw in countries from around the world. In particular, internationally connected businesses have to find ways of managing a wide range of exigencies associated with establishing business operations in areas that are often culturally diverse and subject to social unrest.

Realistically, what are the options for international businesses?

Businesses from the affluent developed countries could decide to divest and withdraw from developing areas, especially from those areas either governed by corrupt and oppressive regimes or subject to high degrees of civil unrest. Many people in developed countries have argued for responses like this. They do so because in part they do not like the fact that low-skilled jobs that once had been performed in factories in Europe, Canada or the United States are now being performed in Asia, Latin America or Africa. They protest additionally against the ways internationally connected businesses seem to impose their own organizational cultures on other peoples. They object more specifically to the ways some of these businesses, sometimes in alliance with local elites, have blatantly exploited the humans and natural resources of developing areas. Many people view the especially large international businesses as imperialistic powers, able to utilize their wealth and influence to dominate underdeveloped areas where they operate (Korten, 1996; Klein, 2000; Barlow and Clark, 2001; Chua, 2003).

Although divestment can and has served at times as a useful tactic in some settings (Sethi and Williams, 2001), as a general and strategic response to the current world situation, this option seems flawed for several reasons. First, most internationally connected businesses are not about to disconnect because they do not see this response as being in their interest. As a result this response seems unrealistic. Second and more importantly, for the most part people within developing areas who work for these businesses do not want them to divest and withdraw. These businesses are viewed at once as sources of jobs that pay better than many alternatives, as sources of tax revenues and as avenues for learning about new and useful technologies (Oxfam International, 2002; UNCTAD, 2002). Third, in spite of the very ambiguous impact of these firms in developing areas, those areas within the developing world in which these businesses operate are generally much better situated economically than those that are less connected. The most economically isolated areas are for the most part the most impoverished areas of the world (Group of Lisbon, 1995; Legrain, 2003). To be sure, economic integration does not by itself guarantee effective economic development. International economic connections have in places aggravated inequalities, over-exploited resources and occasioned economic deprivations (Davis 2001; Oxfam International, 2002, p. 32). Nonetheless, lack of economic ties has not benefited the least developed countries. Severe poverty has doubled in these countries in the past two decades (UNCTAD, 2002).

Aside from certain settings where divestment may serve temporarily as a useful tactic, the fundamental question facing internationally connected businesses in developing areas is not whether or not they should operate in these areas but *how* should they conduct their business in these developing areas (Oxfam International, 2002).

Three fundamental questions

The question of how international businesses should conduct themselves in developing areas can be re-phrased as three different sorts of questions. First, what are the most helpful and effective ways of gauging and promoting sustainable economic development, and what responsibilities do international businesses have with respect to this objective? Second, with respect to business strategy, what orientation ought businesses pursue with respect to their own operations in these areas? Third, with respect to the ethics of firms, what are the social responsibilities of firms and how should these be gauged?

For purposes of discussion, I have represented typical responses to these questions in Table 1.1. The responses to the separate questions may or may

Table 1.1 Typical responses to basic challenges facing international businesses in developing areas

Assumptions	Alternatives A	Alternatives B
Economic development	*Neo-liberal view*: Economic development is gauged by GNP per capita and fostered by trade liberalization and foreign investment	*Institutional view*: Economic development gauged by capacity building, institutional developments and local commerce
Business strategy	Pursue competitive advantage through cost minimization	Foster asset development
The role of ethics	Criticize and reform business practices using standardized benchmarks and social investments	Criticize and reform business practices in relation to models of value-added practices and just exchanges

not be connected. I argue that responses of the second sort, listed under alternative B, operate to reinforce each other. I discuss these alternatives at greater length in the remainder of this chapter.

Questions regarding economic development

How we think about the responsibilities of international businesses in developing countries is influenced by our assumptions about how to identify and foster economic development in these areas. These areas experience extensive poverty. Over one billion people live on less than US$1 a day. Twice that number live on less than US$2 per day. Low income is clearly a major characteristic of many developing areas. How then can these incomes be raised in sustainable ways? If international businesses can make a difference, then at what sort of objectives should they be aiming? These areas suffer from more than low incomes. They suffer as well from under-developed social and physical infrastructures, from huge indebtedness, from poorly developed patterns of local commerce, from lack of access to reasonably priced credit, and from an over-dependence on primary commodities. Given these circumstances, in what ways are international businesses most likely to contribute to the economic development of these areas?

One response to these questions is to focus on policies aimed at raising the average income levels of developing areas. From this perspective, levels of economic development are primarily identified by the overall levels of economic activity – the gross national product – calculated on a per capita basis. Correspondingly, whatever policies raise the overall levels of economic activity are to be encouraged. It is assumed that for under-developed countries to grow they will need to make their overall economies more attractive for investments especially from developed countries. Finally, it is assumed developing countries can attract this kind of investment by reducing government expenditures as well as taxes, by liberalizing trade relations and reducing state corruption (Stiglitz, 2002).

This neo-liberal view has been criticized for several reasons. It gauges development excessively in relation to national income levels. It fails to examine the way overall levels of developments may foster increased inequality between regions, occupational groupings and social classes. As a result, national levels of income may increase while the number of impoverished households does not dramatically change. This view focuses excessively on income and neglects the extent to which sustained development requires the establishment and maintenance of social, physical and economic infrastructures. The neo-liberal view tends to concentrate on means of attracting large foreign investments, which have indeed frequently played an important role for some developing areas; but it often fails to examine factors that either encourage or discourage multiple small investments from domestic sources (Chossodovsky, 1997). The neo-liberal view seeks to impose on developing countries market conditions similar to those prevailing in the early decades of the Industrial Revolution, with market conditions unencumbered by social constraints. In contrast, beginning in the second half of the nineteenth century and continuing into the twentieth century, industrializing countries gradually instituted various policies that created a social minimum, managed the risks associated with markets, redistributed wealth through progressive income and inheritance taxes, and limited the powers of economic conglomerates. As modern markets were developed so were public pensions, social insurance programmes, labour laws, effective tax regimes, well-funded public education and effective property law (Chua, 2003, ch. 12).

A contrasting view of economic development focuses on economic *capacity building*. Economic capacity in turn can be viewed in relation both, one, to *capabilities* of people within an given area to realize basic economic objectives and, two, degree to which the pursuit of these objectives is supported by corresponding *institutional and infrastructure* arrangements.

The United Nations Development Programme (UNDP) measures the development of basic human capabilities by the capacity to:

- Nourish, shelter and clothe people
- Avoid high rates of morbidity and mortality
- Provide educational opportunities
- Participate in community life
- Live with self-respect and the esteem of others.

The ends pursued by these capabilities correspond broadly to the basic human goods set forth in the 'natural law' tradition: the preservation of life, the birth and raising of children, the acquisition and transmission of knowledge and sociability. As we look at development in relation to capabilities, we remain interested in raising income levels but we focus immediately on developing those skills and competencies that enable people to realize these objectives. Thus, areas and countries are judged to be economically more or less developed to the degree that these capabilities are more or less fully cultivated among the people living in these territories (Sen, 1999; Nussbaum, 2000).

There is an institutional argument that complements the focus on the capabilities of individuals. According to this line of analysis, countries are more likely to experience economic development to the degree that they are able to establish reliable and versatile political and economic institutions. Strong, effective, bureaucratically organized government administrations have played a decisive role in the development of countries such as South Korea, Singapore and Taiwan (Wade, 1990; Evans, 1996; Maxfield and Schneider, 1997; Khan and Sundaram, 2000). Countries are likewise more likely to experience sustained economic development in settings where local economic institutions – especially those that facilitate local commerce, credit and sourcing – are also effectively developed. In order for countries to develop economically, people living in these areas, either as individuals or organizations, must find ways to be able to expand what they spend for market purchases. Market liberalization policies that effectively reduce family incomes, by lowering wages, reducing social welfare, inflating prices and/or raising real costs for basic educational and health care services, are likely to have a depressing impact on the possibilities for economic growth (Chossodovsky, 1997; Stiglitz, 2002; UNCTAD, 2002).

From a capacity-building perspective, raising income levels remains a central objective. However, this objective is gauged not primarily in relation to average per capita incomes but rather in relation to the incomes of those households that are the most impoverished (UNCTAD, 2002). Furthermore, it is assumed that this objective is most likely to be realized not only by raising overall national income levels but also, and more decisively by acting to increase the capabilities of these households and to strengthen those institutions and infrastructures that help to cultivate and expand these capabilities. This approach also recognizes that each economic area is at its own particular stage of development. A policy that may work effectively in one culture for an area that has already developed certain infrastructures and capacities may prove ineffective in less well-developed areas influenced by different cultural traditions. Large corporate conglomerates allied with the government fostered Korea's development while Taiwan's economy grew through the efforts of multiple small and medium-sized firms operating on their own. The study of Vietnam's growth in this volume reveals a pattern closer to Taiwan than to Korea. One set of policies cannot be invoked as normative for all settings. If various social and economic institutions are integral to facilitating economic development, then it is important to foster the development of these institutions in ways that are both historically and culturally sensitive.

As we will see, this approach to questions about development nicely complements the asset-development approach to business strategy. Both view alternative strategies and practices in terms of whether they protect and enhance basic assets, in the one case, of the firms and their constituencies and in the other case, of the population generally viewed. Accordingly, as firms organize themselves to protect and develop their assets, they are more likely to act in ways that respect and enhance the capabilities of the constituencies with which they interact, and strengthen the economic and social infrastructures that they encounter.

Questions regarding business strategies

International businesses are not social-welfare organizations. They are expected to pursue what is in their own best interest. There are, however, various ways in which businesses can identify their best interests. Should they primarily be seeking to increase shareholder value on a quarterly basis or expand market share? In developing areas especially, what strategies make best business sense? For heuristic purposes, we can draw a contrast between two distinguishable approaches. The first aims to advance business interests through cost-minimization strategies. The second in contrast seeks to further a business's interests through asset development. Both seek to augment the economic well-being of firms. The first strategy typically seeks to augment current profits by keeping expenses minimal. Working in developing areas meets this objective by offering low labour and maintenance costs and available and inexpensive resources. The second approach to strategy seeks to augment a firm's overall assets over the longer term. Developing areas meet this objective through their potential markets as well as their extensive human and natural resources (Santoro, 2000). In the following paragraphs we analyse these contrasting approaches in greater detail.

Many have argued that international businesses should pursue their own business interests through *cost-minimization* strategies. In principle, cost-minimization strategies call for businesses to operate legally and responsibly in ways that minimize their expenses. This strategy is widely defended as a means for encouraging investments in developing countries, for fostering business enterprises that are indeed competitive, for bringing the resources of modern technologies to developing areas, for avoiding the inefficiencies associated with state-managed enterprises (Porter, 1990). It is assumed that their best interests can approximately be identified either with efforts to maximize shareholder value or at least maintain their market share. If they operate in this manner, they will, it is argued, make the most effective use of their financial, natural, productive, human and social capital. As they operate in economically developing areas, these businesses seek to keep themselves competitive by minimizing expenses, using resources efficiently and building workable, mutually beneficial links with responsible governments. Many different examples of this strategy might be cited.

Many firms in the textile, apparel and toy businesses – Liz Claiborne or Nike, for example – have worked with local suppliers in developing countries to establish workplaces where their products could be manufactured and assembled inexpensively while still paying local labourers at current local rates. Many resource-extraction firms have invested in developing areas where diverse mineral resources are found. While trying to maintain the tacit support of local politicians and community groups and act legally, they seek to manage their operations so as to obtain the greatest return on their investment over the time such operations are active. In the best-case scenario, such internationally connected firms established safe, environmentally responsible operations that pay workers decent wages and also make reasonable tax payments. In practice, however, many firms have not lived up to these expectations.

The strategies of several of the firms examined in this book correspond generally with this kind of cost-minimization approach. Firms such as British American Tobacco in Uganda and Barama forestry company in Guyana operate to develop effective working relations with national governments and to develop reputations as good corporate citizens through selected social investments, and at the same time to minimize expenses and long-range investments beyond narrowly defined business interests.

Cost minimization has been criticized from several perspectives. First, as firms seek to minimize costs in developing areas, they tend disproportionately to exploit their situations to their own advantage. For example, in practice many such firms have exploited workers through low wages, unsafe working conditions, forced labour arrangements and excessive working hours (Sklair, 1989). They often violate environmental standards, or seek to get by with as little compliance as they can. As a condition of their initial investment, they frequently arrange to pay disproportionately low taxes or else manage their internal transfer pricing practices so as to reduce or avoid ordinary tax obligations. In many areas, these internationally connected firms exist within enclaves little related to the larger economy of the areas in which they operate (Klein, 2000). Second, the cost-minimization model ignores the excessive power which especially large businesses can draw upon to serve their own ends. It naively assumes that market forces respond primarily to costs and demands. The model greatly underestimates the barriers that small- and medium-sized enterprises within developing countries face as they seek to compete with these large and wealthy international businesses. The latter typically possess huge head starts in terms of access to capital markets, technological resources and contacts for marketing their products. Large enterprises are typically better placed to influence the decisions of governments and international tribunals adjudicating trade disputes.

The cost-minimization model for how internationally connected businesses ought to operate in developing areas has its defenders and its opponents (Friedman, 2000; Barlow and Clark, 2001). The former have been well represented among economic theorists, defenders of structural adjustment policies and the executives of many international businesses. The latter have been well represented not only by the critics of globalization but also by those who have sought to foster ways of conducting international businesses practices so that they genuinely help developing areas to develop. Advocates of corporate social responsibility as well as those involved in the initiative associated with Business Partners for Development have criticized the cost-minimization model because it assumes too great an isolation of businesses from the societies in which they operate. They have sought to identify alternative models for business practices in developing areas.

The alternative approach to business strategy in developing areas argues that international businesses should seek primarily to develop not only their own assets but also those of their immediate stakeholders. I refer to this as an *asset-development* approach. From this perspective, businesses are expected to invest in developing areas in ways that add to their own long-term value. Rather than attempting above all else to minimize expenses, businesses should seek above all to protect their investments and render them as productive as possible over time. There are number of correlates of this shift in focus from cost minimization to asset development. Insofar as firms are influenced by this approach, they are likely to spend greater amounts in installing appropriate technology. They are also more likely to cultivate skills development among their labour forces and to organize them in ways that render them more productive. They are more likely to work with local supply chains and hence foster a greater social presence among local businesses. Firms following this strategy are also more likely to explore ways of marketing their products locally. Michael Santoro has compared the practices of international firms in China in so far as they have followed either cost-minimization or asset-development approaches. He found that the former, which were represented especially by firms using low-level skills to manufacture for export, paid lower wages and operated with poorer working conditions. In contrast, the latter, represented by firms who also sought to manufacture for local markets, typically paid higher wages, provided better working conditions, invested more in local infrastructures and installed more modern technology in their plants (Santoro, 2000).

It is possible to view the assets of firms in broader or more limited terms. The value of a firm (i.e. its overall assets) ought to be understood broadly to include much more than what might narrowly count as property, namely, financial assets and productive capacity embodied in building, machines and properties. Its value also includes the skills and competencies its work force – its *human capital*. This includes not only the firm's established reputation, but also the goodwill, trust and interconnectedness it cultivates among those with whom it regularly interacts: employees, suppliers, customers, public officials, local community groups, creditors, investors and others – its *social capital*. A firm's value is affected as well by its reliable access to natural resources required and/or taken for granted as bases for its operations – its *natural capital*. Natural capital includes not only the access to resources directly used in the productive process, such as minerals, grains and fibres but also access to potable water, healthy air, useable land and other common resources. Re-stated in slightly different terms, the overall value of a firm is thus the sum of its financial, productive, human, social and natural capital. Consequently, as firms aim at enhancing their value, they can be expected in varying degrees to protect and develop these several sources of economic value in ways that enhance their overall assets, in the broadest possible sense (Bird, 2001).

As an approach to business practices in developing areas, the asset-development strategy provides a broad orientation in terms of which specific questions can be raised and answered about how individual enterprises ought to be most effectively developed and managed. Insofar as businesses adopt this perspective, they are then likely to consider various questions related to marketing, investment decisions, financing, human resources and community relations in terms of whether and to what degree alternatives are more likely to protect and develop their overall assets over time.

We can explore the significance of this approach by reviewing briefly several examples. A small independent foreign petroleum company faced severe security risks in Colombia. Its wells and productive sites were widely dispersed. The costs for hiring security guards under these circumstances were likely to be excessive. As a business decision, therefore, the firm decided to make a series of local investments to strengthen its economic connections with people in the surrounding area. It hired local groups to maintain roads. It sold the excess natural gas at cost to help generate local electrical power. It helped re-organize the local school system and shared the use of buses. As a result of these and other local investments, the company gained the trust and confidence of the local community and thereby greatly augmented its social capital. They also successfully but indirectly addressed their security problems (Fossgard-Moser and Bird, 2003).

Shell has extracted billions of dollars' worth of oil from the Niger Delta since it began operations there in the late 1950s. Throughout its operation, Shell for the most part followed responsible business guidelines, paid reasonable wages, offered thousands of Nigerians opportunities for advancement, paid generous royalties to the central government and invested in local community programmes. Yet the people of the Delta remain almost as impoverished today. For most of this period, Shell burned 85 per cent of the associated natural gas produced by extracting oil. It invested little in local businesses in the delta region. From an asset-development perspective, how might Shell have acted differently? What kinds of additional investments might Shell have undertaken in the past in order to augment both its present-day assets and those of its neighbours in the Niger Delta? Recognizing that these proposed alternatives would not necessarily be easily instituted, it is still interesting to consider how Shell might have attempted together with other local businesses to utilize the flared gas to generate and distribute electricity not only for the Delta but also for larger areas of Nigeria and its neighbouring countries. As it was, significant portions of natural capital were wasted and potential social capital, which might have been developed through these collaborations, was not developed. Likewise, investment in local businesses, which Shell could have helped to initiate, might have fostered a number of economically valuable developments – constructing and maintaining roads, pumping and distributing fresh water, establishing and expanding local systems of credit – all of which would have provided services required for Shell's operations and at the same time benefited the larger local community. If Shell had made these investments, its earnings might have been somewhat lower; it might have paid somewhat smaller royalties to the central government. However, Shell would probably have significantly augmented its social capital, reduced its security threats at least marginally and added at least minimally to the economic well-being of its neighbours (see Chapter 2).

In the late 1980s The Body Shop began to buy some of its supplies from several primary producer groups in the developing world. By the turn of the century it had contracted to purchase both supplies and craft items on an ongoing basis from approximately 40 different producer groups in economically developing areas. The Body Shop not only made sure these groups operated in compliance with the Ethical Trading Initiative guidelines on wages and working conditions; it also worked with these groups to develop relevant marketing, accounting, human resource and production skills. In small but significant ways, it invested in these producer groups both so they could reliably supply The Body Shop with good quality products – and also market their products successfully to other customers. In the process, The Body Shop greatly added to their own assets by building effective and just supply relations and by so reinforcing their market image as a caring and innovative business (see Chapter 13).

Questions regarding fitting ethical approaches

What is the role of ethics with respect to business practices? Is the purpose of ethics primarily to keep business people in line, that is, to police them? Or is the primary calling of ethics to inspire and motivate, to find ways to move business people to think beyond the bottom line? Many believe that the job of ethics is to ride herd on business people, who, it is regularly assumed, narrowly aim at their own personal and organizational interests (Jackall, 1988). So we bring in ethics to expose and limit this self-aggrandizing greed. Alternatively, we may hope to modify or sublimate this pursuit of self-interest by challenging business people to entertain certain ideals and civic projects. We seem to assume that it is acceptable for business people to pursue their ordinary self-interested goals as long as they also champion various social projects, whether these take the form of philanthropy, affirmative action or improved environmental practices. These are two widely shared views of ethics in relation to business: ethics viewed as a means of policing and ethics as a call for social contribution. It is, of course, possible to adopt both views to some extent.

It is also possible to adopt a third view, in which the practice of ethics is much more integrally related to business, as the everyday mindset by which people identify their interests (what is good for them) and address the problems and decisions they face. Accordingly, ethics calls us to live responsibly, taking into account the impact of our choices on others as well as ourselves. From this perspective ethics concerns not only and not primarily conduct that is regarded as exceptional (whether questionable or exemplary), but rather the everyday practice by which we set our basic objectives, we take account of the claims and interests of others and justify these decisions to ourselves and others (Bird, 1996).

In keeping with the policing role of ethics, many have, therefore, argued that businesses operating in the developing areas ought to comply with internationally recognized *benchmarks* for responsible business practices. In recent years a number of such standards have been developed by organizations such as the Caux Round Table, the OECD, the International Standards Organization, AccountAbility and interfaith corporate responsibility associations in Canada, the United States and Britain (Donaldson and Dunfee, 1999; Williams, 2000; Sethi and Williams, 2001). These standards differ mostly in the degree of specificity and the particular concerns that are assigned greatest prominence. These standards are expected to function in two complementary ways: one, as points of reference which businesses can adopt as guidelines for wherever they operate and, two, as checklists by which external groups can monitor business practices. For the most part, these benchmarks have functioned to call attention to ethically questionable practices. They have been invoked to point to environmental abuses, to champion the right of workers to organize, to criticize indentured labour schemes and to protest against the use of children as labourers.[3]

Many morally concerned people have championed benchmarks like these as ways of holding businesses more accountable. They have lobbied for businesses to adopt these standards as part of their operating policies. They have called for investors and/or customers to boycott particular firms that have been proven to violate these standards in excessive ways. They have sought to persuade export-lending banks to utilize these kinds of benchmarks as screens for determining to which internationally oriented businesses they might extend credit (Williams, 2000).[4]

Nonetheless, it is possible to raise a number of questions about this approach. For the most part those who adopt this approach assume that there are universally valid standards for business practices. In taking this position, it can be argued that they may be guilty of seeking to impose particular North Atlantic standards on people with quite different moral and cultural traditions. For example, what counts as acceptable or unacceptable work for children differs considerably: it varies between less and more economically developed areas; between agricultural and urban areas; between areas with well-established public schools and those without such institutions; and between situations where children work alongside their parents and situations where they do not (Akabayashi and Psacharopoulos, 1999; Basu, 1999; Bessell, 1999; Moehling, 1999).[5] Because of their own commitment to certain child labour standards, a number of groups campaigned against the purchase of soccer balls made in Pakistani communities where children, usually working alongside other family members, helped with some of the manufacturing work. In the wake of these protests, local manufacturers in Pakistan moved the stitching of soccer balls from cottages and households to larger factories. As a result, a number of women lost their primary source of income, and their households were less well off (Khan, 2002).

As an exclusive ethical guide for morally responsible business practices, the benchmarking approach can also be criticized for focusing disproportionately on practices that are questionable. What may well get lost to sight in the process are considerations about overall outcomes of the business process. It can be argued, for example, that the most important contributions of businesses in developing countries include both developing job and training opportunities and fostering overall economic development. These are morally valuable benefits; hence, it can be argued that the benchmarking approach represents a too-narrow or too-thin view of morally relevant considerations.

The benchmarking approach to ethics complements the cost-minimization approach to business strategy. When the latter is viewed as the major economic rationale for business strategy in developing areas, the former in turn seems appealing as a moral corrective. If we assume that businesses will operate best in developing areas by seeking their competitive advantage through cost-minimization practices, then we can correspondingly attempt to limit the morally questionable aspects of these practices by seeking to persuade businesses themselves, as well as public regulatory bodies, to adopt particular ethical benchmarks.

In terms of ethics, how then should international businesses conduct themselves in developing areas? Our answer here parallels the answer to questions about business strategy and economic development. Businesses should operate in ways that add fitting value to the constituencies with which they interact as part of their operations. It is by means of these very interactions – with employees, customers, suppliers, creditors, investors, neighbours, public officials and community groups – that businesses constitute themselves. Ethically, then, the first responsibility of businesses is to conduct themselves in ways that not only benefit their businesses as a whole – that is, promote what I have described as the good of their organizations, broadly understood – but also benefit in fitting ways the constituencies without which they would be unable to operate (Bird, 2001). All businesses are socially embedded in societies. They affect societies in multiple ways, as a concomitant of how they interact with their constituencies. In turn, societies impinge upon businesses in multiple ways through the same interactions. International businesses, then, ought to operate in developing areas to enhance the value or good of their several constituencies in ways that are just and fitting, given the contribution and risks that these constituencies face as a result of these interactions. Briefly stated, businesses ought to operate in these areas in ways that *add value and are just.*

Businesses will add value both to themselves and to their constituencies to the extent that their interactions with the latter are *just.* What does that mean? Under the rubric of 'commutative justice', moral philosophers have argued that parties involved in just interactions ought to participate in these interactions voluntarily and fully informed of what can be expected in terms of outcomes and processes. These criteria represent minimal expectations. However, by themselves, they are inadequate. They overlook a number of factors that may render unjust interactions pursued only in these terms. For example, voluntary and otherwise informed interactions can become unjust if one party can exercise much greater power, if the processes of bargaining and agenda setting for negotiation privilege particular parties, and if freedom to pursue alternatives is much greater for some than others. A reasonable account of just interactions requires a fuller statement. Minimally, just interactions are those that meet following criteria:

1. The parties involved participate voluntarily, are fully and reliably informed and are able to represent and bargain effectively for their interests.
2. The benefits that the parties obtain are proportional to the contributions they make, the lost opportunities they forgo and the risks they face.
3. Due consideration is given, first for the way various public goods (reliable social infrastructures, historical precedents, civic peace) make these interactions possible; and second, for the responsibilities of parties involved to support these public goods.
4. Efforts of any one party to excessively dominate these interactions are limited in effective ways either by procedural guidelines, expectations of transparency and/or third party facilitators.

The value-added approach to ethics differs from the benchmarking approach in several ways. Attention shifts from vigilantly policing businesses for violations of basic standards towards a consideration of the ways businesses can be expected to contribute to the well-being of their several constituencies as part of on-going interactions. Vigilance is still called for. However, our primary attention must shift to exploring imaginatively how businesses can operate so that while they maintain or enhance their value, their several constituencies do so as well, and their relations with these constituencies remain interactive and reciprocal. Moral focus about question of compliance with standards about right and wrong conduct is augmented by concerns about the good and goods that can and ought to fostered and achieved.

This shift in attention is illustrated by the way two different retailers in the international apparel business managed their relations with a single workshop in Southern Africa. One firm hired an external group to monitor the suppliers' labour practices.[6] It sought to enforce compliance with its code through external monitoring and public reporting. However, the external monitoring group was unable to develop a working relationship with the supplier. In frustration, the retailer eventually broke off the contract with the supplier. A second retailer adopted a different strategy. In response to the requests from the supplier, they agreed to allow the local firm to utilize its own internal monitoring processes developed in collaboration with a union representing the workers. The monitoring process was viewed as internal activity that allowed for organizational learning and re-commitment to organizational objectives. No public reports were to be issued. This arrangement produced much more satisfactory results, which pleased both the management and the union. The focus had shifted from external policing to internal coaching, appreciation and learning.

The application of the Sullivan Principles by more than 100 US firms working in South Africa in 1970s and 1980s represents another example of a value-added approach. Initially the principles were set forth as very general ideals by which firms committed themselves to work to realize a set of objectives related to improving the conditions of black workers. Firms were monitored privately and received feedback on their performance. There were no public disclosures; firms agreed to work progressively over time to realize higher standards. Over time the Sullivan Principles were gradually altered to become more specific and more demanding. In practice, by endorsing these principles, firms worked gradually to empower their own black workers, and took steps to improve workers' living conditions through various civic measures (Sethi and Williams, 2001).

This shift in focus has several immediate implications for our evaluation of business practices in developing countries. With respect to employees, for example, we are interested in a variety of questions not only concerning adequate remuneration and acceptable working conditions but also about skills development, career opportunities and workers' capacity to exercise discretion over the pace and approach to their tasks. With respect to suppliers, we become especially interested in the degree that firms use local suppliers in ways that further develop local economic and social infrastructures. From this perspective, businesses are called upon to make social investments in the communities in which they operate not strictly out of a sense of philanthropy. Rather such contributions represent a fair exchange to these areas in return for the social dislocations that firms occasion and the social infrastructures that these communities contribute. Overall, if international firms are going to interact with their host areas in a just manner, the benefits they derive from their operations should be balanced with benefits that these areas in turn enjoy.

This value-added or just-practice approach to business ethics complements the capacity-building approach to development and the asset-building approach to business strategy. Each adopts a pragmatic yet teleological approach in relation to certain valued goods. Insofar as international businesses adopt these approaches, we believe that they will operate in ways that are at once good for business, good for the development of these areas and good for their constituencies.

Correspondingly, as international businesses operate in developing communities, they can be expected to review to what degree they add to, maintain, or diminish the overall assets of those communities. Are they adding value or not? And in what ways are they adding? All of the following questions are relevant:

1. In what ways have they added to the *human capital* of their own and their suppliers' work forces? Do workers have opportunities to learn and enhance useable skills?
2. In what ways have they added to or undermined the sum of *social capital* in these developing areas? Have they worked to foster trust and social cooperation? Have they acted to strengthen or weaken economic and social interconnections among these people?
3. In what ways have international businesses added to the *productive capital* of these communities? Have they added to the capacity of these communities to use human and natural resources more productively? Have they worked to transfer relevant technologies?
4. To what extent and in what ways have these firms added to the *financial capital* of these developing areas? Have they responsibly paid taxes and royalties? Do they offer workers and suppliers reasonable wages and prices? Have they explored how they might guard against the tendency for monetary wealth to end in the hands of local elites leaving the poor as impoverished as before?
5. Finally, to what extent and in what ways have these international firms acted to preserve or augment the *natural capital* of these areas? Have they worked to make it possible to utilize given natural resources more effectively? Have they worked to reduce wasteful use of these resources? Have they attempted to make their operations sustainable? In so far as they may have engaged in using up non-renewable natural resources, have they worked to balance this reduction with efforts to increase other assets proportionally?

When we examine the activities of particular international businesses in developing areas, it is fitting to examine their practices through these economic, strategic and ethical lenses. Are the exchanges with their constituents just? Overall have they added value? Many international businesses have significantly added to the overall assets of developing areas. They have helped to reduce poverty. They helped developing areas develop their capacities. They have added value. These are real possibilities. They are also real challenges (Forstater *et al.*, 2002; Prahalad and Hammond, 2002; Prahalad and Hart, 2002).

A cautionary thought about human fallibility and organizational learning

No matter what kinds of codes have been adopted; no matter what sorts of training programmes have been established, or what forms of monitoring have been instituted, no matter what laws have been enacted, or what kinds of moral leadership has been exerted – in practice firms and their constituencies will engage in practices that result in wrongs, ethical shortfalls and hurtful mistakes. Ethical initiatives often make a difference; nonetheless, morally reprehensible actions do occur.

Many firms seek to be good corporate citizens in keeping with current assumptions, but find themselves mired in compromises. These assume myriad forms. Firms seeking to be socially responsible discover they must interact with self-serving or inexperienced government officials. They may face international declines in the prices for their products. They must sometimes lay off thousands in areas where unemployment is already high. They find themselves in the midst of aggravated social conflicts. Their shareholders shy away from investing in areas they regard as excessive risks. Zealous NGOs target them for real abuses that they find it hard to avoid. Doing business in developing areas exposes businesses to many real and serious troubles. Faced with these and many other difficulties as they operate in developing areas, well-intentioned managers do not always readily figure how to act responsibly. They unthinkingly follow models that worked in other countries but are inappropriate where they happen to be located. They misjudge the complexities of their setting. They expect too much or too little. They overlook existing resources. They narrowly seek an immediate advantage. They confuse their own career aspirations with the good of their organization (Jackall, 1988). They deal with symptoms rather than underlying causes. In spite of genuinely good intentions, they do not quite get it right. What seems to matter most is the degree to which those who manage international businesses in developing areas are ready not only to seek to act responsibly but also to learn from their wrongs and mistakes.

The essays in this volume are written neither to blame nor to praise the firms examined. They are written to explore what we can learn from their initiatives, accomplishments and successes, and their missed opportunities, unanticipated difficulties and mistakes – as well as their own reflections on these experiences.

Notes

1. An earlier version of this essay appeared in the Autumn 2003 edition of *Zietschrift fur Wirtschafts- und Untenehmensethik*, under the title 'The Value Added Approach to Business Ethics'.
2. Throughout this essay I refer to 'international businesses' (more precisely, internationally connected businesses) rather than 'multinational enterprises'. The latter term focuses on especially large enterprises and their subsidiaries in developing areas. It tend to exclude from consideration thousands of small and medium-sized foreign-owned enterprises operating in developing countries, as well as firms that have been developed indigenously and are selling on international markets. International businesses include all these enterprises as well as the complex supply chains that connect businesses in the industrialized world with quite varied suppliers in developing areas.
3. The proposed ISO standards for socially responsible business practices differ slightly from others. These standards focus not on concrete business practices but on the management systems for invoking and monitoring socially responsible business conduct.
4. As a complement to the benchmarking approach to ethics, many people have called upon businesses to be involved in social improvements. Businesses have been challenged to take up various social causes, from the sponsorship of cultural and sporting events, to the commitment to help develop local infrastructures (AccountAbility BWB, 2003).
5. While it is tempting to draw parallels between present third-world family labour conditions and the sweatshops of US and European cities 100 years ago, the comparison cannot be pushed too far. The most interesting studies of nineteenth and early twentieth-century sweatshops in Western countries argue that these enterprises gradually (and in some areas even fairly quickly) disappeared with further industrialization. The most effective means for reducing child labour, viewed historically, have been further industrialization and increases in public funding for education. Yet widespread education is not really possible without increased tax dollars made possible by industrialization.
6. Private communication to the author.

References

AccountAbility/BWB (2003): AccountAbility and Business for Social Responsibility with Brody Weiser Burns *Business and Economic Development: The Impact of Corporate Responsibility Standards and Practices*. http://www.economicfootprint.org

Akabayashi, H. and Psacharopoulos, G. (1999) 'The Trade Off between Child Labour and Human Capital Formation: A Tanzanian Case Study', *Journal of Development Studies*, vol. 35, pp. 120–40.

Barlow, M. and Clark, T. (2001) *Global Showdown: How the New Activists are Fighting Global Corporate Rule* (Toronto: Stoddart).

Basu, K. (1999) 'Child Labor: Causes, Consequences, and Cure: With Remarks on International Labor Standards', *Journal of Economic Literature*, vol. 36, pp. 1083–119.

Bessell, S. (1999) 'The Politics of Child Labor in Indonesia: Global Trends and Domestic Policy', *Pacific Affairs*, pp. 353–71.

Bird, F. (1996) *The Muted Conscience: Moral Silence and the Practice of Ethics in Business* (Westport, CT: Quorum Books).

Bird, F. (2001) 'Good Governance: A Philosophical Discussion of the Responsibilities and Practices of Organizational Governors', *Canadian Journal of Administrative Studies*, vol. 18(4), pp. 298–312.

Chossodovsky, M. (1997) *The Globalization of Poverty: Impacts of the IMF and World Bank Reforms* (London: Zed Books).

Chua, A. (2003) *World on Fire: How the Exportation of Free Market Democracy Breeds Ethnic and Global Instability* (New York: Doubleday).

Davis, M. (2001) *Late Victorian Holocausts: El Niño Famines and the Making of the Third World* (London: Verso).

Donaldson, T. and Dunfee, T. W. (1999) *The Ties That Bind: A Social Contract Approach to Business Ethics* (Boston: Harvard Business School Press).

Evans, P. (1996) 'Government Action, Social Capital, and Development: Reviewing the Evidence on Synergy', *World Development*, vol. 24(6), pp. 1119–32.

Forstater, M., MacDonald, J. and Raynard, P. (2002) *Business and Poverty: Bridging the Gap* (London: Prince of Wales International Business Leaders Forum).

Fossgard-Moser, T. and Bird, F. (2003) 'Managing Security Problems Through Community Relations: A Comparative Study of Petroleum Companies in Colombia', unpublished paper.

Friedman, T. (2000) *The Lexus and the Olive Tree: Understanding Globalization* (New York: Random House).

The Group of Lisbon (1995) *Limits to Competition* (Cambridge, MA: MIT Press).

Jackall, R. (1988) *Moral Mazes: The World of Corporate Managers* (New York: Oxford University Press).

Khan, F. (2002) 'Pride and Prejudice: Child Labor and the Pakistan Soccer Ball Industry', unpublished paper.

Khan, M. H. and Sundaram, J. K. (2000) *Rents, Rent-Seeking and Economic Development: Theory and Evidence in Asia* (Cambridge University Press).

Klein, N. (2000) *No Logo* (London: Flamingo).

Korten, D. C. (1996) *When Corporations Rule the World* (San Francisco: Berrett-Koehler).

Legrain, P. (2003) *Open World: The Truth About Globalization* (London: Abacus).

Maxfield, S. and Schneider, B. R. (1997) *Business and the State in Developing Countries* (Ithaca, NY: Cornell University Press).

Moehling, C. M. (1999) 'State Child Labor Laws and the Decline of Child Labor', *Explorations in Economic History*, vol. 26, pp. 72–106.

Nussbaum, M. (2000) *Women and Development: The Capabilities Approach* (Cambridge University Press).

Oxfam International (2002) *Rigged Rules and Double Standards: Trade, Globalization, and the Fight Against Poverty* (Washington, DC: Oxfam).

Porter, M. E. (1990) *The Competitive Advantage of Nations* (New York: The Free Press).

Prahalad, C. K. and Hammond, A. (2002) 'Serving the World's Poor Profitably', *Harvard Business Review*, September, pp. 48–57.

Prahalad, C. K. and Hart, S. L. (2002) 'The Future at the Bottom of The Pyramid', *Strategy + Business Magazine*, First Quarter.

Santoro, M. (2000) *Profits and Principles: Global Capitalism and Human Rights in China* (Ithaca, NY: Cornell University Press).

Sen, A. (1999) *Development as Freedom* (New York: Random House).

Sethi, S. P. and Williams, O. F. (2001) *Economic Imperatives and Ethical Values in Global Business: The South African Experience And International Codes Today* (University of Notre Dame Press).

Sklair, L. (1989) *Assembling for Development: The Maquila Industry in Mexico and the United States* (Boston: Unwin Hyman).

Stiglitz, J. E. (2002) *Globalization and its Discontents* (New York: W. W. Norton).

UNCTAD (2002): The United Nations Conference on Trade and Development *The Least Developed Countries Report 2002: Escaping the Poverty Trap* (New York: The United Nations).

Wade, R. (1990) *Governing the Market: Economic Theory and Role of Government in East Asian Industrialization* (Princeton University Press).

Williams, O. F. (ed.) (2000) *Global Codes of Conduct: An Idea Whose Time Has Come* (University of Notre Dame Press).

2

Wealth and Poverty in the Niger Delta: A Study of the Experiences of Shell in Nigeria

Frederick Bird

The Royal Dutch/Shell Group of Companies has been extracting oil in the Niger Delta since 1958. By 2003 Nigeria's oil export revenues had reached a total of US$290 billion (Litvin, 2003, p. 257). These revenues have benefited Shell and other multinational oil companies like Mobil, Texaco, Agip, Elf and Chevron also operating in Nigeria. They have provided the primary source of revenue for the Nigerian government, helped build a new national capital and enriched a number of high-ranking government officials. But after 45 years the people of the Niger Delta, one of the world's largest wetlands, are practically as impoverished as they were in the 1950s. Natural capital, both in form of oil reserves and of potable and fishable water, has been significantly diminished. Per capita income for Nigerians in 2002 was US$260, less than at independence. Economic analyst Sarah Khan (1994) has called the history of the oil industry in Nigeria 'one of missed opportunities, administrative disorganization and resource mismanagement' (p. 2).[1]

Had Shell managed its operations in other ways than it has done, would the people of the Niger Delta be less impoverished today? Would their resources be less diminished? This chapter explores these questions in retrospect. Although we will focus on Shell in Nigeria for the purposes of this essay, we hope to see what other businesses interested or involved in long-term investments in developing areas can learn from a thoughtful review of Shell's experiences.

First, we will summarize Nigeria's turbulent history, to provide a context for understanding the decisions that Shell took. In 1960, after almost one hundred years of direct colonial rule, Nigeria gained its independence. Later in the 1960s, Nigerians fought a civil war in which approximately one million people died. There have been ongoing ethnic conflicts; Nigerian governments have changed six times as a result of military coups. Clearly, Shell has been conducting its business in Nigeria under conditions of considerable political instability, widespread social unrest, recurring periods of violence and increasingly dramatic contrasts of wealth and poverty.

Second, we will analyse how Shell has worked with the monetary, natural and social resources that it found and subsequently helped to develop in Nigeria. We will argue that Shell for the most part followed current patterns of conventional wisdom as it worked with these resources. It attempted to develop these resources in ways that at the time seemed economically wise, politically practical and organizationally possible. Viewed retrospectively, however, these decisions appear in different light. In hindsight, it seems reasonable to explore alternatives that Shell might have pursued based on what it has learned in the meantime. Our aim is not so much to blame Shell for want of foresight in the past, as to see what companies like Shell can learn in the present so as to further more effectively the economic development of underdeveloped areas like the Niger Delta in the future.[2]

A brief history of Nigeria

Nigeria as a political entity did not exist one hundred years ago.[3] As a British colony, it was initially constituted as a single administrative unit in the early twentieth century, in order to consolidate colonial control of the trade in palm oil. During the nineteenth century the area that was to become Nigeria was inhabited by a number of different self-governing peoples. In the southern area, these included several larger peoples such as Igbo, the Ijaw and the Yoruba. The northern area was dominated by the Hausa-Fulani Caliphate, which was established in 1817. European powers had long taken an economic interest in this area. As early as 1444, the Portuguese had captured and enslaved 235 Africans at present-day Lagos. In 1562–63 the English sailors John Hawkins and his cousin Francis Drake challenged the Portuguese by trading in slaves illegally on the West African coast; and in 1660, when Charles II granted a monopoly to the company of Royal Adventurers of England Trading into Africa (with forts in what is now Sierra Leone), Britain entered a century and a half as a chartered slave-trading power. By 1807, when the slave trade was abolished, Britain had discovered another economic resource: oil extracted from palm trees. The British created a crown colony in the area of Lagos in 1861 and, three years later, a protectorate encompassing the Niger Delta and hinterlands. Initially British merchants purchased the palm oil from traders in the Delta area. While some of these traders sought to secure a higher return by selling directly to industrial customers in Great Britain, British merchants for their part sought to deal directly with the palm-oil growers. The merchants succeeded, aided in large part by British military powers, which conquered not only the Delta but also the Hausa-Fulani Caliphate in the north by 1903. The three regions of Lagos, the Delta and the north were merged into a single colony in 1914.

Britain governed Nigeria as a colony until it became an independent country in 1960. During the years of colonial administration, Britain aided Nigeria's development in several ways. It helped to develop physical and social infrastructures. It fostered trade, mostly between Nigeria and Britain rather than within Nigeria as such (Graf, 1988, ch. 1). It helped to develop a united armed force. It helped to form courts and legislative councils and established schools and colleges. As a result, Nigeria's prospects for independence seemed promising for a country that was constituted by peoples who had never before been joined together as a common political entity. There was sizeable well-educated elite, representing all the major regions. Recently discovered oil resources promised to generate enormous amounts of wealth. However, in spite of these prospects, Nigerians had little or no experience governing a multi-national country or managing a complex modern economy (Ivison *et al.*, 2000; Gagnon and Tully, 2001).

The Nigerians in 1960 established what seemed like a workable federal system of government. Nigeria became a republic headed by a president, Nnamdi Azikiwe and a prime minister, Alhaji Tafawa Balewa. Its federal constitution assigned some self-governing powers to three regions: the Western region, dominated by the Yoruba people; the Eastern region dominated by the Igbo; and the Northern region, dominated by the Hausa-Fulani. The southern regions were largely Christian and the Northern region was largely Muslim. The Niger Delta was divided between the Eastern and Western regions. Each of the three regional governments exerted considerable power. Nigerians' past experiences in self-government had taken place in relation to the various nations and indigenous peoples, and their loyalties were formed largely in terms of these groups. Discontent with the existing arrangement soon arose, as smaller ethnic groups felt themselves dominated by the larger ones. Distrust between the regions increased. There was a general strike in 1964. By 1966 a number of regional and ethnic conflicts came to a head: in January there was a military coup and an Igbo, General Aguiyi-Ironsi, assumed the position as government head. In May he declared Nigeria to be a unitary republic and transformed the regions into territories of the federal government. Following this coup many in the north especially resented the disproportionate influence of the government officials and army officers who were Igbo. There was a movement among Northerners for secession, as well as a mutiny by young Hausa-Fulani officers. Attacks on Igbo occurred in the North and the West. In fear for their lives, thousands of Igbo fled to their own territorial home in eastern Nigeria. In July there was a second coup and Colonel Yakubu Gowon assumed the position as head of state, vowing that the military would govern only for as long as it took to establish fitting conditions for civilian rule. Gowon was a member of a smaller ethnic group from the middle belt area, and was supported by many of the smaller ethnic groups that feared being oppressed by the larger groups in each of the regions. But his government rejected a compromise settlement that would have given the regions greater autonomy, and instead divided the country into 12 states – which effectively strengthened its own centralized power. In May 1967 General Ojukwu declared the Eastern Region, which he governed, to be the independent country of Biafra. The ensuing war between Biafra and the rest of Nigeria continued more than three years and resulted in approximately one million deaths, mostly civilians. However, not all the people within the Eastern region favoured the creation of Biafra. The central government received support from many of the smaller ethnic groups, like the Ogoni, who feared that they would be dominated by the Igbo in the proposed country of Biafra. When the war ended in 1970, Gowon proclaimed that there would be no reprisals, and that military rule would last another six years, in order to stabilize and restructure the federation. No efforts were made to demobilize the army, which had grown to 250 000.

Prior to the 1970s, Nigeria had earned much of its foreign-exchange revenues from the sale of agricultural products such as palm oil, groundnuts and cotton. Beginning in the seventies, Nigeria became increasingly dependent on the sale of oil both for its foreign exchange accounts and the government's own revenues. The Biafran war was fought in part to determine who would control and benefit from the oil extracted in the Niger Delta. In 1969 the government asserted its sovereignty over all petroleum assets in the country, and subsequently moved to become the majority owner of all oil operations, establishing the Nigerian National Oil Company (later re-named the Nigerian National Petroleum Company) and assuming greater fiscal control over Shell, Chevron and the other multinational petroleum companies. The government did not take over actual operations, but served as renters, collecting huge amounts of taxes and royalties.

In 1973, the OPEC cartel, which Nigeria had joined two years earlier, quadrupled the price of oil. In Nigeria, this enormous new wealth funded steep salary increases in the army and the government, diverse public works, and large private and public projects. This surge in new wealth had a number of important but mixed results. It served to increase the powers of the centralized government. It diverted attention away from the needs and opportunities in agricultural production; in fact, agriculture's contribution to export earnings dropped from 60 per cent in 1960 to 10 per cent in 1978. The new wealth also fuelled a marked increase in consumer spending (especially in urban areas) and a sharp increase in the consumption of both imported goods as well as goods manufactured by new ventures established by international businesses. Indeed, most of the revenues from oil production in Nigeria were directly or indirectly consumed rather than invested (Forrest, 1993, ch. 8; Khan, 1994, ch. 8). Much of the recently developed wealth ended up in foreign banks. As a result of its new wealth, Nigeria initially enjoyed a surplus in relation to trade and investment with other countries. By the end of the seventies, however, as domestic spending on imported goods and foreign investments grew, this surplus had turned into an increasingly large deficit.[4]

Meanwhile, political instability increased. In 1974 General Gowon announced that military rule would continue for an indeterminate period. In 1975 Brigadier General Murtala Mohammad seized power partly in order to institute a series of reforms leading to a civilian government. Murtala was a popular leader: he trimmed the budgets of the civil service and army, dismissed or retired nearly 10000 civil servants and set in motion efforts to reduce the army by 60000. He re-divided Nigeria into 19 rather than 12 states. He initiated work on the development of a new capital at Abuja. In early 1976 Murtala was assassinated in an abortive coup. His chief of staff, Brigadier Olusegun Obasanjo, assumed the position of president and prepared the way for a popularly elected government. In 1978 the government enacted the Land Use Act, which declared that all lands in Nigeria belonged to the government. Current owners were thereby treated as if they were leasing their properties from the government. In practice this act served to override the customary land claims of various tribal groups and states. In October 1979 a Second Republic began, with a new constitution designed to reduce ethnic and regional factionalism and created from a consultative process that involved people from all over Nigeria. But the Second Republic itself fell far short of its goals; it became, in the words of the National Concord, 'a government by the rich, for the rich, in the name of the people' (Graf, 1988, p. 95).

In 1980, Nigerians were wealthier on per capita basis than they were before or since, with GNP per person at over US$1000. However, in many ways the social and economic situation in Nigeria was becoming more difficult. The high exchange value of its currency, the Naira, made it easier to buy imports than to sell agricultural or manufactured exports. External debt grew as the agricultural and manufacturing sectors remained underdeveloped. Corruption markedly increased. Between 1979 and 1983 Nigeria transferred US$14 billion into foreign accounts. A sharp decline in oil prices in the early 1980s aggravated these trends. Oil exports declined sharply so that the revenues dropped from US$24.9 billion in 1980 to US$9.9 billion in 1983 (Khan, 1994, ch. 3). Per capita income declined 34 per cent. In spite of continuing sales of oil, the country was becoming poorer and more economically dependent (Ikein, 1990, pp. 71–2; Forrest, 1993, ch. 8).

Economic decline and political instability intensified during the 1980s and into the 1990s. Major General Muhammad Buhari replaced the civilian government on 31 December 1983, ostensibly to reduce the levels of public corruption. Like previous military rulers, he established a legal framework for his government and promised a return to civilian rule; but in April 1985 he was overthrown by General Ibrahim Babangida. By the mid-1980s the government's debt load had grown to the point where more than half its revenues from oil production were being used to pay the interest on foreign debts

(Khan, 1994, ch. 9). In order to help Nigeria meet its increasing debt load, Babangida arranged in 1986 for Nigeria to secure a loan from the International Monetary Fund (IMF). He instituted a series of structural economic adjustments in keeping with the IMF guidelines. These reforms included measures to devalue the national currency, to reduce dramatically government spending and to foster increased foreign investment. However, the reforms did not yield the desired results. Those sympathetic to the IMF argue that these structural adjustments did not work because the government began to abandon them in the early 1990s before they could really become effective (Moser *et al.*, 1997). IMF critics argue that the reforms further weakened the economy by undercutting needed social services, by favouring foreign over domestic manufacturers and by aggravating debt problems. The reforms were more designed to foster international trade than trade within Nigeria, which was really needed (Ikein, 1990; Bangura and Beckman, 1991; Forrest, 1993). By the early 1990s many groups in Nigeria were becoming increasingly upset with the situation in their country: real income levels had been halved over the previous decade; unemployment remained extremely high; the central government seemed increasingly autocratic. Even as poverty increased, huge amounts of wealth were used to build the new capital. Military and economic elites, like General Babangida, had grown increasingly wealthy.

A key development was growing political resistance against various practices of the oil companies in the Niger Delta, especially against the flaring of natural gas and their pollution of freshwater streams. There were protests in 1987 by Iko youth, in 1990 by youth in Etche village of Umuechen and in 1992 by youth in Bori. In some cases, the protesters resorted to force, and were met by force in return, resulting in numerous deaths. Houses were burned. Police forces were directly involved (EAGE, 2000, III).

Most significant for Shell were the highly visible and successful efforts of the Ogoni, who objected to being forcibly included in the eastern region of Nigeria and in the Rivers State without distinct political recognition and representation. Although oil mining in their territory had produced what they estimated to be US\$30 billion, the Ogoni had received next to nothing. They lacked jobs, electricity, fresh pipe-borne water, as well as adequate educational and health services. Their environment had been ravaged. In 1990 Ken Saro-Wiwa, a popular writer and broadcaster as well as a successful entrepreneur, helped to organize the Movement for the Survival of the Ogoni People (MOSOP). A well-organized and articulate movement, MOSOP in its bill of rights, addressed to the government and people of Nigeria, declared the Ogoni to be a distinct nationality within the larger republic. They demanded to be granted political autonomy, representation at all levels of government and the 'control and use of a fair proportion of Ogoni economic resources for Ogoni development' (Paine and Moldoveanu, 1999, pp. 23–4). MOSOP registered with the Unrepresented Nations and Peoples Organization (UNPO) in The Hague.

In November 1992 MOSOP issued a 30-day ultimatum both to Shell and to the government, demanding that the Ogoni be paid US$6 billion for unpaid royalties; that the flaring of gas cease; that all high-pressured pipelines be buried; that a US$4 billion reparation payment be made for environmental damage; and that Shell and the government immediately begin discussions with the Ogoni to resolve these concerns. In January 1993 MOSOP organized a demonstration attended by perhaps as many as 300 000 Ogoni (out of a total population of 500 000). General Babangida met with MOSOP leaders but reached no agreement. Young people among the Ogoni, faced with continuing poverty, high unemployment and the lack of any meaningful discussion or negotiations with Shell or the government, became more restive, expressing increasingly hostile criticisms of Shell. The situation grew tenser, as Ogoni militancy sparked forceful responses by the government. When at the end of April 1993, a Shell subcontractor began digging up farmlands near Biara to bury a high-pressure pipeline, a crowd of youths attempted to stop the operation. Soldiers were brought in to protect the pipeline workers, and in the ensuing clashes some protestors were killed. This incident prompted Shell to close down its operations among the Ogoni until further notice. The company was becoming increasing concerned with what it called acts of sabotage that caused leaks in its oil lines. These latest protests seemed to put Shell's operations at risk (and indeed, Shell has not resumed activities in the Ogoni region of the Delta as of mid-2003).

In May 1993, differences began to surface among the MOSOP leaders. The majority reaffirmed their militant stand; they opposed the laying of a new pipeline and called for the Ogoni to boycott the federal elections called for June. Despite a minority who favoured a more moderate stance, tensions between the Ogoni, Shell and the government increased. Over the course of the summer armed groups attacked and killed over 1000 Ogoni in distinct incidents in July, August, September and October; many more were rendered homeless (Maier, 2000, ch. 4; Okonto and Douglas, 2001, pp. 124–5). The government claimed these attacks were merely evidence of mounting ethnic conflict between the Ogoni and their neighbouring peoples. The Ogoni maintained they were being attacked by federal soldiers and/or militias acting on government orders. In several cases the government's role in these attacks was unmistakable.

The national government itself remained unstable. General Babangida remained in power through 1993. He sought to design a tightly controlled transition to civilian rule, in which regional or ethnic loyalties would play no part. He increased the number of states from 21 to 30, and required that all political candidates belong to one of two newly created national political parties. An election was finally permitted, and on 12 June 1993 the voters of Nigeria elected M. K. O. Abiola, a rich merchant, as their president. Babangida, however, annulled the election. Later that summer, perhaps in response to the protests against his usurpation of power, Babangida retired and handed over the reins to an interim administration headed by Ernest Shonekan.

In November 1993 General Sani Abacha staged a military coup and the situation of the Ogoni became even more aggravated. General Abacha consolidated his power in a number of ways. He suppressed a protest by youth who occupied the Nembe flow station in late 1993. In May 1994 a meeting of Ogoni elders was attacked by a mob; four elders, who had assumed a more moderate political stance, were killed. The police arrested 19 other Ogoni activists, including Ken Saro-Wiwa, who had not even been present at the gathering; they were imprisoned and beaten. In 1995 Saro-Wiwa and eight of the arrested Ogoni were tried by a military court and convicted of murdering or planning the murders of the four Ogoni elders. The trial was manifestly unfair. Witnesses were bribed to testify against the defendants (Soyinka, 1996, p. 146). Unlike cases against General Obsanjo and other arrested political leaders, their death sentences were not commuted to long-term imprisonment. In the face of growing international outrage against the trial and death sentences, Abacha ordered the hanging of Saro-Wiwa and the other prisoners on 10 November 1995, just as the British Commonwealth of Nations was about to begin meetings in New Zealand. As a result, Nigeria was temporarily suspended from the Commonwealth.

Both the government and Shell shared a sense of threat. Shell solicited the government's help in dealing with social disturbance and acts of sabotage (Okonto and Douglas, 2001, pp. 134–7). The government, for its part, was absolutely dependent upon the mineral wealth of the Delta; 90 per cent of its revenue came from the oil extracted from this region. Did the government fear that the Ogoni and other groups would seek to secede like the Biafrans, or set an example to the other peoples who would also seek political autonomy and economic control over the Delta mineral resources? Some sympathetic observers have described the Ogoni as rebelling (Ejobowah, 2000; Maier, 2000); Soyinka (1996) may be closer to the mark when he refers to this situation as an example of ethnic cleansing: the stated aims of MOSOP and other groups were to seek not independence but adequate representation within the Nigerian federation, and a greater share of oil wealth but not outright control. Still, the Government's responses were repressive, violent and autocratic. When in 1994 oil workers struck on behalf of the president-elect Chief M. K. O. Abiola, General Abacha had their union declared illegal. He seized the passport of the writer and Nobel laureate Wole Soyinka. In 1995 Abiola's wife was killed. More than 40 former national leaders were imprisoned, including the former president Olusegun Obasanjo. Unmarked armed forces raided Ogoni villages, killing, wounding and burning. The Ogoni felt they were being attacked by armed forces acting at the behest of the government (Boele *et al.*, 2000; Okonto and Douglas, 2001). Attacks of sabotage against Shell's facilities had increased but were not yet as widespread as they would become in the late nineties. Still, most the Ogoni felt that Shell's operation in this area should remain closed down.

While protests, demonstrations and acts of violence increased in 1998, the political situation in Nigeria changed appreciably. In June General Abacha suddenly died; he was succeeded by General Abdulsalami Abubakar. The latter refused to free Chief Abiola, who still remained the president-elect on the basis of the 1993 election. In early July Chief Abiola died in prison. General Abubakar then arranged for a transition to civilian rule. Different sets of elections were held: first for local government positions, next for state governors and houses of assembly, then for the national assembly; finally a national vote was held for the presidency. On 12 May 1999 the former general and military ruler Olusegun Obasanjo was elected as a civilian president. He quickly introduced a number of reforms. He altered the formula for distributing revenues from oil production so that the producing area received 13 per cent rather 3 per cent in royalties. He established a public commission to review past instances of corruption. He freed political prisoners. But despite these reforms, Nigeria has not yet found a satisfactory political arrangement for balancing the interests of its various regions and peoples. Many people think of themselves primarily as being members of a particular people, tribe or internal nation – like the Yoruba or Igbo, the Hausa or the Ijaw – and only then as Nigerians. Nigerians continue to debate over formulas for sharing tax revenues between the states and the federal government. In an effort to maintain unity, the federal government has asserted its centralizing authority, in the process typically fuelling the efforts of Nigeria's distinct peoples and regions to assert their political autonomy.

While Nigerians live with considerable political instability as well as autocratic assertions of power, Nigeria continues to face major challenges of development, but with declining resources of human, natural and social capital. Its life indicators are grim. By 2000 its population had grown to 106 million, largest in Africa and tenth largest in the world, while income had declined to US$300 per capita from a high of more than US$1000 in 1980. By 2000, Nigerians could expect to live to just over 50 years, an improvement on the life expectancy of 41 years that they had in 1965 but well below a life expectancy of 65 years in Indonesia and 69 years in Thailand. Over 10 per cent of Nigerian children were dying in infancy, and there was a marked increase in the incidence of AIDS. About 60 per cent of adults could read, compared to 85 per cent of adults in Indonesia and 95 per cent of adults in Thailand. Nigeria was spending 1.4 per cent of its GNP on education and health, compared with 10.4 per cent in Thailand. Only half the population had access to fresh water (Guest, 2000, p. 7; *The Economist*, 2001a). In short, after 40 years of independence, Nigeria was in many ways worse off than in 1960. More than half of the vast oil reserves in the Delta had been extracted. The waters of the Delta had become much more polluted, and its fish stocks were more at risk. Civil unrest was on the increase.

Ethnic and religious conflicts had become more pronounced. Crime rates had risen markedly. Attacks of sabotage against oil companies had multiplied. For example, Shell experienced 106 disruptions in its operations in 1997 and twice as many the next year (Ejobowah, 2000, p. 3; Guest, 2000, p. 10). There was an increase in kidnappings and hostage-takings. Of course, it is well to keep in mind that Shell was interacting with approximately 1500 communities in the Niger Delta. Violent incidents, including acts of sabotage, occurred only in some of these communities.

Nigeria has not lacked for resources. The extraction of oil has generated more than US$200 billion in national income over the past 40 years. Unfortunately this wealth has not appreciably benefited the country. It was not been invested as fully as it might have been in developing adequate social infrastructures – schools, universities, hospitals and clinics. It was not invested as extensively as it might have been in developing physical infrastructures such useful and accessible utilities, transportation networks and communication systems. It was not invested productively as it might have been in agricultural, commercial and industrial development; in fact agricultural production has declined. Overall most of enormous revenues produced by oil mining have been diverted into private consumption, lavish public buildings, impractical mega projects and higher incomes and promising careers for a fortunate few. Oil revenues have been treated as windfall earnings to be consumed over the short term rather than invested over the long term. Nigeria's external debt now stands at US$32 billion.

Royal Dutch/Shell has played a major role in Nigeria during the past 40 years. Would it have been possible for Shell to manage its operations differently so that Nigeria would now be less impoverished, more economically developed, socially more ordered, and politically more stable?

Royal Dutch/Shell operations in Nigeria: a brief account

The Royal Dutch/Shell Group is one of largest businesses in the world, with sales in 2000 of almost US$94 billion (*The Economist*, 2001a, p. 56).[5] Technically Shell is not one company but a group of more than 200 separate companies involved in exploration and production of petroleum, distribution and marketing of refined products, chemical manufacturing and other activities listed under the broad category of 'Renewables'. Overall, these companies employ more than 100 000 workers and operate in more than 120 countries. A six-person Committee of Managing Directors directs the Royal Dutch/Shell Group through two legally independent but collaborating holding companies in the Netherlands and Great Britain.

Shell has been involved in Nigeria since its initial explorations in 1937. It discovered oil in 1956 and began commercial production in 1958. Although the oil fields in the Nigeria Delta are small, there are a large number of them, many lying offshore. As such, it has been necessary to link the various fields through increasingly complex networks of pipelines, and to continuously explore for new fields in the area. Once oil was discovered, Shell and other international oil companies rapidly expanded their operations: drilling wells, laying pipelines, constructing refineries, building port facilities, developing flow stations and exploring for new oil. They created many new but short-term jobs, typical for the start up and construction phase of mining companies, as well as many more permanent positions. They contributed taxes and royalties to the government.

During the Biafran war, Shell withdrew temporarily from the Delta, but expanded during the 1970s and 1980s. Its status within the country was redefined by the government. Royal Dutch/Shell had begun its Nigerian operations largely as an international business in partnership with British Petroleum (BP), staffed by a mixture of foreign and domestic workers. The Nigerian government moved to nationalize their operation, buying out BP and demanding a larger portion of the royalties as well as taxes. Currently, the Shell Petroleum Development Company of Nigeria Limited (SPDC) operates a joint venture, which holds a 30 per cent share, while the Nigerian government holds a majority of 55 per cent through the Nigerian National Petroleum Company (NNPC). The remaining shares are held by Elf (10 per cent) and Agip (5 per cent). SPDC currently operates more than 1000 wells, 87 flow stations and more than 6000 kilometres of pipelines in the Niger Delta. Through SPDC, Shell directly hires about 4000 employees and contracts with about 5400 more. All the employees are Nigerian (except approximately 250 expatriates). Sixty per cent come from the Delta (SPDC, 1999).

This joint-venture structure was intended to respond both to greater governmental financial control and to the ongoing history of governmental instability and autocracy. Shell long assumed that its primary responsibility was to be a good corporate citizen, in the traditional sense: to operate an effective and honest petroleum company, managed in a businesslike way, obeying the laws, meeting its tax obligations and maintaining its autonomy against government intervention. Shell officials committed themselves not to condone bribery and not to get involved in politics. Moreover, from the beginning Shell began making social investments on a modest scale. Even before they struck oil, they had set up a scholarship fund for Nigerian students studying in Britain. They contributed to building local health clinics and schools. They drilled water wells to help some local communities obtain fresh water. In the mid-1960s Shell began an agricultural extension programme. In the 1970s they helped local farmers obtain new disease-resistant strains of cassava cuttings. They trained and hired local workers, most of whom came from the Delta. They addressed their security needs by hiring their own guards and by calling upon the state and federal governments to offer them extra protection.

Despite these well-intentioned efforts, Shell met increased hostility from peoples living in the Delta, who raised many complaints about the way their environment was being degraded. Levels of pollution in the rivers and swamps had greatly increased, with adverse effects upon fishing. Fishermen often had to travel much further and spend greater effort to return with smaller catches. Farmlands were dug up for new pipelines, sometimes without appropriate consultations and negotiations. Increasing numbers of oil spills and leaks occurred (in part because old pipelines had corroded), polluting lands and water; these were not always cleaned up quickly. Shell burned off almost all the natural gas that was extracted along with the oil. In the mid-nineties 87 per cent of the associated natural gas was being flared in Nigeria. This compared unfavourably with flaring rates of 21 per cent for Libya and 0.6 per cent for the United States (Okonto and Douglas, 2001, p. 67). Delta residents complained especially about the way this flaring polluted the air they had to breathe. They felt that they were experiencing more illness because the air was contaminated by chemical produced by the constantly burning gases. Of course, by burning these gases, Shell and the other petroleum companies were wasting a huge natural resource which, if it were properly used, might have produced additional billions of dollars – a concern villagers voiced indirectly when they complained about the absence of electricity, which might have been produced by gas generators. However, few voices were raised publicly about the loss of this immense opportunity.

Although Shell's operations provided wages and job opportunities for several thousand workers, the numbers employed were insignificant in a Delta population of some seven million. Some workers were hired full-time; others received contractual work. Yet the highest-paid positions seemed to go either to foreigners or people from other parts of Nigeria, even as local rates of unemployment and underemployment were steadily growing. Shell's social investment projects generated similar responses: those who benefited were appreciative, but many others felt overlooked and left out. Many of Shell's social investment projects never became fully operational. In the years between 1992 and 1997, only 36 of the 64 roads that Shell helped to build had become functional. Only a little over half its efforts to support the building of town halls (15 out of 28 projects) came to fruition, though the success rate for school building construction projects was higher (156 out of 286 projects). Water projects were the most disappointing: in only 24 per cent of their drilling attempts (28 out of 115 projects) were Shell-sponsored efforts able to find potable water that met national standards (due to contamination by iron). The fact that so many Delta villages lacked adequate fresh water sources made this situation particularly aggravating. In their experience, the oil business polluted their air and water, tore up their lands and disrupted their traditional ways of life and sense of community. Yet if Shell could succeed with the complex enterprise of mining petroleum that generated so much wealth for others, then why could Shell not succeed with these seemingly simple social projects that might have helped some of the people most adversely affected by the oil production business?[6]

Above all, Shell's social-investment projects, however well intentioned, did not address the chief source of resentment among the various peoples of the Delta: the fact that wealth produced by the oil business went to others. Military dictators and high-ranking officers got rich. Extravagant public buildings were constructed. Many business and professional people in far-off Lagos enjoyed high salaries. Much of the oil revenues were being spent in other parts of the country with which the Delta people had almost no sense of connection. Foreign companies were thriving. But the Delta people remained impoverished – far worse off in the nineties than they were in the early eighties, and afraid that the Delta oil reserves would become depleted before they would experience any real benefit.

In the early 1990s, officials at Shell had not yet become aware of how difficult the situation was becoming from the Delta peoples' perspective. In modest ways Shell officials were becoming more socially and environmentally conscious. They were now regularly undertaking Environmental Impact Assessments before each new project. Their spending on social investment projects increased to US$23 million per year by 1996. At Shell's urging, in 1992 the federal government had created the Oil Mineral Producing Area Development Commission (OMPADEC) to serve as a vehicle for investing oil royalties for economic and social development projects in the Delta and other oil-producing areas in the northeast. However, the government rendered OMPADEC ineffective by budgeting only 3 per cent of oil revenues to it.

During the 1990s, Shell became increasingly embattled. The number of voiced complaints grew; relations with the Ogoni became especially strained. Security became more of a problem; there was an increase in the acts of sabotage against pipelines and other facilities. When Shell agreed to compensate all damages suffered from accidents or spills that were not caused by vandalism, it was accused of narrowly construing this standard for its own advantage. As vandalism increased, Shell's responses were mixed. The company asked for added protection from the state and federal governments, while strengthening its own security measures. After a large public demonstration organized by MOSOP, Shell agreed to withdraw at least temporarily. At the time, however, Shell did not seek to enter into direct consultations or negotiations with MOSOP, declaring that 'MOSOP's demand for a greater share of oil revenue from the government, political self-determination and ownership of oil beneath their land are [*sic*] political. SPDC as a commercial organization does not – and should not – be [*sic*] held accountable for actions that are the responsibility of a sovereign government' (SPDC, 1997, p. 8).

Shell seemed to stand by passively as the government and unidentified armed gangs launched attacks against the Ogoni, and as the Ogoni in turn protested. Shell officials voiced little public concern about the several attacks on Ogoni villages and people; they seemed to view these instead as expressions of ethnic conflict (SPDC, 1997, p. 2). Shell remained publicly mute as Ken Saro-Wiwa and eight others were seized by the police, imprisoned without formal charges, tried and condemned by a military court on charges of murder. Shell initially sent a lawyer to the court, assuming the trial would consider all of the recent civil disturbances in the area, but their lawyer withdrew after day one when it was clear that this was being restricted to a murder trial. But Shell spoke up during the trial and after. The company publicly rejected several charges by its critics, denying that it had had any involvement with the military, or provided arms for militia, or bribed witnesses. Using quiet diplomacy, Shell privately asked for a fairer trial and for clemency. The Chair of Shell wrote a letter to General Abacha pleading for clemency for the men who had been sentenced. And once the men were executed, Shell publicly expressed shock and outrage at the hangings.

With respect to the trial as well as the troubles experienced by the Ogoni, many people around the world felt that Shell was in some ways complicit, for what it had done (e.g. contributing to the pollution), for what it did not do (mounting a more overt protest of the trial) and for what it was suspected of doing (in some way encouraging or supporting the raids on the Ogoni). In several ways SPDC sought to defend itself and improve its status among the Delta people. In 1996, together with NNPC, Elf and Agip, Shell committed to the construction of a liquefied natural gas (LNG) plant at the cost of US$3.8 billion. It offered US$220000 in humanitarian aid to the Ogoni and the Adoni, a neighbouring people with whom the Ogoni had reputedly been in conflict. Shell supported the position of a recently held Constitutional Convention, which proposed that beginning in 1998, 13 per cent of Delta oil royalties (increased from 3 per cent) be invested in the area through OMPADEC. Shell arranged for a thorough environmental survey of the Delta, the same kind of assessment that had recently been undertaken by the World Bank. The company also sought to obtain a more objective account of its activities. They paid for a number of European reporters to come to Nigeria and review Shell operations, reporting on these as they saw fit. They increased their social investment budget from US$22 million to US$36 million. They made a number of overtures to foster better relationships with the Ogoni although they still did not formally consult with the leaders of MOSOP. They began replanting paths they had cut through the forest for seismic testing.

In the meantime Shell International had begun to respond to the international furore over the Ogoni protests and executions as what they referred to as a 'wake-up call'. Shell had just attempted to sink the Brent Spar, a floating storage platform in the North Sea; threatened with a well-organized boycott of its products in Europe, Shell relented and towed it to shore. Now with the events in Nigeria, Shell realized it had suffered a sizeable blow to its reputation. Shell officials felt they had acted conscientiously and complied with relevant laws in both cases – they felt they were not morally compromised, as the public saw them. Treating the situation as one calling for serious 'reputational management' (Paine and Moldoveanu, 1999, p. 5), they initiated a series of multi-stakeholder consultations. In 14 countries they held roundtable discussions with community groups, academics, employees and executives. In an initiative referred to as 'Society's Changing Expectations', Shell solicited criticism and advice. They were viewed, they learned, as being too Eurocentric, too arrogant, too cavalier about environmental concerns and too secretive.

In response, Shell International launched three significant reforms over the next several years. First, they rewrote their 1976 statement of business principles, acknowledging their accountability not only to employees, customers and society generally but also to shareholders and all those with whom Shell did business. While reaffirming its pledge to stay out of politics, Shell acknowledged a responsibility to speak out on issues that it deemed relevant to its businesses. They also affirmed the importance of transparency in all its activities, especially audits. Shell reiterated its opposition to bribery in any form, and asserted that Shell companies must respect, and support respect for, human rights. In recent years Shell has reinforced the importance of these revised and augmented business principles, which it has translated into more than 50 languages, and invoked more frequently in relation to business strategy and practices. Shell also has produced printed guidelines on issues of human rights and bribery, providing useful advice for Shell employees on how to put these principles into practice in complex and possibly confusing situations. And it has stood behind these principles: in 2000 four employees were dismissed when they were caught making or receiving illegal payments (Royal Dutch/Shell Group, 2000).

Second, Shell has recognized in a much more serious way the importance of environmental and social issues. It has increased staff working in these areas, and now regularly undertakes environmental assessment before all new projects. Shell has initiated an annual auditing process that is public and includes assessments not only of its business and financial performance but also of its social and environmental performance. Shell has worked to develop key indicators for gauging the social performance of Shell companies. Since 1997, its annual reports set aside space to evaluate how well the Shell Group of Companies is performing in relation to social and environmental indicators. Each Shell company is expected to submit an annual letter judging its own performance in relation to this common set of indicators. Companies are urged to use benchmarking standards such as the ISO 14001 or the Caux Principles. In particular, Shell has lent considerable support to the development of international Sullivan Principles, modelled after the standard written by the Rev. Leon Sullivan for companies doing business in South Africa. Furthermore, through an open internal communication network called 'TellShell', anyone connected with Shell is invited to voice his or her criticisms and comments. A sampling of these comments, both negative and positive, is included in each annual report. As a result of these practices Shell's annual reports seem more candid, transparent and realistic with respect to their failings and successes.[7]

Third, Shell began to re-orient its outlook on social investments. Typically, such aid assumes the form of providing philanthropic grants for cultural or social projects where community groups are passive recipients. Shell began to think less in terms of community assistance and more in terms of community development. In this perspective, businesses act less as distant donors than as collaborating partners with community groups (IBLF, 1996; Sagawa and Segal, 2000). They become involved so as to help such groups to determine their own priorities. They support activities beneficial to both the communities and the businesses. In keeping with this shift in orientation, Shell has initiated a wide range of consultations both at the global level with governmental agencies, international NGOs and foundations (in search of complementary funds and jointly sponsored programmes), and at the local level with local community groups and voluntary associations.

In the late 1990s Shell in Nigeria initiated changes corresponding to these new priorities. It expanded its community projects, spending US$52 million in 1999 compared to US$22 million just four years earlier; even more was spent on various environmental projects, including efforts to clean up spills and manage waste better. It spent much more on building and repairing roads, and modestly improved its success with water projects. It decided to build or repair a number of health clinics and hospitals as well as a number of classrooms and schools, and offered even more scholarships. It worked with women's groups and helped to establish micro-credit associations. It provided sand fill to reclaim land in several areas, and continued to provide agricultural extension services. It upgraded the gas plant and flow station at Alakiri to meet ISO 14001 standards, continued to replace older, corroded pipelines and buried its new lines. And Shell was far more likely to undertake these projects by consulting with local communities and finding local partners to manage them. For example, in 1999, it developed experimental partnerships with 13 pilot communities. In 2001 it joined with the World Bank and Diamond Bank of Nigeria to lend money to indigenous contractors so that the latter could develop the capacity to provide competent services as local suppliers (Royal Dutch/Shell, 2001). Beginning in 1998, SPDC began holding annual stakeholder conferences with representatives from local and state governments, community associations and international NGOs. More than 700 attended the workshop in March 2002. Participants asked Shell to play a greater role in helping to supply fresh water, respond more quickly to oil spills, address the problems of restive youth and expand agricultural services. The conversations were wide-ranging and reciprocal (SPDC, 2002a). By 2002 Shell expanded and varied its involvement in community development programmes. It helped operate 32 health facilities, provided extensive agricultural assistance and supplies, helped a number of community cooperatives, provided scholarships to thousands of secondary and college students, adopted a more collaborative approach to fresh water problems by establishing working committees with local communities and invested considerable sums helping to develop roadways in the Delta region (SPDC, 2002b).

Also, a LNG plant began operating in late 1999. It was finally constructed, after negotiations between Shell and the government, which reached back to the late 1970s. The Nigerian Liquefied Natural Gas Company (NLNG) was formed in 1985 with NNPC holding a 60 per cent share, followed by Shell with 20 per cent share and Agip and Elf with 10 per cent each. However, in their zeal to get the LNG plant up and running, SPDC and their partners did not examine ways to manage more effectively the social unrest occasioned by the local economic bubble Shell had created. Building the NLNG plant created 13 000 new jobs for the two to three years of the construction phase. The sudden influx of workers gave rise to undesired side effects, including a rapid increase in teenage pregnancies and escalating conflicts between indigenous residents and newcomers. The wages effectively inflated prices for consumer goods and rental apartments. Still the LNG plant has led to more efficient use of Nigerian petro resources. In the Delta, Shell began a concerted effort to use more gas for its own operations, to supply several factories and to refurbish and expand an electrical generator station formerly used by the national electrical power authority. Since building the LNG plant, Shell has spent hundreds of millions equipping its facilities to gather and transport gas (SPDC, 2002b, pp. 44–6, 51).

Overall, SPDC has faced very mixed responses to its attempts to develop better relations with the people of the Niger Delta. Large numbers of individuals, households and villages have been helped directly and have expressed their gratitude; yet many others continued to complain. A number of community projects, including a majority of the fresh water projects, failed to become functional (*The Economist*, 2001b). Expressions of anger with Shell have continued. Acts of sabotage increased from 100 in 1996 to 325 in 1998 (SPDC, 1998, p. 13). The number of oil spills declined in 2000 but increased again in 2001 (Royal Dutch/Shell, 2001). In 1999 there were 45 hostage-taking incidents and 45 again in 2001 (SPDC, 1999, 2002b). Although Shell had managed to hold some talks with MOSOP leaders, the influential Ogoni organization remained suspicious. They were not yet ready to invite Shell to re-enter their territory to continue their operations. During 2001 there were a number of incidents in which Shell facilities were attacked in Ogoniland. In one case, experts had to be flown in to cap a wellhead that had blown when its seal had been broken (SPDC, 2002b, pp. 27, 28, 42, 43). This dissatisfaction continued to find political expression. In 2003 the Nigerian House of Representatives ordered SPDC to pay the Ijaw people US$1.5 billion over ten years to compensate for hardships and environmental damage caused by their operations since 1956. The Ijaw in turn were asked to work with SPDC to reduce acts of sabotage. The federal elections in

April 2003 occasioned widespread unrest and violence, directed in part against the ruling government and partly among rival ethnic groups, as well as against the large oil companies. The main refinery at Warri was temporarily closed and oil production was greatly reduced. In spite of Shell's varied attempts at greater social involvement, the situation as of this writing (2003) remains unstable.

Ethical reflections on Shell's operation in Nigeria

We can learn a great deal from reviewing Shell's experiences in Nigeria if we see Shell as facing dilemmas in deciding how to manage its overall assets, that is, the natural, human, social, technological and financial resources entrusted to it (Bird, 2001). International businesses operating in developing areas face a range of characteristic dilemmas involving how they should manage their relations with autocratic or unstable governments, how they should manage security, handle expatriate issues or work with cultural differences, to name just a few issues. The dilemmas are real, and the answers are not simple.

Most businesses make mistakes, some quite serious. Unless we seriously examine these mistakes, we are likely to learn little from them.[8] We can learn much more about how we should manage these operations in the future if we thoroughly and candidly review the practices for their problems as well as their successes. It is significant that Shell responded to its wake-up call by devoting much time and resources consulting with others and soliciting criticisms. The troubles Shell faced and continues to face in Nigeria, especially with respect to the Ogoni people, clearly occasioned these consultations and reforms. However, the factors giving rise to these troubles were deep-seated and revolved around matters of greater importance than the particular actions that Shell took or failed to take at the time of this crisis. In large part, this crisis occurred because over a much longer period of time Shell had not managed the overall resources entrusted to it in Nigeria as effectively and responsibly as it might have done. In the paragraphs below I will consider a number of dilemmas Shell faced in Nigeria, and how it managed the natural, financial and social capital with which it was working.[9]

Financial and productive capital

Shell's operations generated enormous wealth during the past 40 years. However, very little of this wealth benefited the people of the Delta; their per capita income grew until the 1980s, but since then it has continued to decline.[10] We can then reflectively inquire if Shell might have managed its business so that more of this wealth was used to strength the economies and raise the income levels of the people of the Delta. This remains a genuine dilemma, in that Shell was not the only actor. We know the extensive role that governments in Nigeria played in shaping how this wealth has been consumed and expended. We know how fluctuations in the international price of oil affected the extent of this wealth. We can examine the mixed impact of Nigeria's structural adjustment policies in the 1980s. In addition, nonetheless, it is important to explore how Shell might have responded to these exigencies in ways that rendered the people of the Niger Delta less impoverished.

In retrospect, it is possible to consider ways by which Shell might have acted more imaginatively. To be sure, oil production is a high-tech activity, which does not easily provide job opportunities for largely unskilled or semi-skilled indigenous people living in rural areas. Nonetheless, we can ask whether Shell worked as industriously and imaginatively as it might have done to hire and train local workers as well as to invest and help to develop local suppliers capable of providing logistic and semi-technical services. Shell indicates considerable current interest in these objectives (Royal Dutch/Shell, 2001; Shankleman and Moser, 2002); they were, however, at best only marginal concerns over much of the 40-year period. It may well have cost Shell decidedly more initially in time and money to seek out and to train local workers and provide start-up economic and technical assistance to local suppliers. However, over the long run, these arrangements would have enabled modest portions of wealth to enter the Delta economies on a sustainable basis. They would also have strengthened Shell's relationships with local communities. It may well have been less expensive in the long run to take these kinds of initiatives if, as a result, these initiatives strengthened local communities and fostered better community relations for Shell.

Shell might have explored ways in which the Delta peoples might gain a greater share of wealth in the form of royalties for the minerals extracted from below the surface of their lands. Nigerian law certainly did not require Shell to make such payments. Still, it could be argued that these people had a reasonable moral claim to mineral rights, even if they could not make legal claims. In law their property rights have been underdeveloped (De Soto, 2000). However, in other political jurisdictions these mineral rights might well be held in part by the people who have traditionally claimed such lands as their own. Initially, Shell may well have seen this lack of legal rights as advantageous. It is more convenient to deal with one government than hundreds or thousands of local property owners. However, this under-developed legal right left the people of the Delta impoverished. It therefore is instructive to inquire whether Shell might have sought to honour some partial or shared mineral-rights claims of the Delta people. In the 1990s Shell did lobby to augment the share of royalties assigned to OMPADEC, the government commission assigned to receive and invest oil royalties in oil-producing areas. In other settings, such as Papua New Guinea, Quebec and Alaska, mining companies have taken a variety of initiatives to transfer royalties directly to long-range investment funds managed by local communities. To be sure, any efforts by Shell to assert and strengthen the mineral rights of Delta residents would probably have been resisted by Nigeria's federal government. Still, Shell might have pursued the possibilities of strengthening the land titles and at least modest mineral-rights claims, seeing that it was in the company's own interest to cultivate better relations with its neighbours, as well as enhance its image worldwide.

Shell probably could have invested more productively in its community projects. Much of the wealth produced by oil production in Nigeria assumed the form of grants, most of which went to the federal government as royalties, though some of the grant money went to state and local communities. For most of the past 40 years Shell made such grants to local communities. But grant-giving suffers from several problems. First, recipients are transformed into dependants, who tend to focus their energies more on gaining larger and more secure grants rather than on utilizing their resources more productively. Second, recipients tend to consume rather than to invest these transfers; and to the degree that this new wealth is spent on consumption, it is unlikely to help foster sustained economic development (Auty, 1993, 2001). Given these concerns, the challenge for businesses operating in developing areas, like Shell in Nigeria, is to explore ways of productively investing as much of their wealth as possible with the aim of developing and sustaining local economic enterprises and infrastructures generally. Only now is Shell attempting to shift from a charitable to business model – from community assistance projects where they bestow grants to community development programmes in which the company works as a partner (Shankleman and Fossgard-Moser, 2002). To this end, Shell recently has markedly increased the amount it spends on community programmes. The particular challenge is to find ways of spending this money so that it operates more like productive investments.

Shell might have explored further strategies to reduce its Nigerian taxes through greater investment in the local economy. Often businesses in these settings seek to reduce their tax burdens by re-investing as much as possible of their earnings in the development and maintenance of their own operations. They might choose, for example, to upgrade their equipment, to invest in internal training programmes, pay for land or water remediation, pay for local rights-of-way and support similar projects, many of which would substantively enhance the economic conditions of local populations. Shell might have chosen to help to start and then to invest in a variety of local suppliers to help build roads, develop local electricity grids and work at developing reliable freshwater supplies, which, as resources required for its own operations, could also be made available to local communities. In these ways Shell would have added to internal company expenses, reduced earnings on its books and therefore paid lower taxes. They would also, most importantly, have transferred funds directly through business transactions, rather than grants, into the local economy. Investing in these kinds of internal improvements and local transactions needs to be distinguished from bloated transfer pricing, where multinational businesses have been found to deliberately inflate prices charged for internal purchases, in order to reduce their tax burdens. Shell has been accused of deliberately seeking to reduce its tax bills by some forms of internal investment and clever accounting (Okonto and Douglas, 2001, pp. 98–105). The issues here are indeed complex. Nonetheless, given the political history of Nigeria and the fact that the federal government diverted so little of its revenues on a reliable basis to help oil-producing areas, Shell would have been morally justified to explore ways to reduce its taxes by investing in transactions that would strengthen the local economy.

Shell might have made further attempts to buffer Nigeria against dramatic fluctuations of the international oil market. The mining industry in general faces the dilemma of how to manage dramatic fluctuations in earnings, caused by international commodity price fluctuations and boom–bust extraction cycles. Marked increases in earnings can create economic bubbles that distort the economies of communities and states. Nigeria clearly suffered from such fluctuations. The huge increase in oil wealth in the 1970s gave rise to unsustainable levels of spending and borrowing. When international oil prices crashed in the early 1980s, Nigeria was left with huge debts as well as an under-developed agriculture sector. Even though overall economic policies were the responsibility of the federal government, it is reasonable to ask whether Shell might have acted to moderate the spending spree of the 1970s or the economic vulnerability of the early 1980s. Might Shell have acted to reduce or limit the windfall character of their earnings? Shell might have buffered the steep increase in their earnings by a series of internal and partnered investments in the physical, social and economic infrastructures in the Delta. To be sure, Shell may have been able only in very modest ways to buffer its earnings in this manner. Nonetheless, this strategy would have served at once to conserve its own assets and augment those of the Delta.

Natural capital

Currently Shell widely publicizes and makes good on its commitment to environmental responsibility by requiring members of the Shell Group to evaluate their performance in relation to a number of standard environmental criteria. Shell employees and constituents are invited regularly to voice criticism of sub-standard practices. Here I will review Shell's environmental performance in Nigeria not primarily in terms of their compliance with certain benchmarks but rather in terms of how well they utilized and conserved the natural resources with which their operations were entrusted. At issue is how well Shell has treated the rivers and swamps, the sub-surface ground water, the oil it has extracted or expects to extract and its associated natural gas and the atmosphere. These resources represent the Delta's natural capital. By 2000 the Delta's volume of natural capital, insofar as it was reflected in the status of these resources, was of much less value than it had been 40 years earlier.

First, Shell has been roundly criticized for operations that have contaminated surface waters and degraded lands within the Delta (EAGE, 2000; Okonto and Douglas, 2001, ch. 4), although the extent of this damage has been debated (SPDC, 1997, 1998; Paine and Moldoveanu, 1999). The overall effects of oil production have made it more difficult to obtain reliable sources of fresh water from surface sources. Of course, the lack of reliable freshwater sources is a national problem in Nigeria, and it is impossible here to estimate the precise degree to which oil companies have aggravated the shortages. Shell has helped to drill hundreds of freshwater wells through its community assistance programmes. Unfortunately, these wells frequently have not been successful, due to lack of diesel or electrical power to run sub-surface pumps, inadequate local maintenance or sub-surface water supplies that were either inadequate or contaminated. Shell also has undertaken scattered efforts to reforest and to dredge and clean waterways. The net effect, however, has been that the renewable resources within the oil producing areas of the Delta are in a worse rather than a better condition after 40 years; their value has been diminished by environmental practices that have contaminated waterways and despoiled lands, undermining local fishing and farming. Thousands of residents have seen their livelihoods greatly reduced. Shell has an obligation to compensate for the ways in which its operations may have reduced reliable freshwater sources, and to enhance the physical infrastructures of the Delta as resources that it has regularly counted on. But compensations and restorations have been meagre, if not minimal (Human Rights Watch, 1999, pp. 102–3; Okonto and Douglas, 2001, ch. 4; Marong, 2003, ch. 4).

Second, while Shell has drilled and transported oil in an effective way, it has allowed some to be wasted either through leaks due to faulty equipment or through acts of sabotage which they might have more effectively discouraged or prevented. Shell has often been slow in its response to oil spillage through leaks due to faulty equipment, arguing that much of this damage was occasioned by acts of sabotage. No doubt that is true; but it is not a fully adequate response, for two reasons. Most observers argue that the proportion of oil spillage caused by old pipes and poor maintenance is much greater than Shell acknowledges (Human Rights Watch, 1999; Okonto and Douglas, 2001, ch. 4; Marong, 2003, ch. 4). Shell bears some responsibility for how its installations and activities affect the lives of people inhabiting lands contiguous with Shell's operations, whatever the cause of the spillage. Even in settings where some individuals may have deliberately caused breaks in pipelines or blowouts at wellheads, it is not clear that the much larger number of people not directly involved should suffer without compensation when their lands and livelihood are damaged.

Third, and most significantly, Shell has destroyed a vast quantity of natural capital by flaring almost all of the associated natural gas released by 40 years of oil production. Delta residents have understandably complained about the way this flaring has polluted the air they breathe, contaminated the water they drink and damaged the lands they farm. The flaring of associated gases has thus diminished the *human* capital of the people of the region and it is reasonable that Shell support health clinics to help people affected by such environmentally occasioned maladies. Natural gas is a non-renewable resource; ideally, its sale could be used to substitute for and strengthen other forms of capital. Thus, for example, the people of the Niger Delta might have used their share of gas royalties to invest in education and training, thereby augmenting their supply of human capital. Or they might have invested in productive capital, in the form of local industry. Shell could have used the gas to generate electrical power for millions of Nigerians and produce income for those involved in the various stages of its extraction, transmission and utilization. But as a result of burning this gas, the Delta people have suffered a triple loss: first, a considerable portion of their natural capital is diminished without adequate compensation; second, they have had to forego the opportunities which adequate compensation during this period might have occasioned; and third, they have suffered the additional costs to their health and their environment.

Or course, there were barriers to effectively utilizing the resource of associated natural gas resource. Building the LNG plant in the late 1990s required US$3.8 billion, 12 000 extra workers and three years. Further, it required considerable funds, labour and cooperation to transport the gas by pipeline to potential users. It was also necessary to secure reliable markets; but in the 1980s the market remained uncertain. Local use of the gas, on the other hand, required building generating stations and electricity grids. Furthermore, Shell and other oil companies may have been discouraged for other than market reasons. At the time, Nigeria's public utilities responsible for electricity were unreliable; there were no national laws against flaring; there was extensive political instability and social unrest; and local politicians and business people with whom the oil companies would have had to collaborate were not readily prepared to come to terms. Yet, Shell and others may simply have seen the LNG options as outside the domain of their business interests as they understood them at the time. However, in retrospect these rationales seem not to justify inaction. The investments in liquefaction, power generation and power grids would have paid in the long term. Efforts by Shell and other oil producers to help develop viable energy grids would have helped to strengthen physical infrastructures, which in turn would have served to strengthen business and social networks. Shell needed to consider the long-range benefits of these projects for itself and the people of the Delta.

Social capital

'Social' capital refers to the networks of social relations – to the trust that facilitates social cooperation, as well as to the commitments that lead people to volunteer time, goods, hospitality and forbearance to others. Social capital finds expression in community good will, especially to others not already connected by bonds of kinship (Putnam, 1993, ch. 6). Social capital is valuable because it fosters cooperation, civic engagement, volunteerism and community development. In its absence, people are likely to act with much greater suspicion, fear and self-aggrandizing behaviour. In settings of low social capital, people are likely to act both to exploit immediate advantages and to protect themselves from attacks or self-aggrandizing conduct by others.

The question is whether or not Shell conducted its business so that the existing expressions of social capital in the Niger Delta were fostered and grew, or were undermined and depleted. It appears that during the period when Nigeria was becoming independent, modest amounts of trust and good will existed within the separate nations and peoples, but not much between these groupings. Primarily, loyalty existed within families and larger kinship groups. Then over time, Nigeria's history of military coups, civil war, ethnic rivalry and economic exploitation served to erode any larger expressions of trust and good will. Yet within their own groupings, both Muslim groups and Christian groups have fostered some larger feelings of community. As well, MOSOP and the corresponding associations among other peoples have occasioned loyalties, collaborations and common identification within these movements.

For most of their history in Nigeria, Shell did little to cultivate and honour these communal sentiments and activities. Like many businesses, Shell has taken the formation of social capital for granted. To be sure, Shell has acted in modest ways to augment the human capital of the people of Nigeria and the Delta, offering employment and training opportunities to thousands of Nigerians. Yet Shell has recruited for senior positions from across Nigeria, while offering less skilled positions to people from the Delta, a practice which has bred resentment. Shell has also failed to pay sufficient attention to social-capital formation in two other dimensions of their activity.

First, Shell's community programmes, though substantial, have been flawed in approach. Shell has contributed thousands of secondary and university scholarships, as well as school buildings, health clinics, agricultural assistance, road building and water projects. Over the past decade the budget for these community-assistance programmes has nearly tripled. Nonetheless, from the perspective of Nigerians, these contributions have seemed to be spotty, given the large and steadily increasing population. Ironically, the programmes also may have unwittingly occasioned envy and distrust by helping a favoured few, while leaving others to resent their bad fortune. Such unequal access reduces social capital. Some Shell-funded community programmes suffered as well from poor quality, especially roads and clinics (Okonto and Douglas, 2001, chs 5, 7). Of course, such criticisms have been made about public works and public projects throughout Nigeria. For the most part, Shell has sought to assist people with their problems, lending its programmes a philanthropic social-service character. However, community-assistance projects leave recipient groups dependent. They rarely strengthen local social networks; they seldom augment social capital. They ignore the existing personal, interpersonal and associational resources of communities, and so fail to find ways of utilizing and building upon such strengths (Kretzman and McKnight, 1994; McKnight, 1995). Acknowledging the merit of this critique, Shell has begun to shift its community programmes away from philanthropic assistance and move them more towards forms of partnering favouring community development.[11]

Second, Shell has managed its security needs in ways that have diminished the social trust that it otherwise might have enjoyed, especially during the past dozen years. Like every other business, Shell is responsible for protecting its facilities and employees. It is admittedly difficult to provide protection in settings of social unrest and erratic violence. Shell has received severe criticism of its security practices (Soyinka, 1996; Boele *et al.*, 2000; Maier, 2000, chs 4, 5; Okonto and Douglas, 2001, ch. 6). Setting aside Shell's alleged complicity in violent assaults on the Ogoni (SPDC, 1997), it seems that its normal security practices were problematic. For the most part, Shell seems to have addressed security concerns as marginal problems, which might be satisfactorily handled for them either by contracting for guard service or calling on the state police to offer added protection. In the past, Shell seems to have failed to recognize fully what it now acknowledges: namely, that the management of security is inevitably an integral aspect of *community relations*. As we can now see in retrospect, Shell's handling of security directly affected the way in which it was regarded by the Delta communities. When Shell called upon the state police, it failed to consider fully how these forces had been employed in the past and how ruthlessly they might act. Shell discounted reliable evidence that the police or militia hired by some still-unidentified sources were acting brutally – in some cases, killing innocent residents and burning villages. Why did Shell choose to regard these incidents primarily as mere examples of ethnic conflict or criminality? Clearly ethnic conflict was present; but these Ogoni protests also reflected anger at pollution, poverty and poor infrastructure (EAGE, 2000; Maier, 2000, ch. 4; Okonto and Douglas, 2001, chs 6, 7, 8). It seems clear that the security arrangements Shell put in place severely aggravated its relations with local communities.

Shell, working with international NGOs, has recently been attempting to spell out much more clearly the terms of engagement that should be followed by security forces. It would, therefore, be particularly fitting to inquire about advantages and disadvantages of alternative ways of addressing these security needs. Security issues are not likely to diminish in the near future, given the steady expansion of the population, the high rates of unemployment, continuing poverty and the pervasive (if unevenly expressed) feelings of distrust towards both Shell and the Nigerian government in general. Shell's ways of managing its security problems have had the effect of reducing in some measure the trust, commitment and community goodwill that would have been an asset not only for Shell but also for the local communities. Managing security issues effectively represents an ongoing dilemma. Using Shell's experiences in Nigeria as a point of reference, it seems important for international businesses like Shell that are operating in developing countries to reconsider these matters not only in relation to concerns for protection, of people and property, but as integral features of how businesses interact with their communities.

Conclusion

Our concern in this essay has been to explore what might be learned by reviewing how Shell managed the monetary, natural and social resources with which it was entrusted. The context of our concern is the contrast between the increase in monetary wealth created by the oil production in the Niger Delta, the continuing poverty of the Delta residents, as well as the reduction in natural and social capital occasioned by the oil business. We have been interested in exploring what might be learned from reviewing this history so that these kinds of operations might prove more beneficial and less impoverishing to developing areas. If companies like Shell are going to be well placed in the future to act responsibly with respect to these assets, they must learn all they can by critical examinations of their own pasts.

During the past four and half decades, Shell operated in ways that produced enormous wealth but left the people living in the immediate vicinity of their operations poorer in financial, productive, natural and social capital. It does not seem that Shell consciously sought to exploit these comparatively powerless people; rather Shell did not consider many of the alternative strategies for protecting these vital forms of capital in Nigeria, either because it could not justify these strategies in terms of short-term financial performance, or because it defined its business interests and responsibilities more narrowly than they do now. Historically, Shell in Nigeria has had to balance returns to overseas investors and the Nigerian federal government, which both assigned tax rates and holds a 55 per cent interest in the joint venture SPDC. But while the Nigerian government had considerable power to determine basic rules within which Shell managed its financial wealth, Shell, like other businesses in these kinds of settings, has retained room to manoeuvre.

International businesses these days are frequently extolled as potential 'partners for development', along with both governments and the associations of civil society (IBLF, 1996; Sagawa and Segal, 2000). In addition, businesses are expected to be 'good citizens' (McIntosh *et al.*, 1998). What might it have meant for Shell if it had adopted this kind of civic calling in Nigeria several decades ago? Given the overall political instability of Nigeria, what sort of options did Shell really have? It is impossible to answer these questions with any kind of certainty. Nevertheless, it seems clear that Shell in Nigeria might have pursued a number of courses as a part of a long-range investment strategy. For example, it might well have worked more with local utilities on the long-range project of increased electrification. Shell might have begun earlier to work with local municipalities to develop reliable freshwater supplies. It might have lobbied for public policies that would have been in the long-term best interest of its local constituencies, such as increased taxation powers for local governments and increased investment in social and physical infrastructures. They might have explored the possibility of managing a very difficult security situation through greater cooperation with organized and unorganized local constituencies. As 'good citizens', international businesses are expected in various ways to be engaged civilly and probably politically. What has yet to be clearly delineated are guidelines that distinguish between engagements that are acceptable – non-partisan, legal, transparent, publicly engaged and communally involved – and those that are not because they are partisan, covert or illegal.

As the Royal Dutch Shell Group now acknowledges forthrightly in its annual report, Shell companies must take into account the social and environmental impact of their operations. It is not enough simply to maximize returns on financial investments. It is not sufficient merely to conduct environmental and social impact assessments. Shell's basic responsibility is to maximize returns on invested wealth not only for shareholders, but for other stakeholders as well, in proportion to the value of their contributions, their legal claims and the risks to which their investments have been exposed. To this end, Shell has acknowledged its need to learn from its experiences in Nigeria and elsewhere.

Notes

1. The research is based not only on the works cited but also on a number of interviews with officials of Royal Dutch/Shell at their International offices in London. For comments and criticism on earlier drafts of this essay, I am grateful to William Buenar Puplampu, Frank Chalk, Egberet U. Imomoh, Joe Smucker, Marco Mingarelli, Farzad Khan, Alhaji Marong and other members of our research team in Montreal.
2. Shell is currently applying standards like these as it develops frameworks for new mining operations in the tar sands area of Alberta (Shankleman and Fossgard-Moser, 2002).

3. This historical survey is primarily based on the studies by Graf (1988), Okonto and Douglas (2001) supplemented by the works by Guest (2000), Boele *et al.* (2000), Ikein (1990), Forrest (1993), Wiwa (2000) and Khan (1994).

4. For comparative studies of countries with abundant mineral resources and weak patterns of development, see studies by Ascher (1999) and Auty (1993, 2001).

5. This account of Shell is based on case studies by Paine and Moldoveanu (1999), Boele *et al.* (2000), Okonto and Douglas (2001), Ikein (1990) and Forrest (1993), as well as a number of Shell Reports (Royal Dutch/Shell, 1998, 1999, 2000, 2001; SPDC, 1997, 1998, 1999).

6. The data cited in this paragraph come from an internal Shell memorandum.

7. In early 1997, as it was just beginning to initiate these changes, Shell faced a share-holder resolution put forward by the Pension and Investment Research Council and the Ecumenical Council for Corporate Responsibility, calling for an external audit-ing of the company's performance. In spite of being formally opposed by Shell, this resolution received 10.5 per cent of the vote, with 6.5 per cent abstaining (Paine, 1999). Although Shell's auditing process had become more multidimensional, open and participatory, many shareholders felt external auditors should be used.

8. I recognize that it is much easier to conjecture about alternatives than to put them into practice. Indeed, the alternatives considered here might well have to be fundamentally altered or relinquished in response to given exigencies. I have attempted to be realistic about these alternatives and have outlined them retro-spectively, using as points of references practices that have more recently been attempted by Shell or other international businesses.

9. I am purposefully not evaluating Shell's performance in Nigeria in relation to cur-rent benchmarks of fitting business conduct, such as codes of human rights or the Caux Principles. Rather, I am evaluating its performance from a teleological perspective, examining how well Shell might have acted to realize particular goods, in this case measured in relation to specific clusters of resources.

10. I realize that a strong case can be made for distributing a reasonable share of the wealth produced by oil industry for the welfare of Nigerians generally. I do not suggest that the wealth generated by oil production should go exclusively to help the Delta peoples; but clearly, as the Ogoni Bill of Rights suggests, they deserve a much fairer share than they have received.

11. There is considerable enthusiasm among businesses for the idea of developing viable partnerships with community groups (IBLF, 1996; McIntosh *et al.*, 1998; Sagawa and Segal, 2000). However, it is important not to minimize the difficul-ties attendant on this approach, as long overdue as it may be, in a setting like the Niger Delta. Viable partnerships and workable collaborations with community groups require continuing sensitivity to local political realities, which are likely to be contentious and changing. These issues are considered in other essays related to our larger research project, especially the essay on mining operations in northern Quebec (included in this volume), Colombia and Madagascar.

References

Ascher, W. (1999) *Why Governments Waste Natural Resources: Policy Failure in Developing Countries* (John Hopkins University Press).

Auty, R. M. (1993) *Sustaining Development in Mineral Economies: The Resource Curse Thesis* (London and New York: Routledge).

Auty, R. M. (ed.) (2001) *Resource Abundance and Economic Development* (Oxford University Press).

Bangura, Y. and Beckman, B. (1991) 'African Workers and Structural Adjustment: The Nigerian Case', in Ghai, D. (ed.), *The IMF and the South: The Social Impact of Crisis and Adjustment* (London: Zed Books).

Bird, F. (2001) 'Good Governance: A Philosophical Discussion of the Practices and Responsibilities of Organizational Governors', *Canadian Journal of Administrative Sciences*, vol. 18(4), pp. 298–312.

Boele, R., Fabig, H. and Wheeler, D. (2000) 'Shell, Nigeria, and the Ogoni: A Study of Unsustainable Development'. Submitted to the Annual Meeting of the Academy of Management, Toronto.

De Soto, H. (2000) *The Mystery of Capital* (New York: Basic Books).

EAGE (2000) Essential Action and Global Exchange, 'Oil For Nothing: Multinational Corporations, Environmental Destruction, Death, and Impunity in the Niger Delta', *Essential Action* [website] (updated 25 Jan. 2000). http://www.essentialaction.org/shell/report/intro.html

The Economist (2001a) The World In Figures (London).

The Economist (2001b) 'Helping, but not Developing: Nigeria and Shell', 12 May, p. 52.

Ejobowah, J. B. (2000) 'Who Owns the Oil? The Politics of Ethnicity in the Niger Delta of Nigeria', *Africa Today*, vol. 47, Winter, pp. 29–47.

Forrest, T. (1993) *Politics and Economic Development in Nigeria* (Boulder, CO: Westview Press).

Gagnon, A. -G. and Tully, J. (eds) (2001) *Multinational Democracies* (Cambridge University Press).

Graf, W. (1988) *The Nigerian State: Political Economy, State Class, and Political System in the Post-Colonial Era* (London: James Carry).

Guest, R. (2000) 'Here's Hoping: A Survey of Nigeria', *The Economist*, January, pp. 1–16.

Human Rights Watch (1999) *The Price of Oil: Corporate Responsibility and Human Rights Violations in Nigeria's Oil Producing Communities* (New York).

IBLF (1996) Prince of Wales International Business Leaders Forum, *Business as Partners in Development: Creating Wealth for Countries, Companies and Communities*, in Collaboration with The World Bank and the United Nations Development Programme (London).

Ikein, A. A. (1990) *The Impact of Oil on a Developing Country* (New York: Praeger).

Ivison, D., Patton, P. and Sanders, W. (eds) (2000) *Political Theory and the Rights of Indigenous Peoples* (Cambridge University Press).

Khan, S. A. (1994) *Nigeria: The Political Economy of Oil* (Oxford University Press).

Kretzman, J. P. and McKnight, J. L. (1993) *Building Communities From the Inside Out: A Path Toward Finding and Mobilizing A Community's Assets* (Evanston, IL: Institute for Policy Research, Northwestern University).

Litvin, D. (2003) *Empires of Profit: Commerce, Conquest, and Corporate Responsibility* (New York: Texere).

Maier, K. (2000) *This House Has Fallen: Midnight in Nigeria* (New York: Public Affairs).

Marong, A. (2003) 'Law and Sustainable Development in West Africa: A Case Study of the Petroleum Industry in Nigeria', PhD thesis, Faculty of Law, McGill University (Montreal, Quebec).

McIntosh, M., Leipziger, D., Jones, K. and Coleman, G. (1998) *Corporate Citizenship: Successful Strategies for Responsible Companies* (London: Financial Times).

McKnight, J. (1995) *The Careless Society: Community and its Counterfeits* (New York: Basic Books).

Moser, G., Rogers, S. and Til, R. van with Kiblake, R. and Lukonga, I. (1997) *Nigeria: Experience with Structural Adjustment* (Washington, DC: The International Monetary Fund).

Okonto, I. and Douglas, O. (2001) *Where Vultures Feast: Shell, Human Rights, and Oil in the Niger Delta* (San Francisco: Sierra Club Books).

Paine, L. S. and Moldoveanu, M. (1999) 'Royal Dutch/Shell in Nigeria' Harvard Business School Cases N9-399-126; N9-399-127 (Boston: Harvard Business School Press), pp. 1–27, 1–2.

Putnam, R. D. (1993) *Making Democracy Work: Civic Traditions in Modern Italy* (Princeton University Press).

Royal Dutch/Shell Group (1998) *Profits and Principles – Does there Have To Be a Choice? The Shell Report 1998.*

Royal Dutch/Shell Group (1999) *People, Planet, and Profits: An Act of Commitment: The Shell Report 1999.*

Royal Dutch/Shell Group (2000) *How Do We Stand? People, Planet, Profits: The Shell Report 2000.*

Royal Dutch/Shell Group (2001) *People, Planet and Profits: The Shell Report 2001.*

Sagawa, S. and Segal, E. (2000) *Common Interest, Common Good: Creating Value Through Business and Social Sector Partnerships* (Boston: Harvard Business School Press).

Shankleman, J. and Fossgard-Moser, T. (2002) 'Athabasca Oil Sands Project (Muskeg River Mine): 2001 Social Performance Baseline Review' (London: Shell International).

SPDC (1997) Shell Petroleum Development Company of Nigeria Limited, *Ogoni and the Niger Delta* (Lagos, Nigeria).

SPDC (1998) Shell Petroleum Development Company of Nigeria Limited, *People and the Environment* (Lagos, Nigeria).

SPDC (1999) Shell Petroleum Development Company of Nigeria Limited, *People and the Environment Annual Report* (Lagos, Nigeria).

SPDC (2002a) Shell Petroleum and Development Company of Nigeria Limited, 'Proceedings of the SPDC Integrated Environment and Community Development Stakeholders' Workshop' (Lagos, Nigeria).

SPDC (2002b) Shell Petroleum Development Company of Nigeria Limited, *People and the Environment Annual Report 2001* (Lagos, Nigeria).

Soyinka, W. (1996) *The Open Sore of a Continent: A Personal Narrative of the Nigerian Crisis* (New York: Oxford University Press).

Wiwa, K. (2000) *In the Shadow of a Saint; A Son's Journey to Understand His Father's Legacy* (Toronto: Vintage Canada).

3
A Political and Economic History of Ghana, 1957–2003

Bill Buenar Puplampu

Introduction

Ghana lies along the Gulf of Guinea in West Africa. It has a population of about 20 million in 10 administrative regions. The capital is Accra, with population of about 2 million. The country is named after the old West African Empire of that name which flourished some 600 miles north. The 250-mile-long coastline is dotted with more than 100 castles and forts, testifying to a long history of Western interest and involvement. The first Europeans to set foot on the shore, around 1475, were the Portuguese. They built their first castle in 1482 and named the region 'Gold Coast' for the vast quantities of gold they found. They were followed by the Dutch, the Danes, the English and the Swedes. The castles and forts served variously as slave posts, trading posts, army garrisons, colonial residences and territorial markers. By the 1850s, only the Dutch and British were left. When the Dutch withdrew in 1874, the British proceeded to make the Gold Coast a Crown colony. At the time, the Asante were a dominant political and empire force in the central and forest regions of the area. A proud and warlike people steeped in tradition, custom and wealth, the Asante were not subdued easily. The British made friends with more compliant coastal peoples such as the Gas and Fantes. Between 1817 and 1896, several wars, negotiations and treaties between the British and various Asante kings brought the Asantes into partial submission, and their king was exiled to the Seychelles. For the next 50 years, the British enjoyed colonial control, and exploited natural resources such as timber and gold.

By the late 1940s, in the aftermath of the Second World War, the drumbeats for political independence were beginning to sound in the Gold Coast. The country achieved independence in 1957 and was renamed Ghana. Its independence ushered in a wave of other liberations from colonial rule across Africa. It has, however, been spared the aggravated civil strife and socio-economic upheavals that other countries in Africa have suffered. Ghana has never had a civil war as was experienced by Nigeria in the early

1960s and Côte d'Ivoire in 2002–03. It has not experienced the famine of Ethiopia, nor the political strife and upheaval of Kenya or the Democratic Republic of Congo (DRC). But neither has it achieved the economic growth and social-infrastructure development attained by Southeast Asian countries, which attained independence at about the same time.

Ghana's economic development has been disappointing largely because its political development has been uneven. As one observer has put it, any 'economic progress made…hinges on what political solutions can be found – and when' (Games, 2002). Its political and economic experience spans the entire spectrum of African possibilities. The eloquent and charismatic Osagefo Dr Kwame Nkrumah led the country to independence in 1957. His rule, however, degenerated from the euphoria of independence into a highly personalized one-party state under the Convention People's Party (CPP), marked by tight state control of the economy as well as social life. After his overthrow by the military in 1966, Ghana experienced a further four coups d'état (in 1972, 1978, 1979 and 1981), two short-lived attempts at constitutional rule (1969–72 and 1979–81) and a period of greed, corruption and social chaos. The era of military adventurism, dictatorship and constitutional conversion of Flight Lieutenant Jerry Rawlings (1979, 1981–2000) was marked by efforts at economic reform under the watchful eye of the World Bank. Debts in excess of US$6 billion once made Ghana a 'black beast' of international financial institutions, but by the end of the 1990s, Ghana was being paraded by the World Bank as an example of successful 'structural adjustment'. The New Patriotic Party (NPP) assumed power in 2001 through a peaceful election (December 2000), on a platform of 'positive change', free trade, private-sector growth and personal freedoms.

Four major socio-economic periods coincide with the changes in the country's political leadership. A closer look at this turbulent history will demonstrate the major lesson Ghana has learned: that economic reform and prosperity cannot be achieved without attendant political development.

Nkrumah and the Convention People's Party (CPP), 1957–66

At independence in 1957, Ghana was politically inexperienced in statecraft and economically underdeveloped. British colonial rule had not allowed the fundamental organs necessary for institutionalizing democratic life under indigenous leadership to grow. To be sure, there was a significant crop of the educated elite, as well as wealthy traders, cocoa farmers and powerful traditional chiefs. Education was fairly well established (especially in the southern half of the country), due partly to the efforts of missionaries and colonial administrators, as well as Ghanaian social leaders. The country's economy was sustained through exports of cocoa, timber and minerals like gold and diamonds. But it lacked the technical capacity to generate employment, produce new consumer goods and create wealth. In the social sector, health, water and transport services were at a very rudimentary stage. Most roads and railways led to the capital and the port at Takoradi, linking the primary and cash crop producing areas. The vast majority of the Ghanaian population, as well as the greater part of the country's geographical territory, remained underdeveloped. This socio-economic backwardness, coupled with a general sense of the inequities created by the period of colonial domination, created a situation where the post-independence national agenda was dominated by economic emancipation, which was understood to be dependent on industrialization.

Kwame Nkrumah deserves pride of place among African nationalists for his early insistence on the importance of industrial development and economic independence. Nkrumah was a charismatic, visionary idealist, but also knowledgeable and pragmatic enough to operate on the international stage, form alliances, secure funding and advocate Pan-Africanism. He was responsible more than any other individual for popularizing 'neo-colonialism' as the source of independent Africa's troubles and the gap between promise and performance of the new states. Ghana at the time of independence had foreign reserves in excess of 200 million pounds sterling. However, these reserves were quickly whittled away as the euphoric new government sought to implement major capital investment in schools, roads and buildings. It also supported independence movements across Africa. The economy's fragile base in mono-crop trading became unstable with a decline in export earnings, while expected foreign investments did not materialize. The government had to rely heavily on the country's depleted external reserves to finance both imports and development programmes.

The pragmatic Nkrumah quickly realized that the only way forward was to align the country's economy with the fortunes of major Western industrial concerns. The government established state-owned enterprises (SOEs) to control major activities of the economy: finance, procurement, distribution, manufacturing, farming, fishing and basic service. A key effort of the Nkrumah era, which yielded fruit was the direct investment made by the Kaiser Aluminum Corporation of America in building the Akosombo Hydro Electric Dam. Here capitalism converged with development rhetoric. Kaiser was looking for a source of cheap energy and labour for processing bauxite from its Jamaican fields into aluminium. Nkrumah recognized that his drive for industrialization was dependent on energy, whose development the colonial government had neglected completely, despite knowing as early as 1949 that the Volta River was viable for hydroelectric power. After much discussion, the US government under Eisenhower, the Ghana government and Kaiser agreed to fund the building of the Akosombo dam (1961–65), and to the construction of a major bauxite-smelting plant by the Volta Aluminum Company (Valco) at Tema on the Atlantic coast at the Gulf of Guinea.

However, Nkrumah neglected the development of democratic institutions, choosing instead, the machinery of one-party rule to deal with internal problems. Dissent and repression were exacerbated by economic difficulties. By 1965 the economic crisis was rather severe, and the material conditions of the majority of Ghanaians were showing serious signs of deterioration. Nkrumah actively courted political ties with the Soviet Union, and his Soviet-influenced world statesmanship was frowned upon by the United States. His government was overthrown in 1966, and his vision was shattered as he was banished into exile in Guinea. To Nkrumah's credit, however, much of the infrastructure Ghana enjoys today – roads, telephone, railways, harbours and airports, as well as social infrastructure such as schools and hospitals – were laid down during his leadership. But as Baah-Nuakoh (1997) notes, much of the economic progress of the period centred on an artificial industrial drive. There was a gap between the agricultural base, which would provide raw materials and the industrial base using various sophisticated machinery to process goods, a gap which the SOEs did not fill. Despite the profusion of industries, the development of physical infrastructure and the rhetoric of economic independence, Nkrumah's socialist model of economic planning and management failed to deliver.

The wilderness years, 1966–81

The overthrow of Nkrumah's government ushered in a period in which military coups alternated with popularly elected governments seeking to return Ghana to its democratic ideals. In 1966 the army and police constituted the National Liberation Council (NLC), which gave way to the popularly elected government of the Oxford don, Dr Kofi Busia and his Progress Party (PP) in 1969. Both sought to win the confidence of foreign investors – variously by devaluing the currency (1971), realigning internal prices to those prevailing in the world economy, deregulating prices, liberalizing external trade and other monetary measures. They tried to restore the primacy of private enterprise as the engine of development, while attempting to deal with a bloated state sector, state-determined wages and salaries, poorly performing SOEs and state subsidies for consumer goods and social services. These efforts caused the standard of living of Ghanaians to deteriorate further, provoking some of the fiercest battles the state ever had to fight with workers. By 1970, workers were joined by university students and those petty bourgeois who could not cope with the draconian monetary policies.

Due to the political immaturity of the country, popular dissent and discontent were interpreted as reason to change government before the end of its constitutional mandate. Busia's government lasted just two-and-a-half years. It was overthrown on 13 January 1972 by Colonel Ignatius Kutu Acheampong, who established the National Redemption Council (NRC) and declared that Ghana would establish a 'Union Government' of army, police and civilians, pursue self-reliance in agriculture and refuse to pay its foreign debts. For a brief period, Ghana experienced food sufficiency and considerable relief from the crushing and humiliating weight of foreign debt. Donor agencies, governments and international banks accommodated this resurgent economic nationalism and rescheduled debt payments. Acheampong's regime also insisted upon reserving of state partnership in some key foreign-owned enterprises. It also sought collaborations between private Ghanaian capital and foreign investors: for example, the Norwegian conglomerate Scancem/Norcem set up a cement venture named Ghacem Ghana Limited with significant government involvement. As the only cement producer in the country, Ghacem monopolized the market and to this day remains the largest in this region of Africa, despite the arrival of competitors in the past three years.

But overall, the personal weaknesses of Acheampong, the incompetence of the army in conceiving and carrying out political and economic policy, and avaricious profiteering by the merchant class caused significant corruption, lack of national purpose, dwindling foreign investment and economic stresses on the ordinary people. Popular discontent once again led to a palace coup in 1978. General Akuffo, a Sandhurst Military Academy graduate, established a new government. But the moral fibre of Ghanaian society had been severely compromised by greedy army officials, corrupt civil servants and traders who profited from selling hoarded goods. Shops were empty; prices were high; nepotism, favouritism and sycophancy reigned as the only established means of personal progress and economic security.

This boiling pot of economic and social decadence produced a fourth military uprising. On 4 June 1979 – a date burned on the political consciousness of Ghanaians – people woke up to hear a terse and angry voice on the radio, declaring that 'the ranks have taken over'. The charismatic young Flight Lieutenant Jerry John Rawlings, half-Scottish and half-Ghanaian, led the junior ranks of the army in establishing the Armed Forces Revolution Council (AFRC). The AFRC proceeded to inject a sense of moral rectitude into Ghanaian society by appropriating assets presumed to have been acquired by dubious means. Newly established tribunals required people to account for their wealth. A number of high army officers who had served in previous military governments were tried and summarily executed on charges of corruption. The AFRC lifted the ban on political activity and several parties were formed. The period of June–September 1979 was marked by extreme stress produced by uncertainty, internal military activity, public floggings and renewed party political activity.

Elections were held in August and in September 1979. Rawlings' AFRC ceded power to Dr Hilla Limann's People's National Party (PNP) – but with the threat to return if the country again became unstable. The constitutionally elected civilian government tried in vain for two years to grapple with demands for employment, a living wage, housing, education, health services and other improvements in the midst of a chaotic social order.

The PNP was dominated by the professional politicians, traders and other merchants who had been deprived of their livings through the long years of military rule. They set about enriching themselves while grappling with political and economic chaos. At the end of 1981, Rawlings and his 'boys' fulfilled their promise to return.

From 1966 to 1981, little real economic progress was made. The two civilian regimes were so short-lived that they were unable to achieve anything of substance. The five military regimes, for their part, lacked the economic and social strategy by which to launch the country into economic progress. According to Baah-Nuakoh (1997), the economic models of the time mixed centralized planning and capitalism. Damachi (1976) describes this mix as a confused implementation of 'socialism-capitalism', 'undistorted capitalism' and 'self-reliance'. Because the political atmosphere was so adversarial, each successive government sought to do away with its predecessor's achievements. Economic planning therefore followed a very inconsistent pattern and economic infrastructure development was severely limited. Various attempts were made to privatize state farms and industries, reduce government subsidies for university education and privatize medical practice. Many of the SOEs set up by Nkrumah became moribund, as workers were not paid for long periods. A blueprint for sewage system for the whole country was designed but never implemented. Price controls were eliminated and reintroduced. External economic factors also contributed to Ghana's woes. By 1974, the depression in advanced economies produced by the global oil crisis reduced the demand for Ghana's primary products of cocoa, timber, bauxite and gold. Inflation spiralled upward to 73 per cent by 1978 (Baah-Nuakoh, 1997).

The Rawlings era, 1982–2000

In December 1981, Flight Lieutenant J. J. Rawlings took control once again. His Provisional National Defence Council (PNDC) was received by Ghana's underclass as a populist response to the national crises of the previous decades, one, which would pave the way for a restored democratic order. By the close of 1984, however, it had become clear that the regime was digging in. The PNDC insisted that a sound economic base needed to be established before thought could be given to democracy based on a multi-party system. The PNDC was resented and resisted by lawyers, students, some journalists, political pundits and the Catholic Secretariat. The PNDC responded by fostering an atmosphere of intimidation, suspicion and fear. At the same time, it set about to implement a serious programme of economic reform, which was sorely needed. There was excess money supply, with inflation running upwards of 90 per cent; corruption was rampant and foreign exchange reserves were depleted. Rawlings at first sought to impose price controls, rationing and a socialist path of centralized development. In early 1983, the government confiscated all large-denomination ¢ (cedi) notes in order to reduce the bloated money supply. The government also engaged in strident anti-western rhetoric. But these drastic measures failed; they produced even higher inflation, and more queues for medicine, food and transportation.

The Rawlings administration changed its economic strategy in late 1983. It adopted economic reform and structural adjustment programmes proposed by the World Bank. This laudable micro- and macro-economic programme included deregulation, privatization, restructuring of the financial and non-bank system, civil service reforms and a gradual return to constitutional rule through District Assembly elections in 1988. Given the PNDC's abysmal human rights record and Rawlings's personal lack of patience with the democratic sentiments of many Ghanaians, this partial return to democracy is believed by some to have been forced on the Rawlings regime by the World Bank.

Rawlings and the PNDC succeeded in restoring sound economic management and a measure of political stability. By the late 1980s, the World Bank was lauding Ghana as a successful example of structural adjustment. But by 1990–91, many Ghanaians, the donor community and even members of the government recognized that the PNDC could not hold on to power in its pseudo military form. Rawlings, known by now as the 'benevolent dictator', decided to constitutionalize his rule by forming a political party and submitting to popular elections. A new constitution was approved by referendum in early 1992, and Presidential and parliamentary elections were held at the end of the year. The election was boycotted by the opposition, and won by Rawlings' National Democratic Congress (NDC). Nonetheless, the election gave birth to Ghana's fourth Republic – an important landmark in the country's successive attempts to institutionalize a democratic order. In 1996, another election returned the NDC to power, albeit with a much-reduced parliamentary majority.

The Rawlings era brought a degree of political stability, which fostered slow but certain socio-economic development. Deregulation of the financial system in 1990–95 opened up the economy to banking, insurance and other financial-service providers. A first ATM card system was introduced. Artificial controls on foreign currency trading were lifted and the cedi floated freely. From 1989 on, the government began to divest more than three hundred SOEs (DIC, 1999). International businesses purchased many of these SOEs, and the government earned more than ¢900 billion (about US$110 million). For example, the Anglo-Belgian AFGO Group took over cargo-handling at Ghana's International Airport. Carson Hair Products (French) established itself in Accra, while Gafco, a Belgian firm, bought a food-processing SOE. From this process was born Ghana's only multinational business – Ashanti Goldfields. Its sale brought in much needed foreign capital. Through the 1990s, Ashanti expanded into Guinea Bissau and Tanzania, and has become perhaps the largest gold-mining firm outside South Africa.

The Ghanaian government retains 20 per cent ownership as a way of retaining involvement and the Ghanaian character of the enterprise. Meanwhile, donor inflows funded a number of major building and road construction projects. In one significant move, the Rawlings government opened up the ports and skies of Ghana to free trade in 1996. The ports at Tema and Takoradi were modernized in an ongoing process of renewal. These initiatives notwithstanding, the NDC by 1999 seemed to have lost its grip on economic management.

Major economic indicators fell short. GDP grew only by 5 per cent per year in 1995 and 1996. The money supply grew by 34 per cent – far beyond the target of 5 per cent. Inflation was running at almost 38 per cent, rather than a predicted 20 per cent. The national budget and balance of payments were running deficits rather than surpluses. And despite major efforts at reforming the health and educational sectors, Ghana still lacked major hospitals and schools. Eighteen years after Rawlings' reforms began, basic social indicators such as infant and maternal mortality, educational enrolment, literacy and poverty levels still came in well below international standards (ISSER, 2001).

The NPP and Kufuor, 2000–03

By late 1999, Ghana's economy was in serious trouble. Its position as the world's leading producer of cocoa was lost to neighbouring Côte d'Ivoire. By the end of 2000, the cedi had depreciated by over 100 per cent. Rising oil prices and lower revenues from exports harmed private investment and household necessities. Rawlings' administration, weakened politically by corruption, submitted to the multiparty democracy of the ballot box. Elections were held at the end of 2000, and voters heeded the call for 'positive change' preached by the New Patriotic Party (NPP). Led by John Agyekum Kufuor, a lawyer, the NPP took power in a smooth transition. For the first time in Ghana, one elected administration took over from another elected administration.

The NPP draws its ideological roots from the Progress Party tradition of Dr Busia. This tradition espouses free trade, private sector growth, liberal economies and strong democratic institutionalization based on freedom of speech, religion and association. The new government has sought to stabilize the economic environment through sound microeconomic management, macroeconomic targets and other encouraging policy initiatives. The clearest evidence of its efforts so far can be seen from the relatively stable exchange rate. President Kufuor has launched initiatives to develop cassava, textiles and garments and information technology through the private sector. In 2002, a new Bank Act granted a significant measure of autonomy to the Central Bank. Corporate tax law was changed somewhat in 2000, and while the government imposed a 'national reconstruction' levy on major companies, it may reconsider this new tax. The President has travelled widely, to persuade international businesses in Europe, the United States and Asia that Ghana is a stable, peaceful and free country, safe for direct investment. The government recently published a glossy book setting out its achievements in development of real infrastructure and economic stability (Ghana Ministry of Information, 2002). The judicial system has been upgraded with a fast track system to ensure the expeditious rule of law.

Conclusions: reflections on Ghana's political–economic history and nationhood

The four eras described above suggest that Ghana has perhaps experienced the full range of African political and economic possibilities. Despite the turbulence of its uneven political development, Ghana has been able to avoid the major civil strife and socio-economic upheavals that have afflicted other African nations since independence. Five factors, some perhaps unique to Ghana, help explain this moderate history. First, Ghana's people are not tribally polarized; tribal affiliation does not confer automatic rights to political power. To be sure, there has been some tribally based civil strife. The mid-1990s have seen serious clashes between the Kunkumba and Nanumba peoples in the North over land and cattle grazing rights. More recently, in March 2002, a chieftaincy dispute led to the murder of a sitting chief, also in the North. But the nation as a whole is not polarized; the Akan majority (about 42 per cent) has not laid claim to political power by virtue of their numbers. Since the independence struggles of the 1940s and 1950s, all the main political parties in the Gold Coast/Ghana have had a broad base, rather than reflecting a purely ethnic divide, as in Rwanda or Burundi. Second, the traditional authority residing in the institution of chieftaincy derives more from control of land and traditional respect than from financial clout and political control. The chiefs therefore have tended to act as a unifying force. Third, anecdotal evidence suggests that Ghanaians tend to intermarry among tribes and clans (Assimeng, 1990). The boarding secondary schools set up throughout the country by missionaries and successive governments have served as social melting pots where many Ghanaians make lifelong friends and associations from all parts of the country. Fourth, the country's most valued resource, cocoa, is not controlled by the government or any one group. It is grown in the forest zones of the Volta, Eastern, Ashanti, Central, Brong Ahafo and Western Regions in family holdings, which vary greatly in size. Fifth, religion has not been a divisive force at the national level, partly because religious affiliations are not confined to specific geographic areas. While the North is typically Muslim, it has a significant Catholic population and an increasing Protestant/Charismatic following. And even though the rest of Ghana is largely Christian, nearly every city and town has its 'zongo' – the Muslim quarter typically inhabited by people of northern descent.

For these and perhaps other reasons, Ghana has developed more as a cohesive African nation than many others. But cohesion alone does not make for development. As Games put it, political solutions are critical for national development. This notion is critical to development in Ghana and in Africa generally. Economic progress, involvement of international business and social development cannot be discussed or envisaged outside of political progress and stability. Ghana has traversed, politically speaking, from one form of governance to another, and only recently has ballot-box democracy gained the ascendancy. Still, the prospects for Ghana's development remain precarious in large part because its economy remains dominated by the export of primary products. Cocoa, timber, gold and diamonds still account for much of its earnings, rendering its socio-economic development hostage to commodity markets located in Western cities. It is still unable to raise sufficient internal revenue to finance its budget and developmental projects. The country therefore depends precariously on donor inflows to achieve government-spending targets. As recently as 2003, Ghana's budget was nearly thrown out of gear by its failure to secure an International Financial Consortium (IFC) loan of about US$1 billion.

In conclusion, it can be said that despite the vagaries of its political and economic experiences in the 46 years since independence Ghana has considerable potential to grow its economy and achieve stature and standing within the community of nations. It is being lauded now as the one island of stability and peace in a region of chaos and conflict. The country in its role as Chair of the Economic Community of West African States (ECOWAS) has helped broker peace for war-torn Liberia, Côte d'Ivoire and Sierra Leone. These efforts, along with political stability, financial deregulation and a generally peaceable populace, have placed Ghana in a position to attract investor capital from overseas, as evidenced by the keen interest being shown in Ghana's gold mining multinational firm, Ashanti, by South African and Canadian mining giants such as Anglogold and Placer Dome. However, if the experience of the Southeast-Asian tigers (as discussed by Hill, 1998) is anything to go by, Ghana must work on and consolidate its political systems. It must fine-tune its approach and philosophy to international business, making sure that its agreements and interactions with foreign firms serve its best interests. It must improve its regulatory business and corporate processes to make both indigenous and foreign business participation hassle-free. It must consolidate the rule of law, build grass-roots democracy through local government agencies and create an environment in which the institutions of state function irrespective of the political party in power. It must seek to generate within itself the wherewithal to raise its own funds for development, and expand its enterprise culture where citizens are keen to build businesses and create wealth – legitimately. Such an enterprise culture can facilitate the diversification of the country's export base, while moving it away from primary produce to value-added manufacturing industry. Ghana must resolutely decide that donor inflows, welcome as they may be, cannot secure development. Development can and will come from stable politics which enable private enterprise, both foreign and local, to flourish.

References

Assimeng, M. (1990) *The Social Structure of Ghana* (Tema: Ghana Publishing Corp).

Baah-Nuakoh, A. (1997) *Studies on the Ghanaian Economy*, vol. 1 (Accra: Ghana Universities Press).

Damachi, U. (1976) 'The Development Path in Ghana', in U. Damachi *et al.* (eds), *Development Paths in Africa and China* (London: Macmillan Press).

DIC (1999): Divestiture Implementation Committee *Factsheets* (Accra: Ministry of Information).

Games, D. (2002) 'Holding the Centre', *Business in Africa*, February, pp. 36–41.

Ghana Ministry of Information (2002) *Two Years of Positive Change* (Accra).

Hill, C. W. (1998) *International Business: Competing in the Global Market Place* (Boston: McGraw-Hill).

ISSER (2001): Institute of Statistical, Social and Economic Research *Ghana Human Development Report* (Legon: Ghana University).

4

Capacity Building, Asset Development and Corporate Values: A Study of Three International Firms in Ghana

Bill Buenar Puplampu

Introduction

This chapter examines the operations of three international firms operating in Ghana in order to explain how their actions intersect the developmental aspirations and host-country concerns of Ghana.[1] Our position is that the core values of these firms and the positions they espouse about human and social development greatly influence the way they use the human, social, financial, productive and natural capital Ghana has made available to them. Are these firms engaged in building local capacity, developing local assets, integrating themselves and generally ensuring that they add value to the Ghanaian context – and are *just*? For each of the three companies, this chapter will address four questions particularly sensitive in the Ghanaian context. First, are the firms conducting human resource management and skill development in such a way as to build local capacity? Second, do their governance and management structures involve local people? The use of expatriate managers creates the impression of foreign ownership, domination and concrete ceilings, which cap the progress of local managers. Third, do they integrate their supply chains within the economy of Ghana? Fourth, do they demonstrate social responsibility by providing support for the underprivileged, whether through charity or human resource investments in schools? This chapter will conclude with a number of prescriptive suggestions for international companies doing business in developing areas.

By Ghanaian standards, the three international firms are large. Each has more than one thousand employees (directly or indirectly), as well as extensive linkages, through suppliers and contractors, with several hundreds of thousands more people in nearly all of the 10 administrative regions of Ghana. Perhaps the only comparable Ghanaian-owned organizations are two banks, which each have staffs of over 2500 and operations all over the country. While the three companies studied here have operations centred on the coast, their linkages to Ghanaian society differ markedly. Volta Aluminium (Valco) is centred in the industrial and port city of Tema on the southeast coast. It is important to the power sector throughout the country. It has the most employees, although they are sometimes seasonal. The plants of British American Tobacco, Ghana (BATG) lie in the industrial and port city of Takoradi on the southwest coast, and it has extensive reach into farming communities. Unilever Ghana (Unil) has the highest number of permanent employees. Its factory operations are localized at the city of Tema, and its Swanzey Estates. Plantations and elaborate distributor network give it the largest direct reach throughout Ghana. Valco, BATG and Unilever Ghana Ltd differ in another respect: while Unil faces competition from firms such as PZ and Nestle, Valco and BATG have no real competitors. Still, these three firms operate in a vibrant private enterprise environment where other firms, both local and foreign, compete for human and physical capital, as well as market resources and shares. Their behaviour in terms of treatment of employees, wage and compensation levels and social responsibility often sets the tone for what other companies do.

Unilever Ghana Ltd (Unil)

In Ghana, Unilever had its origins in the United Africa Company (UAC), which began trading in consumer goods in what was then the Gold Coast in 1787. UAC developed further interests in manufacturing, real estate and eventually textile manufacturing. The textile interests were recently sold to the Vlisco Group of Belgium. The umbrella company, Unilever International, was formed in 1930 when the Dutch margarine company Margarine Unie merged with British soap maker Lever Brothers. The companies merged because they were competing for the same raw materials; they were marketing household products on a large scale, and they used similar distribution channels. The newly formed Unilever introduced improved technology to the production and distribution of products such as soaps, margarines, fish, ice cream and canned foods. The business grew and new ventures were launched in Latin America. Today, Unilever NV and Unilever PLC, headquartered in Rotterdam and London, are the parent companies of one of the largest consumer-goods businesses in the world. The entrepreneurial spirit of the founders and their approach towards their employees and communities remain at the heart of Unilever's business. International by design, it is rooted in 90 countries and employs about 306 000 workers worldwide. Despite this size, Unilever aspires to be an integral part of the societies in which it operates. Local companies are run predominantly by local people who understand and are in tune with the needs and values of the communities in which they operate. Unilever considers itself a multi-local multinational. In West Africa, Unilever operates in Ghana, Côte d'Ivoire and Nigeria.

Unil (as Unilever Ghana calls itself) organizes its products in three groups: home care, personal care and foods. It also has an industrial wash business known as Diversey Lever. The company prides itself on innovation and brand creativity. Its home-care products include major brands such as Key Soap (second-largest-selling laundry bar soap in the world), Omo and Sunlight. This category of product accounted for almost 40 per cent of sales in 2000, in large part due to the re-launch of Key Soap with better perfume and enhanced washing abilities. Personal-care products include brands like Pepsodent, Sweetie (a bath soap) and Rexona Deo Stick deodorant. The sales volume of these products grew 27 per cent in 2001, due to innovation and pricing strategy. Unil introduced Pepsodent in a new, powdered form, which enabled it to make greater inroads into the rural areas. Ten million cakes of Sweetie were sold in its first 12 months, for about US 10 cents each. Similarly, Rexona Deo Stick was introduced in 2001 as the first affordable deodorants on the market; more than one million units were sold within the first two months. The foods category saw a growth in volume of over 30 per cent in 2001, and contributed 32 per cent of the group's operating profit. Frytol, its brand of cooking oil, achieved significant growth through the launch of a new theme-based ad campaign and the fortification of Frytol with Vitamin A. Unil effectively dominates the fast-moving consumer goods market. Anecdotal evidence suggests that one in every three television ads features a Unil product.

Unil's governance and local involvement

Unil has six functional departments: Finance, Marketing, Customer Service, Supply Chain, Human Resources and Plantations. An executive director heads each. Unil is governed by a board and an executive committee (Exco) in which Ghanaians are well represented. The board chairman, at least two of the executive directors and the three non-executive directors are Ghanaian. Exco, consisting of the chair and executive directors, is the executive arm of Unil. It takes major decisions affecting the conduct of the business and the company's relations with the outside world. Unil runs a generally open and inclusive governance system. Exco is unashamedly bullish in its focus on working for the benefit of the company. There are over 90 Ghanaians in three levels of management (Work Levels 1–3). All levels of managers (from WL1–3) have access to the board and its chair. They are grilled on various managerial activities and initiatives. They are involved in all aspects of the managerial function, from planning and coordination to leading major projects such as product design and launch. The culture is that of a high-pressure professional environment in which one has to learn to speak up to be heard. Perhaps as testimony to the success of this approach, the Ghanaian chairman was recently assigned to oversee all the national operations in West Africa. The Ghanaian operation is also much valued and respected in the global Unilever world.

Unil currently has six expatriates as managers and directors: two Nigerians, and one each from Sweden, Zimbabwe, Britain and Belgium. Unilever has always had expatriate staff, which is indicative of its multinational character. Unil has taken a unique approach to compensating expatriates. Other companies typically view compensation from home base, enhancing the expatriate's home salary and adding a range of benefits such as school fees for children. Unil expatriates, in contrast, are given the same basic salaries as their local equivalents receive, and are at par with locals in terms of benefits; for example, an expatriate director receives the same car as a Ghanaian director. But the expatriates are compensated additionally for moving out of their home countries. Moreover, the reasons for rotating expatriates into Ghana differ. For a number of international firms, expatriate presence is used as a control mechanism (Puplampu, 1993, 1995a). For Unilever, control does not seem to be the key issue. Expatriates are posted to Unil as part of global staff internationalization processes, just as Ghanaians get posted to countries such as India, Malaysia and the United Kingdom. Where control is the dominant ethic, expatriates almost always hold senior positions. This is clearly not the case with Unil, where day-to-day responsibility is exercised by senior managers who are nearly all Ghanaians.

Unil's human resource management

Unil employs about 90 managerial staff in a workforce of about 800 (about 1300 if contract and distal workers are included). Both managers and workers are made to feel responsible for the performance and reputation of the company. They experience relentless demands to meet a set of 'high-pressure' performance requirements in which excuses for non-delivery are severely frowned upon. Strict adherence to company codes is required. Some managers and workers complain that the environment is 'stressful'; others acknowledge they have no choice but to work hard because the consumer goods market is fast moving. Any lapses might cost the company dearly in volume and market share. Innovation is encouraged, but some employees feel it is not rewarded sufficiently. In some respects, Unil is rigorously fair. Company policy is to recruit, employ and promote employees on the sole basis of expertise, qualifications and abilities needed for the work to be performed. In addition, Unil ensures safe and healthy working conditions for all employees. Its factory has a medical doctor (who is also responsible for all sites). The factory environment is visibly clean, with safety markings separating vehicular access from pedestrian access and walkways. Unil has a continuous programme to enhance the teamwork, communication, feedback and skills of all employees. This is not to suggest that Unil is without problems. In 2002, workers went on strike for higher wages. The strike was resolved and workers returned to work. Unil uses contract workers at some of its packing plants, and it is not uncommon for regular workers to strike in solidarity with contract workers who may be having difficulties with their agency.

Unil is perhaps second to none in Ghana with its focus on employee development. Its Human Resource (HR) department is clearly distinguished from other functions in the organization and headed by an executive director. Usually in Ghana, HR is subsumed under 'Finance & Administration', an arrangement that tends to lead to the unsystematic management of people. Unil, in contrast, has clear policies for recruitment, retention, development and performance management. It has procedural manuals derived from policy and experience, which guide human-resource operations. It has a dedicated training facility separate from the factory, complete with training rooms, restaurant, lounge and a training administrator. Its training programmes are so well known nationally that any Unil-trained manager is snapped up eagerly by other organizations. The Unilever recruitment and selection model, which uses competency assessments, is also very well known. There is anecdotal evidence that some organizations wait to interview any candidate who has been through the final stage of Unil recruitment, since such candidates will have been exposed to the highest corporate standards.

According to current strategic human resource management trends (Kamoche, 1996), the human resource function should be represented at the highest echelons and allowed input into strategic and policy decisions. This is the case with Unil. This results from a value system that sees people as key – as attested by human resource officers at Unil and other organizations in Ghana. There is a real drive at Unilever Ghana to search for and influence the development of Ghanaian managerial talent. It works closely with academics at the country's premier university to bring corporate requirements to bear on teaching and learning at the university level. Indeed, the forward-looking Executive Chairman of Unil, Dr Ishmael E. Yamson, is also the Chairman of the Council of the University of Ghana.

Unil's rootedness in the local economy

Unil is the largest producer and distributor of 'fast-moving consumer goods' in Ghana. In 2001 it paid about US$3.3 million in taxes (UNIL, 2001, p. 29). Unil, which is listed on the Ghana Stock Exchange, has integrated itself into the Ghanaian economy by attempting to establish mutually beneficial relations with its suppliers, customers and business partners. It makes extensive use of local consulting firms in areas such as management development and recruitment. It draws upon small-scale local entrepreneurs, such as a third-party manufacturer who makes the Annapurna iodized salt under the Unil label. It makes extensive use of local truck and haulage firms for distribution of all its products. The packaging used is mostly made in Ghana. Its warehouses are rented from local contractors. All its key distributors are Ghanaian. These distributors receive awards from the company at annual ceremonies, where those who expand Unil's markets receive considerable rewards. In 2002, the media reported prizes including double-cabin pick-up trucks, or cash prizes greater than US$5000. In a developing country, such rewards serve as significant motivators.

Unil sources most of its major raw material, palm oil, from plantations in the country. Unil owns the Twifo Oil Palm Plantation Limited (TOPP), and has controlling interests in Benso Oil Palm Plantations Ltd. Apart from their obvious commercial advantages, these plantations are a means to develop rural areas and provide income-generating opportunities for the rural folk. An out-grower scheme ensures that apart from the plantations, rural folk with their own oil palm farms have a ready market for their good produce. In short, Unil's philosophy of securing its essential raw materials from Ghana's rural communities has yielded fruit – it has now achieved full back-ward integration into this key raw material base and has thus contributed significantly to development and income generation of many rural areas of Ghana's Western Region.

Unil's corporate citizenship

At the heart of Unil's approach to doing business is the drive to serve con-sumers in a unique and effective way. The company's purpose is to meet the everyday needs of people everywhere, anticipate the aspirations of its cus-tomers and respond creatively and competitively with branded products and services, which raise the quality of life. In the words of one Human Resource Director, 'We are a humble organisation producing everyday things for everyday people'. For example, Unil has worked with UNICEF, Ghana's Ministry of Health and other governmental agencies to raise awareness of iodine deficiency disorders. The company has championed eradication of these disorders through consumption of Annapurna Iodised Salt. Unil increased supplies by upgrading the refineries of its third-party salt proces-sors and installing automatic packing machines. Annapurna Salt, now clearly visible in urban open-air markets, generated sales of about US$1 mil-lion in 2001. Unil's definition of being a successful business involves achiev-ing growth by balancing short- and long-term interests. For example, Unil is committed to brands and production processes that have a low negative impact on the environment. This standard challenges the company to con-tinuously improve the environmental performance of its manufacturing process.

Unil has established an atmosphere in which it is known as a trusted cor-porate citizen and an integral part of society. It is committed to developing the human resources of Ghana. In 2001, for example, its corporate founda-tion spent US$110000 on scholarships for 60 senior secondary school stu-dents, 12 university undergraduates and two postgraduate students for studies in the United Kingdom. It funds chairs at the country's three premier universities. It recognized the 16 best graduating students from the public universities and polytechnics. It organized a two-day entrepreneurial workshop for small-scale entrepreneurs to upgrade their skills. As part of a comprehensive HIV/AIDS communication programme it appointed 75 peer group counsellors to work in their communities, especially in the rural areas where Unil has its plantations. It has teamed up with a local NGO to develop a workplace HIV/AIDS programme. Recently, workers, management, directors as well as the Chairman marched in the city of Tema, to raise awareness of AIDS. On a lighter note, Unil sponsors entertainment programmes, which appeal to both urban and rural dwellers, all the while promoting its products. The most popular of these is the 'Key Soap Concert Party', which takes place every week at the Accra National Theatre and which has provided employment for many local stand-up comedians and drama groups. Unil's Annapurna Salt is linked to its campaigns with UNICEF and the Ministry of Health to raise awareness about iodine deficiency. It is not surprising therefore, that in a recent Corporate Image Survey commissioned by a Norwegian/German firm in Ghana, Unil came out at the top of a group of seven major companies in Ghana (*PsyconH.R*, 2002).

What seems to account for Unil's approach to business in Ghana? The company is driven by a clearly articulated philosophy. Its first responsibility is to the success of the business, to deliver superior returns to its shareholders and employees. To this end, it demands that all employees attain a high level of effectiveness. Its second responsibility – subordinate to the first – is to the community. It feels that it must meet the everyday needs of people with a range of affordable and innovative products; its products and practices must have low negative environmental impact; it must care about its employees, business partners and must show proactive community involvement. These are the values articulated at various forums by the Chairman, the directors who were interviewed, as well as by Unil managers. Unil is unequivocally committed to maintaining competitive advantage by keeping its products innovative and affordable; by developing its employees' job skills; by recruiting and grooming local staff for full involvement in the Ghanaian economy, and for being among the very best in Unilever's global setting.

Volta Aluminium Company Ltd (Valco)

Volta Aluminium Company Ltd, widely known as Valco, is the world's largest producer of primary aluminium. It is located in Tema, a port city on the southeast coast of Ghana. Valco is owned by Kaiser Aluminum (90 per cent) and Reynolds Metals Company (10 per cent). It processes bauxite into aluminium ingots; 200 000 tons of ingots are produced annually. Some 90 per cent are exported to Europe and the Americas, while 10 per cent are supplied to Ghanaian customers. Aluminium processing is a power-intensive industry. Electric power is provided by Ghana's Volta River Authority (VRA) hydroelectric dam situated at Akosombo, some 70 kilometres northeast of Accra, the capital. At peak strength, Valco's workforce numbers about 1300.

From 1949 to 1956, the then Gold Coast colonial government explored how to develop the Volta River, which stretches some 350 kilometres from its source in the northwest of the country to the estuary at Ada in the southeast. In 1953 a commission was established to harness the hydroelectric power of the river. By this time, the Gold Coast had a government with an African majority, and by 1956, when the commission recommended construction of a dam Ghana was in the process of becoming independent. Even after independence in 1957 the fate of the project was still uncertain because of the cost – US$350 million. By 1958, Ghana's electric power company was generating only 35 megawatts, not enough to serve Ghana's residential, commercial and industrial needs. President Kwame Nkrumah wanted his country to industrialize, but needed the guarantee of a large consumer of electricity to attract financing for a dam and hydroelectric project at Akosombo. Kaiser Aluminum, with huge bauxite deposits in the West Indies, wanted to locate a processing plant where both power and labour could be obtained cheaply.

Dr Nkrumah raised the issue with US President Dwight D. Eisenhower during an official visit to the United States in July 1958. As a result of their talks, a US firm of consulting engineers, the Henry J. Kaiser Company, was commissioned to reassess the project. It recommended that the aluminium smelter be built at Tema, 18 kilometres east of Accra, and on the coast by the fast-growing port rather than further inland, as originally proposed. They also recommended that processed bauxite, or aluminium oxide (alumina), should be imported until revenue made it possible to mine and refine the local bauxite. Finally, Kaiser recommended that a 500-mile network of electrical transmission lines should be installed, covering the whole of southern Ghana. While this report gave impetus to the project, Ghana could not provide the needed financing until Kaiser made a commitment to purchase, in dollars, at least 300 megawatts of electric generating capacity. The Ghana government provided a written promise that the smelter would not be expropriated and exempted the company, henceforth to be known as Valco, from duties and taxes on imports and exports. The Valco shareholders contributed about 10 per cent of the initial cost, with the Export–Import Bank contributing about 25 per cent and the Ghana Government 65 per cent in the form of international loans. Construction of the dam started in early in 1963. Ghana set up the VRA to operate the Akosombo Dam. By 1965, hydroelectricity started flowing through the power lines. The VRA sells power to Valco and the Electricity Company of Ghana (ECG) and mines such as Ashanti Goldfields. Commercial production of smelted aluminium started at Valco in 1967; the smelter was enlarged in 1970 and again in 1974.

Kaiser and Reynolds, both of the United States, supply aluminium oxide to Valco for processing into aluminium. Valco is paid a fee for the processing, a fee determined by a long-range contract. The aluminium produced by Valco belongs to Kaiser and Reynolds and is sold according to their wishes. About 10 per cent of the aluminium produced each year is sold to Ghana's

Minerals Commission, which in turn supplies the local users. Not only does this locally sourced aluminium save Ghana over US$20 million in foreign exchange each year, but it also supports a vibrant local industry, which has grown on the back of Valco's processing. Companies such as Aluworks, Pioneer Aluminium Company, Wire Weaving Industries, Naco Louvre Frames and Eastern Aluminium Company produce cooking pots, roofing sheets and other such items for sales of US$50 million per year. Instead of having to import aluminium, these firms buy from Valco through Ghana's Minerals Commission (MINCOM), an umbrella regulatory agency that oversees the sale and export of various metals and minerals in and out of Ghana. MINCOM operates much like Ghana's Cocoa Board, which also oversees the purchase, sale and export of cocoa beans in and out of Ghana.

Valco's governance and local involvement

Valco's local presence has changed in two major ways over the past two decades. Valco management and governance structures have been indigenized, and the enclave mentality created by expatriates has been reduced. About 99.3 per cent of Valco's workforce is Ghanaian. Until 15 years ago, expatriates dominated its operations. The changes have been progressive and drastic. Until the late 1980s resident directors tended to be Americans; the current director is a Ghanaian economist, Dr Charles Mensah. The number of expatriates in various management and technical positions peaked at 200, and has declined to only 12 among a total managerial staff of some 220 today. This process of gradual replacement has been achieved in large measure by hiring engineering and physical-science graduates from the country's Kwame Nkrumah University of Science and Technology. Corporate values have played a role; Valco believes in technology transfer to enable Ghanaians run the company. Another factor is relevant: an expatriate presence, over time, is expensive to maintain. Valco found that it is cost-effective to reduce expatriate numbers, thus keeping personnel costs down.

Also during the past 15 years, the enclave character of Valco's presence in Ghana has been reduced. Until the late 1980s expatriates lived in clearly identifiable flats and bungalows in specific areas or sections of the Tema municipality. They had their own clinic and sports club. Their apartments were distinctly different, modern and well laid out. They also drove identifiable cars, which tended to be imported and registered at about the same time. American expatriates drove around town in characteristic baseball caps. By now, the drastic reduction in the number of expatriates has helped reduce this enclave atmosphere. Many of the flats have been sold and now house affluent Ghanaians. Ghanaian managers of equivalent standing have the same benefits, for example, including the same cars as expatriates. The baseball caps are not as conspicuous as before.

There are clear reasons for the current crop of expatriates in managerial, technical and directorship positions: they are brought in for their expertise, and to protect foreign stakeholder value. Valco puts its mainly American expatriates through a significant orientation process before they leave the United States. Any expatriate who does not show the capacity to adjust – to operate within the laws of Ghana, to stay out of local politics, to be professional in their dealings with Ghanaian employees and to be good corporate citizens – is not sent on to Ghana. Despite such sensitivity, one significant inequity remains. Valco differs from Unilever in its approach to expatriate compensation. Since expatriates are recruited on the American job market, their salaries are pegged at the equivalent American level; and this creates a considerable disparity with the local managerial pay scales.

Valco's human resource management and rootedness in the local economy

Valco has a Human Resource Department, with units responsible for personnel, industrial relations (IR), compensation and other matters. It organizes training and development for staff. Every employee has 20–30 hours of training a year. This training includes on-the-job skill reviews, management development and in some instances sponsored courses. A number of Ghanaian Valco engineers who have reached managerial level are pursuing an executive MBA programme at the University of Ghana's School of Administration with corporate support.

Valco has become increasingly rooted in the local economy. Since 1998, Valco has used local contractors in its operations. It has divested most of its support services, including transportation, laundry and catering to local suppliers. Through its annual purchases of about US$1 million, it has created a huge market potential for local suppliers. For example, Kingdom Transport Services (KTS), a well-known intercity bus company, has seen considerable growth since it bought out Valco's bussing operations. KTS now takes workers to and from the factory, and has expanded its intercity transport network. In 1998, Valco lent its expertise to the VRA, to bring an energy crisis under control.

Valco is somewhat integrated into the Ghanaian economy at the back end. While it secures its raw material from the Caribbean, it purchases locally generated hydro power. The terms of this exchange have tightened over the years, reflecting an integration that was somewhat disadvantageous to Ghana. In 1985 the Government of Ghana under Jerry Rawlings demanded to renegotiate the tariffs Valco was paying to VRA. These tariffs, negotiated when the dam was built in 1965, were increasingly seen as uncompetitive. Further, the VRA was strapped for cash just as the Akosombo Dam was approaching retrofit stage – a process known in energy circles to be quite expensive. Professor Akilakpa Sawyer, then Vice-Chancellor of the University of Ghana, led Ghana's negotiation team. In the end, these negotiations led to upward adjustments of Valco's power tariff by as much as 30 per cent. Since 2000 there have been further efforts to renegotiate the tariff. These have been unsuccessful, since the Akosombo Dam has suffered from persistently low levels of water due to low and erratic rainfall patterns since the late 1980s. In May 2003, for example, Valco was facing the possibility of shutting down since the hydro power situation was so precarious.

Valco's corporate citizenship

The contribution of Valco to the economy of Ghana has been enormous. As of 1997, Valco had injected more than US$1 billion into the economy through 30 years of taxes and payments. According to its resident director, Valco is the largest corporate taxpayer in the country; its tax bill runs 10 per cent higher than the taxes paid by both Unil and Ashanti Goldfields Company, Ghana's sole multinational. Valco also has paid more than US$700 million to the VRA since 1967. During the past 35 years, the fortunes of Ghana and Valco have been intertwined through the Akosombo Dam.

Valco also has contributed more than US$43 million through the Valco Fund to support educational, medical and other social-economic projects of benefit to Ghanaians. Recent projects include equipment for Korle-bu Teaching Hospital and the University of Ghana Medical School; buses, scientific equipment and textbooks for educational institutions; a hostel for the School of Medical Sciences; and a Postgraduate Block for University of Ghana in Legon. US$20 000 is given to each of the country's three main universities annually. Valco also has a scholarship programme for children of Tema, Manhean and Kpone, three communities next to its smelter. It organizes annual training programmes for teachers of Technical Schools and Polytechnics. So far, more than 70 teachers have benefited from a programme aimed at improving the technical and human resource base in the country. Valco also provides grants to promote inter-schools and colleges soccer to unearth talents for the national football teams. Finally, Valco is environmentally sensitive. It has treatment plants to process both solid and liquid waste. An in-house environmentalist monitors the impact of waste disposed into the Tema environment, and Valco collaborates closely with the Ghanaian EPA.

All of these activities reflect Valco's basic corporate values. Valco believes in protecting and obtaining value for money for its stakeholders' investments, but also extends its sense of responsibility to other shareholders. Valco believes it is fair to expect an international firm to pay realistic and competitive wages to its local employees. It believes that its involvement in the community should not create a culture of dependency. It believes that it should be an environmentally friendly organization, but – given its experiences and initiatives – these wider commitments seem more tenuous than at either Unil or BATG.

British American Tobacco, Ghana Ltd (BATG)

The international British American Tobacco Company Ltd (BAT) registered its Pioneer Tobacco Company (PTC) subsidiary in the Gold Coast in 1952, well before independence. The next year, work started on a factory building at the industrial port city of Takoradi on the southeast coast and production of the first cigarette brand, 'Tusker', commenced in 1954. This enterprise very quickly made Ghana self-sufficient in cigarette manufacture. It still has no competitors in terms of local production of cigarettes. Disparities in wholesale excise duties on cigarettes between Ghana and neighbouring countries such as Togo and Côte d'Ivoire have resulted in cross-border smuggling of cigarettes into Ghana. BAT Ghana used to export to Sierra Leone, but the political situation there led to a down turn. The headquarters moved from Takoradi to Accra in 1959 to be closer to the financial and governmental nerve centres of the country. Factory operations continued in Takoradi. PTC was renamed BAT Ghana in 1999. The international BAT group originally owned the company in entirety. However, the ownership structure has changed. Today, BAT International owns 46 per cent of the shares. The rest is divided between a variety of corporate and individual shareholders including Unilever Provident and Managers Trust Funds, Ghana's Social Security and National Insurance Trust, Ghana Re and others.

BAT Ghana's main business is the production of finished cigarettes, as well as the export of processed leaf. Its brands currently include Rothmans King Size, Diplomat, London Menthol and London Filter. Its factory remains in Takoradi, Ghana's second-largest but older port city. It has leaf stations, or tobacco growing farms, in several districts and towns in the central, western, Brong Ahafo, Volta and northern regions of Ghana. With gross sales of about US$34 million in 2001, the company paid taxes in excess of US$15 million, estimated to be 2.5 per cent of total government tax revenue. The company's own data suggest it has contributed 10–34 per cent of Ghana's GDP annually over the years (BAT, 2001). The company believes that despite the growth of the anti-smoking lobby worldwide, it will continue to grow through aggressive brand drives, investment in people, proactive supplier-community relations and social responsibility.

BATG's governance and human resource management

BATG is governed by a 10-member board, including six executive directors who are involved with day-to-day executive and managerial administration. On the board, the chair, the company secretary and three other non-executive members are Ghanaian; so are all the rest, except for the finance director, who is British, and the managing director, who is Nigerian (recently appointed in 2003 to replace the retiring Ghanaian MD). There are thus only two expatriates out of 310 permanent staff. In addition to the permanent staff, BATG has 55 contract and 90 occasional staff, and many hand-pickers who are employed on a daily basis at the leaf stations. BATG also provides work for 14 distributors, 250 sales staff, over 8000 registered retailers and about 2000 registered tobacco farmers in a wide range of rural communities. Due to the health implications of working in a tobacco-processing environment, each staff member has a free full medical check once every two years. In the past few years the company has invested over US$250 000 in developing the skills of its employees. It has initiated on-line performance and career reviews – an innovation in Ghanaian human resource management circles. BATG claims that it has never had any major industrial relations dispute in its 50-year history in Ghana, despite the fact that its workers are organized by the Industrial and Commercial Workers Union (ICU), one of the most militant unions in Ghana. (Even major international banks and firms such as Unilever Ghana have upheavals in their industrial relations.) One reason perhaps is BATG's careful management of salary levels. Salaries are managed at line level; determinations are based on employee capacity and regular salary market surveys and are adjusted to match the cost of living. BAT commissions regular surveys of employee compensation from the local PricewaterhouseCoopers firm in Ghana. These surveys help the company to pitch its salary regimes amongst the best in the country.

BATG's rootedness in the local economy

BATG has pioneered a mutually beneficial relationship with its main suppliers, the farmers who grow tobacco leaf. This relationship is reasonably cordial and transparent, unlike what appears to pertain with the cotton-growers who feed the textile industry in Ghana. BATG recognizes the need to achieve quality and regularity of dependable supply. It provides extensive agricultural extension services to the 2000 farmers from whom it buys exclusively. Six hundred are judged to be the best farmers, based upon the quality and consistency of their supply, and farming practices. A yet more select group of 'master farmers' numbers about 192; these own the largest tobacco farms and are considered the most dependable suppliers. Leaf markets are located in major cities like Kumasi (capital of the Ashanti region), Tamale (a major city in the north) and Takoradi, the port city where the factory is located. The farmers who own their farms lease them to BATG for up to 10 years at a time so as to ensure supply. The farmers are provided with seeds or seedlings to produce both air- and flue-cured tobacco leaf. They are provided expertise in soil management. BATG also offers loans, fertilizers and pesticides, and guarantees purchase of good leaf at prices previously negotiated and agreed to with the farmers and their associations. Because of such extensive support, these farmers have also turned out to be more efficient food-crop farmers even though they focus on cash-cropping tobacco. By rotating these crops both to sell and to consume, the farmers are busy all year round, and assured of market for their tobacco. In a good year, a good farmer can make US$15 600, which by Ghanaian standards is a significant return. The farmers have associations at the district, regional and national levels which provide them negotiating clout and a framework by which to monitor their own activities. All these initiatives arise from BATG's determination to engage farmers and the farming communities in a responsible manner. The farmers have significant social standing in their communities and their children are eligible to participate in BATG's scholarship programmes for primary and secondary school education. Through these initiatives, social dislocation as a result of tobacco plantations is virtually unknown. In essence, BATG appears to believe in its farmers. This involvement with the farmers has a direct spillover effect on the communities, with projects ranging from road rehabilitation to construction of market sheds and assistance towards rural electrification.

There seem to be some differences between the experience of BAT Uganda (BATU) and BATG in their relations with the farmers. In a paper included elsewhere in this volume, Sam Sejjaaka's points out that Ugandan tobacco producers of the Alur people are migratory or settler farmers, who do not own the land on which they farm. As a result, they do not appear to have any commitment to farming practices that allow for cultivation of the preferred type of tobacco; one BATU manager complains that they 'just won't change' (see pp. 116–118). Further, BATU considers that the farmer cooperatives are corrupt. As Sejjaaka notes, not all BATU's suppliers are this way; Uganda's Banyoro farmers appear more prosperous and perhaps more prudent. The critical ingredients seem to include the farmers' ownership of land and their roots in the community, as well as the company's view of the farmers. The Ghanaian farmers are rooted in their communities. They own their farms; they use their own labour, which in some cases consists of family members, but more and more appears to involve hired labour from the community. Apart from owning their farms, they have a multi-tiered cooperative association and they also seem to have the respect of BATG. They use the agricultural extension services to help them become better farmers in terms of both tobacco cash cropping as well as food cropping. In the words of the human resources and leaf-station directors, the farmers 'are hardworking and diligent' and have a 'concern to provide good education to their children'. They take advantage of the scholarships offered by BATG. As a result, the company extends its definition of employee to include the farmers. BATG adheres to corporate values, including human rights and environmental values, to which BATU only appears to pay lip service.

BATG's corporate citizenship

Three clear values emerge from the story of BATG: the company's concern for its employees and suppliers; its sense of environmental responsibility; and its community involvement. First, the relationship between BATG and its farmers is comprehensive. It generates benefit for both the company, which is able to buy quality leaf from reliable sources, and for the farmers, who get earn regular incomes, receive agricultural support, are encouraged to grow foodstuffs in-between time, and obtain the same educational support offered to the dependents of BAT's regular employees. Second, BATG's corporate citizenship is visible in its efforts to renew the forests of Ghana.

Tobacco production in Ghana is heavily reliant upon the use of wood fuel for curing the leaf. Increasingly, BATG farmers are being required to meet their wood fuel requirements from managed woodlots, rather than from the indiscriminate harvesting of firewood. Each farmer is required to plant up to 500 trees each year, with seedlings provided by the company. BATG itself has put more than 3700 hectares under Teak timber cultivation to renew its fuel supply as well as reforest depleted areas in Ghana. The company also has aggressively forested more than 3000 hectares in the middle belt of the country with 4.1 million trees, to help check the southward spread of the Sahara desert. And it has reforested the banks of Weija Lake, a large reservoir in southern Ghana and Volta Lake behind the Akosombo dam – the largest artificial lake in the world. Rural communities along its banks engage in intensive farming, which has resulted in silt and sand filling in the lake and reducing water levels, thus affecting hydro power generation. BATG's efforts have been recognized at the national level and in 1991 and 1996, the company was honoured with the National Agro-Forestry Award. In further effort, BATG is encouraging the use of palm kernel shells in the furnaces for curing tobacco. It has built an ultra-modern, fuel-efficient furnace at Wench in the Brong Ahafo region. All the pesticides supplied to farmers for use on the plantations are registered with the Environmental Protection Agency (EPA). To ensure compliance, crop residues are examined every year in laboratories in the United Kingdom and United States.

Third, BATG actively supports various social causes in Ghana. This is not surprising, given that the tobacco industry is under attack globally by health activists and environmental lobbyists. Ghanaian sensibilities have forced tobacco advertising out of sports activities; there are hardly any TV or radio ads promoting tobacco products. It is not surprising that BATG has initiated innovative social programmes to put its corporate profile in a positive light in the public domain. It has supported higher education in Ghana by funding a chair at the Institute of Renewable Natural Resources at the Kwame Nkrumah University of Science and Technology. It has also sponsored an annual University of Ghana lecture series. The lectures in 2002 were delivered by the eminent Kenyan scholar Ali Mazrui and focused on the intellectual-political legacy of Dr Kwame Nkrumah and the political legacy of Flight Lieutenant Jerry Rawlings; two years earlier, UN Secretary General Kofi Annan was honoured at these lectures. BATG also has provided scholarships to needy students and made regular donations to Ghana's Trust Fund, which sees to the welfare of needy people in the community. When interviewed, BATG's directors and managers stress that these initiatives are necessary for good corporate citizenship. While it is difficult to gauge the genuineness of these efforts – in contrast to simply an effort to divert attention from tobacco – BATG is doing what other proactive companies are doing, and its efforts do meet real needs.

A recent incident tested BATG's social sensitivity. In March 2002, the company put up a huge poster advertising one of its cigarette brands at a major market complex in Accra. The imposing poster was considered too accessible for young people, and so generated much controversy. Significantly, there is no law banning cigarette advertising in Ghana, and the industry is self-regulating. BATG, which complies with worldwide standards requiring the posting of health warnings on all billboards and cigarette packs, quickly removed the poster and has not replaced it. The company asserts that cigarette smoking is a choice for adults to make. It has urged retailers to mount posters saying 'I don't sell cigarettes to children under 18'. The efficacy of this campaign appears in doubt since a 2002 radio report asserted that underage smoking is a problem in secondary schools, where children's attitudes are formed and where they get access to cigarettes through adults. The campaign seems to have lost its drive, but at a recent stockholder meeting, BATG claimed once again that it views smoking as an adult choice and would therefore seek to comply with all regulatory requirements, while actively seeking to grow its business.

Achieving competitive advantage by building capacity and developing assets

What can be learned from these companies? How can an international firm contribute to the development aspirations of a developing country in which it operates? Where should it draw the line between business and politics, social concern, interference and or poor stewardship of investor capital? This study assumes that the main responsibility of international firms in Ghana lies in enhancing the competitive advantage of their parent companies. This, however, cannot be achieved outside of the competitive advantage of the host nation. The competitive advantage of a nation lies in its ability to achieve synergies between the activities of firms as agents of productive enterprise and governments as regulators, social service providers and representatives of the people. Porter's notion of competitive advantage (Porter, 1990, 1998) implies a commitment by international firms to assist the development of their host locales. For over a hundred years, prominent business leaders from Andrew Carnegie to Lord Seiff have repeatedly made the point that business cannot be useful for society if it neglects its primary focus (CSP Task Force, 1980; James and Parker, 1990). But it is also agreed that a narrowly economic role is an inadequate measure of a firm's responsibility to help its host society develop its own competitive advantage.

Developing the competitive advantage of a host nation requires, at the micro level, that guest firms leverage and upgrade all the possibilities available to them within the nation. They need to both develop assets and build capacity, which are two distinct activities. Developing assets involves using the basic raw-material base of a country in such a way as to ensure long-term rootedness and involvement of a firm in the locale. It requires integrating the firm vertically and horizontally into the economic activities of the country through distributor and supplier relations as well as various forms of technology transfer. Capacity building, in contrast, involves focusing consistently and deliberately on improving – through education, healthcare, wealth generation, etc. – those key human capacities which enable people to take their socio-economic destinies into their own hands (UN, 1998; HD Report, 2000; Asenso-Okyere, 2001).

This study of three international firms in Ghana has examined their practices in terms of both concepts. What does it mean to build local capacity? In Ghana, this overused phrase denotes anything from talk-shop seminars to teaching market women basic bookkeeping. It starts with the idea that the social stability, which makes it possible for a business to operate and enjoy a reasonable measure of predictable profit-taking, is a valuable resource that has been fought for by the Ghanaian people over time. An international business should conduct itself so as not to insult this effort and sacrifice. Rather, it should build upon it by helping the people acquire the skills that progressively enable them to deal positively with their life circumstances. This study has reviewed the practices of three firms that serve most positively to build both capacity and assets in four areas. The most obvious places to look are in human-resource practices and governance structures; here the three firms have sought to increase the human capital of Ghana by developing and promoting their employees all the way up through the higher echelons. This study also explores how these three firms have rooted themselves in the Ghanaian economy, to show how they are engaged in building local assets. Finally, it reports on their practices of corporate citizenship – their environmental, educational and other 'social responsibility' programmes – as measures of both asset and capacity building.

Corporate values and behaviour

Various researchers, including Loughlin and Barling (2001), have argued that our values, beliefs and attitudes significantly influence our behaviour. Here we are looking at corporate behaviour, where the claim seems to hold true. To evaluate whether a firm is to be commended for its involvement in a developing society, we have to consider the links between a corporation's values and its behaviour. What does the firm really treasure? Its development orientation is a function of how it sees its core values. The extent to which the three surveyed companies build assets and capacity appears to be linked closely with their corporate values. The three firms all express their values clearly, and these values seem congruent with what they actually do. All the firms studied here have capacity-building and asset-developing strategies. They have all built factories and are using Ghanaian expertise to the highest levels. But there are differences in their values, which impact upon how they behave and, carry large implications for the development of Ghana.

Consider Valco in contrast to BATG regarding asset building. Valco has voiced a commitment weighted primarily to shareholder returns and secondarily to environmental responsibility, while BATG has affirmed a stronger commitment to the environment and community welfare. Valco had to be pressured into tariff renegotiations in 1985. Had this pressure not been brought to bear, it most likely would have continued paying low tariffs, despite the VRA's increasingly precarious financial situation. The point here is not to criticize Valco, but to point to how its value orientation disposes it to particular behaviour. Similarly, Valco commits itself to ensuring that its aluminium production does not impact the environment negatively. It complies with all EPA standards, and that is where its commitment ends. BATG, in contrast, espouses 'service to the community', and carries out massive forestry in an area (Weija Lake) not directly related to its core activity. Finally, consider their use of natural resources. BATG grows its raw material on plantations in Ghana. Through this backward integration into the Ghanaian economy, BATG has helped Ghana attain complete self-sufficiency in tobacco production and cigarette manufacture. Unil has also achieved similar levels of backward as well as forward integration, through an elaborate system of front-end supply-chain distributor networks. Valco, in contrast, does not utilize Ghanaian bauxite. It ships the raw ore in from fields in the Caribbean, and so its backward integration into Ghana's economy is limited. Again, the value Valco places upon its shareholders can be seen. Its shareholders have interests in the ore-producing areas of the Caribbean. As a result, Valco's commitment to asset development is rather limited.

Consider all three companies regarding capacity building. All three companies have moved more and more Ghanaians into the higher and more technical levels and functions. But there are differences. Valco started its operations in Ghana with a heavy expatriate presence, to ensure shareholder value. Later, Valco declared that it wished to avoid a dependency culture and so carried out progressive and drastic reductions in the number of expatriates. The expressed values of Unil and BATG extend further. Unil has committed itself to employee development, and has a coveted place in the minds of Ghanaians as an employer of choice. It is committed to full involvement with Ghana's educational system, to develop its human resources. BATG has expressed a concern for its farmers, and has developed very cordial relationships with them.

These contrasts suggest that corporate values are important in determining corporate behaviour. A key question here is what accounts for these differing value emphases? Researchers on corporate leadership note that leaders often determine the qualitative direction, strategic focus and actual behaviour of a firm (Puplampu, 2003). This appears especially true in the developing world, where much of the organizational and economic activity is driven by persons and personalities rather than by systems and established procedures. The directors interviewed for this study voiced a strong commitment to the development-oriented values of their firms. Of course, if leadership does not commit to real practices, then values are merely empty suppositions, abstract guarantees of intention without form or substance. The challenge is for the top of the hierarchy to find ways of merging profit with development responsibility – and increasingly for a public audience.

Business executives in Ghana are having to increase their sponsorship drives, relate more to their communities, take closer look at the image of their companies, attend state functions, give speeches and make donations. The top executives of Valco, BATG and Unil constantly find themselves making speeches about how government policy impacts business, or what business expects of institutions of higher education, what should be done about HIV/AIDS and so forth. They are often called upon by government for advice.

The impact of corporate leadership in realigning the behaviour of firms is underscored by Aykac and Gordy (1993), who argue that the role and responsibilities of corporate executives is moving beyond the parameters of traditional commerce. The boundaries of traditional business strategy and responsibility are shifting progressively to a broader, less clear-cut agenda. Directors and managers of international firms – operating in Ghana, at least – are experiencing this shift more and more, following the end of the cold war, the emergence of democratic governance and the increasing potential for quick movement of capital and logistics to most parts of the world. They are strongly encouraged to take the lead in social responsibility. According to Nicholson (2000), the firms, which succeed at community involvement '…create values of true community, where people of many kinds can be fulfilled … what they share is a business drive consolidated around a unified value set … where respect is the key' (p. 266). He describes respect in terms of treating customers, employees and the community *right*. One may ask, what does *right* mean? Social exchange theorists like Adams (1965) would suggest that behaviours within an exchange must meet mutual transaction and goal needs, must be recognized and seen as relevant. In other words, it is necessary for a firm to understand what its constituents see as right treatment, and commit to interacting with them accordingly. This is what leads societies and regulators to set standards, such as the Ghana Securities Regulatory Commission's November 2000 circular on corporate governance (GSRC, 2000). Standards are a reflection of what is valued and present an organization with a compelling reason to oblige (Nicholson, 1993, after Heller, 1988). These factors and social expectations make it difficult for directors and managers to stick to traditional business roles. Such inflexibility could easily lead to loss of image, resulting in the loss of market and profits. Within this context, their initiatives for social responsibility and the environment, their links with government, their image with regulatory agencies and so on become key strategic business issues. The three firms studied seem to have leaders who have managed to bridge the divide between development concerns and strategic business thrusts.

Capacity building and asset development – achieving both international profits and national development

International firms do business in developing areas to tap markets, resources, labour or power at acceptable costs. Nations as well as international firms pursue their competitive advantage: when developing areas invite investment by international firms, they are looking for firms which will directly and indirectly contribute in tangible ways to development; in such an exchange, both parties look for returns. The aim of Kaiser in establishing Valco was to secure power that was competitively priced and labour that was cheap; its partnership with Ghana provided both. The Ghana Government, for its part, achieved a critical development aspiration: hydro-electric power generation that has now powered industry for over 35 years. The aspiration for socio-economic development, however it is defined, is at the heart of every well-meaning government of a developing country.

Firms become good corporate citizens when they aim at mutually sustainable profit maximization and development, over mere profit taking. As long as governments continue to provide the climate in which the firm can safely do its business, the firm ought to be actively involved with the ongoing development of both the capacities and assets of its host country. Consider, for example, how McDonald's contributed to the development of Russia. It found that it could not rely on local bakeries to produce to the standard required. Yet instead of importing buns it built bakeries; it indirectly managed ranches, potato farms and vegetable plots, achieving a nearly complete vertical integration into the local food industry (Hill, 1998). Such integration meets the development aspirations of the country by building local capacity and developing local assets. It clearly demonstrates the firm's commitment to and rootedness in the country. And it benefits the firm. Unilever's operation in Ghana shows that it makes business sense to seek profits by building up the locale. Unil has pursued a strategy that aims at economic integration and the development of people. And it declared post-tax profits and dividend payments of US$6 million in fiscal 2001 – significant by Ghanaian standards.

Conclusion

The emerging political economy of international business involvement in developing areas is one in which image, involvement and community sensitivity are important. Often people in developing countries are aware that they have wealth, but this wealth is untapped; so when an international firm enters the scene, with its capital, equipment and expertise, expectations of its social involvement to lift up the life conditions of the people are often rather high. Unil, Valco and BATG all have made strenuous efforts to root themselves in Ghana. They have been in the country for over 35 years, with no intention of leaving. Their successes have yielded societal dividends in the form of taxes, employment and economic stability of the community. It seems reasonable to conclude that, where an organization sees its long-term future as located in the country of operation, it would make efforts to manage its local employees well and it would also seek to enhance their competencies and expertise. These three firms have managed the human capital available to them in innovative and beneficial ways, through comprehensive human resource practises and governance arrangements. They have progressively reduced dependence on expatriate expertise.

Unil and BATG also have achieved a nearly complete vertical integration into the economy, and have managed the natural resource endowments well. They have achieved a backward integration through plantations and out-grower programmes and forward integration through distributor networks. Production facilities have also been built which serve as real, tangible legacies. This integration has created sustainable capacity and expertise, which could easily survive the companies in the unlikely event that either Unil or BATG should ever fold up. The front-end logistics of vehicles, stores and other arrangements for distribution networks could easily be turned over to other uses or users. Plantations are unlikely to run out of possible buyers of oil palm; it is a critical resource for making soaps, detergents, margarines and other industrial products on a global scale. Tobacco is a more specialized industry; but the same can be said of BATG's plantations, although to a lesser extent. Valco's major failing in terms of asset development is that its initial agreements with Ghana proscribed the exploitation of Ghanaian bauxite. If Valco were to discontinue its operations, Ghana would face a significant uphill task building a system to mine and cart bauxite to the plant at Tema. Valco also has not provided enough assistance for developing alternative power sources, and so risks the shutdown of its aluminium plant. All three firms, however, have made efforts to manage the social capital and goodwill available to them through consistent and long-term support for afforestation, farming communities, higher education and trust funds dedicated to the needy.

If an international firm wishes to operate equitably, responsibly and with sensitivity to the economic and social needs of its host country, it needs to follow three 'rules'.

First, the firm needs to articulate a set of values and or guiding principles, which make clear that practices that are responsible are also strategically sound. In Ghana, the expressed values of the firms appear to have a direct bearing on their behaviour. 'We value employee development' translates into significant staff-development programmes; 'we believe in sound environmental management' translates into programmes of forestation. Firms that have not articulated clear values are unlikely to have the internal moral structure and order needed to confront and manage the range of ethical dilemmas they are likely to face.

Second, international firms must wherever possible root themselves by involving local people in the governance and management of the firm. They must commit to helping develop the human capital of the country. Reducing expatriate staff and engaging in sound people management demonstrates such commitment. Tokenism, in contrast, plays with the minds of local people, as when meagre donations are given, or the odd one person is appointed to a visible position while real power and authority are reserved for expatriates or the head office overseas.

Third and finally, good corporate citizenship requires vertical integration, both front and back. Should the firm wind down its operations, it will leave structures and capacities in the community, which would enable the people to carry on. In an equitable exchange between an international firm and its host nation, the demise or departure of the firm should not cause the demise of the host community.

Note

1. Interviews were conducted between June 2000 and June 2002. For each of the three firms, four senior officials were interviewed about history, company policy, practices and procedures, lapses and strategic initiatives since incorporation in Ghana. Additional management staff were interviewed at each of the three firms. Overall, the interviewees included managing directors/chief executive officers/ resident directors; human resource managers/directors, public relations managers; administrative managers; and leaf station directors. Further, a number of lower level employees were interviewed at random in each company. These unstructured interviews centred on perceptions and feelings regarding the companies' treatment of employees and opportunities available for advancement and fulfilment.

References

Adams, J. (1965) 'Inequity in Social Exchange', in L. Berkowitz (ed.), *Advances in Experimental Social Psychology,* vol. 2 (New York: Academic Press), pp. 267–99.

Asenso-Okyere, K. (2001) *Wealth Accumulation, Utilization and Retention,* Professorial Inaugural Lecture, University of Ghana (Accra: Ghana Universities Press).

Aykac, A. and Gordy, M. (1993) 'The Emerging Corporatism: Business Executives as Social Managers', in B. Sutton (ed.), *The Legitimate Corporation* (Oxford: Blackwell), pp. 211–23.

BAT (2001) BAT Ghana: Annual Report (Accra and Takoradi: BAT Ghana Limited).

CSP Task Force (1980): Task Force on Corporate Social Performance *Business and Society: Strategies for the 1980s* (Washington: US Department of Commerce).

GSRC (2000): Ghana Securities Regulatory Commission *Corporate Governance* Circular # 3 (November) (Accra).

HD Report (2000): *Ghana Human Development Report* (Accra: UNDP/ISSER).

Heller, A. (1988) *General Ethic* (Oxford: Blackwell).

Hill, C. (1998) *International Business. Competing in the Global Market Place* (Boston: McGraw-Hill).

James, S. and Parker, R. (1990) *A Dictionary of Business Quotations* (London: Routledge).

Kamoche, K. (1996) 'Strategic Human Resource Management Within a Resource Capability View of the Firm', *Journal of Management Studies*, vol. 33(2), pp. 213–34.

Loughlin, C. and Barling, J. (2001) 'Young workers' Work Values, Attitudes and Behaviours', *Journal of Occupational and Organisational Psychology*, vol. 74(4), pp. 543–58.

Nicholson, N. (1993) 'Business Ethics – of Academic Interest to Organisational Psychology?', *The Occupational Psychologist*, vol. 21, pp. 31–7.

Nicholson, N. (2000) *Managing the Human Animal* (London: Texere).

Porter, M. E. (1990, 1998) *The Competitive Advantage of Nations* (NY: Free Press).

PsyconH.R (2002) 'Corporate Image Survey', Unpublished Consultancy Report (Accra).

Puplampu, B. (1993) 'Differential Perceptions of Expatriation between UK and Ghana', PhD Thesis (London: University of East London).

Puplampu, B. (1995) *Towards a General Theory of Expatriation*, Working Paper Series (London: University of Westminster Press).

Puplampu, B. (2003) 'Of Ants, Mice and Men – An Organisational Psychologist's Views on Corporate and Institutional Leadership in Ghana', Interfaculty Lecture, University of Ghana, Legon, March.

UN (1998): United Nations A Vision of Hope: 50th Anniversary Publication (New York: UN).

UNIL (2001) Report and Financial Statement (Accra: Unilever Ghana Limited).

5

A Political and Economic History of Uganda, 1962–2002

Samuel Sejjaaka

Introduction

Uganda, the 'Pearl of Africa', sits astride the equator in Eastern Africa. At the time of independence in 1962, after 68 years of British rule, Uganda had one of the most vibrant and promising economies in Sub-Saharan Africa (World Bank, 1993b). Favoured with a good climate and fertile soils, the country was self-sufficient in food, and agriculture was the single largest export-earner. However, its potential for growth has been curtailed by more than 20 years of civil strife, especially between 1966 and 1986. The resultant economic mismanagement and civil war have had disastrous effects on the once-promising country.

During this period, the population grew from 9.5 million in 1969 to 21 million in 2000, and half the population is 15 years old or younger. It ranked 150th out of 173 countries on the human-development index in 2002. Uganda has a per capita GDP of US$1208 – well below the per capita income of Ghana at US$1964. Fifty-five per cent of its people live below the extreme poverty line of less than a dollar a day. With per capita health expenditures of only US$18, it has been severely affected by HIV/AIDS, although a thorough awareness campaign has reduced its incidence from 13 per cent in 1990 to 5 per cent in 2003. The average Ugandan can hope to live only to 44 years of age.

Independence and the post-independence era, 1962–71

Uganda was made a protectorate of the British Empire in 1894. The colonial administration was headed by a governor, and the protectorate's affairs were carried out by public officers appointed by the Colonial Office in London. Only after 1940 did the British actively exploit the resources of Uganda, but by the 1950s, their regime had become a lame duck, as Uganda accelerated towards independence. The British lost effective power because their colonial state failed to serve as a factor of cohesion, despite its administrative, judicial and coercive power (Thompson, 2003). While colonial rule bequeathed to Uganda the essential apparatus needed to define a modern nation-state, it failed to reconcile the competing expectations of the different feudal and tribal societies that made up the territory of Uganda.

Historically, the people of the central region, Buganda, were viewed as collaborators in the colonization of Uganda. They made tremendous strides in developing their infrastructure, educational and other social services. Other groups have both envied and denigrated Buganda as a basis for their own political advancement. Buganda's demands for a special position in the post-independence period were seen as manifestations of a bogus superiority, which had to be subdued by the so-called republicans. To this day it has been difficult to sustain effective civilian administration in Uganda because of the problems in reconciling the interests of different regions and peoples. Even rational political demands such as creating a federation of autonomous regions were viewed as suspect because they were spearheaded by Buganda. The Ugandan state remains fragile, with tensions simmering just below the surface.

In 1962, Sir Frederick Mutesa, the Kabaka or ruler of the territory of Buganda, was elected the first President of Uganda. As a monarch, he found it difficult to take orders from the national government, which was headed by a commoner, A. Milton Obote. In 1964 there was a referendum to decide whether two counties, which Buganda had annexed, should be returned to the neighbouring territory of Bunyoro. Bunyoro won, but Mutesa refused to sign the transfer instrument, thereby creating a crisis for the government. From that point matters deteriorated rapidly. Until 1966 Uganda managed to maintain a degree of stability, but in that year matters came to a head, as the Buganda government resolved to expel the Ugandan government from its soil (Ibingira, 1980). This event played into the hands of Obote, whose national government responded by sending soldiers to the Kabaka's palace to 'investigate' the presence of arms. The soldiers (headed by Idi Amin) overran the palace and forced the Kabaka into exile. Obote proceeded to suspend the constitution crafted for the independence of Uganda and declared himself executive president, head of state and government and commander-in-chief of the armed forces. Most of the officers and men used in this exploit were from the same ethnic group as Obote.

This 'Uganda crisis', as it came to be known, had an immediate and enduring political impact. By using the army to overthrow the status quo, Obote introduced and entrenched the military as coercive arbiter of conflict in Uganda (Henstridge, 1995). Obote became increasingly dictatorial. To deal with dissent, he introduced draconian laws like the Emergency Powers (Detention) Regulations in 1966. He also used state security institutions to cow his political opponents; these included members of his cabinet, four of whom were arrested during a cabinet meeting. His new constitution, ratified in 1967, concentrated power in the Presidency and the National Assembly.

Radicals viewed this constitution as a positive effort to create a strong and effective central government, but the country now was divided between traditionalists and non-traditionalists. Obote subdued the National Assembly, which was now largely composed of members of his party, the Uganda Peoples Congress (UPC). The country was now effectively a one-party state and Obote confirmed this shortly by banning all opposition parties.

At the time of independence in 1962, Uganda had one of the most vigorous and promising economies in Sub-Saharan Africa, and the years following independence had amply demonstrated this economic potential (World Bank, 1993a). The country was self-sufficient in food, and the agricultural sector earned ample foreign exchange through the export of coffee, cotton and cocoa, despite traditional methods of production. A vibrant manufacturing sector supplied basic inputs and consumer goods. Mining in the south supplied copper and cobalt for export, and the country enjoyed a positive balance of trade. Fiscal and monetary management was sound, and the domestic savings rate averaged about 15 per cent of GDP. There was a strong local administrative system that provided effective supervision of economic activity by disciplining all those who were not productive. The locals needed little coercion to produce, since consumption was predicated on what they produced (Thompson, 2003).

Obote, like several African heads of state, had become enamoured of socialism, and proposed at a UPC party conference in 1968, as part of his modernization philosophy, that Uganda 'move to the left' in ideology and practice. He laid the groundwork for socialism in his 'Common Man's Charter' (1970), which began by declaring that the main purpose of government was 'the realization of the real meaning of Independence, namely, that the resources of the country, material and human, be exploited for the benefit of all the people of Uganda in accordance with the principles of socialism' (Obote, 1970, p. 1). Article 38 declares furthermore that 'the guiding economic principles must be that the means of production and distribution be in the hands of the people' (p. 9). In effect, Obote's 'Charter' offered a blueprint for a mixed economy, in which government controlled the commanding heights. The blueprint was put into effect beginning Labour Day (May 1), 1970, when Obote announced his intention to nationalize oil companies, Kampala Bus Services, the Kilembe mines, banks and other companies.

The nationalization strategy, which was poorly conceived, had a serious impact on the economy. First, it precipitated the flight of capital because there were no indigenous managers to run the nationalized companies. Expatriate managers therefore had to be retained, but they found it tempting to repatriate their profits from this increasingly volatile environment (Kasozi, 1994). Second, the government launched ambitious programmes to build hospitals and schools in various parts of the country, but this spate of construction left the country seriously indebted. Third, several parastatal corporations were created under the auspices of the Uganda Development

Corporation (UDC) to take on some of the activities of nationalized companies. The UDC had been created in 1952 as a vehicle for investment, not for nationalization of existing business firms. The new parastatals were given monopolies over the marketing of export, produce and commodities, but proved inept and corrupt. Fourth, the cooperatives and trade unions, which had been strong up to that point, were throttled by incessant interference and legislation such as the Cooperative Act of 1970 (Kasozi, 1994). Obote's 'Africanization' programme failed dismally to create a local property-owning (business) class to take over management of the economy. In effect, Obote's policies disenfranchised the non-citizens who ran the economy without empowering the African natives who, hitherto, had not been allowed to participate in commerce, industry and large-scale agriculture. The experiments in socialism, the enlargement of the bureaucracy and the ambitious investment in infrastructure without regard to budgetary or economic fundamentals began to eat away at the economy. The situation was compounded by innuendoes of corruption in government, and by growing violence.

Amin's economic war, 1972–79

Obote used the army to abuse the population with impunity. His dictatorial tendencies and Buganda-phobia alienated large sections of the army, public services and regional authorities as well. More importantly, he lost the trust of the business community and the Western bloc by nationalizing businesses in which multinational companies were stakeholders. By 1971, discontent and corruption in the army, arising mainly out of inequitable promotions and poor care for soldiers crystallized into a *coup d'état*. It has been suggested that there was foreign involvement in this coup. Whatever the immediate causes, the coup brought to power Idi Amin, a former corporal in the British colonial army who had been used by Obote to quell several riots. Amin did not actually participate in the coup, but used popular indignation against Obote to gain power. The United Kingdom and Israel first recognized Amin as the legitimate ruler of Uganda, largely because of their economic interests. The Israelis provided his forces with training and logistical support, and the British convinced other Commonwealth member states to accord Uganda recognition. There was considerable International Monetary Fund (IMF) involvement in the first budget of the Amin government and the conduct of fiscal policy was, initially, not wholly outrageous (Henstridge, 1995).

Then, in one fell swoop, Idi Amin set the conditions for economic decay, which he oversaw until his overthrow eight years later. In 1972 he declared an 'Economic War' against 'imperialist' forces and the large Asian community in Uganda. Increased defence spending, financed by bank borrowing, made the national budget untenable. Annual inflation rates shot to double digits (World Bank, 1993a). Like Obote, Amin believed that it was important to address the social inequality that prevailed in the country by economically empowering Ugandans. At this time, Uganda's Asian population had extensive control over the economy as artisans, shopkeepers, industrialists and professionals. In particular, they controlled local and international trade. Amin expelled the Asians, and in this way continued the wave of nationalizations that Obote had begun. Increased insecurity and persecution of white-collar workers resulted in an additional mass exodus of professional managers of all nationalities and persuasions. The vacuum that was created by his actions marked the beginning of Uganda's economic collapse.

Amin did not relax the economic regulations instituted by Obote; rather, he presided over the social and economic destruction of Uganda. On the social side, the people were markedly traumatized: official murders, torture and abductions became the order of the day for all types of crimes. Estimates of how many people died as the violence escalated range from 50 000 (Kasozi, 1994, p. 104) to 500 000 (World Bank, 1993). The social disorder occasioned by Amin's regime jeopardized transactions and assets, and diminished the social capital of Uganda (Collier and Pradham, 1998). Because essential commodities were scarce, there developed a wide disparity between official prices and actual market prices. The black market prospered, to the benefit not only of smugglers, but public officials, who through personal influence could obtain (and re-sell) 'allocation chits' for sugar, beer, salt and even foreign exchange. The government reacted by setting up an anti-smuggling unit. Economic crimes such as overcharging, hoarding, smuggling, corruption and dealing in foreign currency became punishable by torture or public execution. The net effect was to further emaciate the economy, as the biggest culprits were influential public officials who were not punished.

Uganda became a pariah state and faced various international embargoes. It had been a charter member of the East African Community (EAC), a trading bloc that included Kenya and Tanzania. The EAC collapsed, further isolating Uganda. Key industries relocated to Kenya. Services such as air transport and telecommunications, which had benefited from the existence of the EAC, also suffered. The rail transport system collapsed and this further increased the costs of inputs. Production, as measured by constant-price GDP, declined by 13 per cent between 1971 and 1986. In absolute terms the economy declined by 1 per cent per year (Collier and Reinikka, 2001), even as Uganda's population was growing rapidly. Many factories collapsed due to lack of inputs, which were imported, and due to the absence of vertical or horizontal linkages between economic sectors. All sectors, with the possible exception of subsistence agriculture, suffered from the lack of imported inputs. Between 1970 and 1979, the per capita income of Uganda fell from US$225 to US$148. The debt–export ratio grew from 51.1 per cent to 142.2 per cent, and agriculture's share of GDP rose from 48.5 per cent to 70.5 per cent as the manufacturing sector collapsed.

For eight years, as Amin ran roughshod over the populace, there were several uprisings and attempted coups. Plots and mutinies in the army occurred in 1972, 1974, 1975, 1976 and 1979. In 1972, the remnants of Obote's army and other exiles attempted an ill-fated attack from Tanzania. Yoweri Museveni, who later was to become president, led one of the groups. Brave men and women risked their lives to end Amin's brutality, but most of the opposition was uncoordinated. Amin himself turned the tide, when in 1978 he ordered his troops to attack the Kagera Salient, a border region of Tanzania. The Tanzanians retaliated, and were joined by an umbrella coalition of Ugandan exiles, the Uganda National Liberation Front (UNLF). Kampala, the capital city, fell on 11 April 1979 to the advancing Tanzanian forces and the ragtag army of exiles.

The post-Amin era, 1979–86

Between 1979 and 1980, Uganda had three governments. Two were created under the banner of the UNLF, whose diverse composition of exiles and rebel elements and lack of cohesive objectives plunged Uganda into further chaos and violence. The UNLF had been formed as a guerrilla organization in Tanzania; two weeks later, it found itself at the head of the country (Kanyeihamba, 2002). There was no national army, but rather several armed groups. The largest, the Kikoosi Maalum, was allied to Obote. The second, led by Yoweri Museveni, vehemently opposed Obote's return to power. The scene thus was set for further conflict. The first UNLF president, Yusufu K. Lule, managed only 68 days in office before he was forced out by the conspiracies that involved both the UNLF and Julius Nyerere, the president of Tanzania. The next president, Godfrey L. Binaisa, lasted until May 1980, when he was removed by Paulo Muwanga, again with the tacit approval of the Tanzanian forces. Muwanga's regime returned Milton Obote through elections of questionable validity.

Obote's 'second coming' heralded a period of terror in Uganda as he sought to hold state power regardless of the cost. Several armed opposition groups, which included the National Resistance Movement (NRM), rejected the results of the election and took up armed rebellion on the pretext that Obote's regime was illegitimate. As many as a million people may have lost their lives in the civil war that resulted (Kasozi, 1994). For another five years, unspeakable atrocities were visited on the Ugandan people, both through the machinery of state and through sabotage by rebels. Grave violations of people's rights and misgovernment were the order of the day. Obote had learnt his lesson regarding the military, and he let them have their way; when soldiers were not paid, they were free to go marauding in the population. The state had dissolved into anarchy and all civil institutions had broken down.

Not surprisingly, economic mismanagement continued during the second Obote regime. Disparate ideologies in the factionalized UNLF hindered the articulation of meaningful economic policy. There were attempts at stabilizing the macroeconomic framework, but given the continuing war, these were largely unworkable. During the war that ousted Amin, Uganda's infrastructure and industrial plant had been largely destroyed: out of 930 enterprises registered in 1971, only 300 remained in the early 1980s, with an estimated capacity utilization of just 5 per cent (Livingstone, 1998). Such was the sorry state of Uganda at the time of 'liberation' from Amin's excesses. The destruction continued after 1979. The Luwero Triangle, the food basket of the central region, was destroyed in a kind of 'scorched earth' policy (Kasozi, 1994, p. 185). The lack of political stability made it impossible to initiate or implement economic recovery.

The government attempted to regulate the foreign exchange market through a two-tier pricing system. Essential goods and services were to be purchased at an official rate, while non-essential goods and services at a market rate. The system soon broke down because strategically positioned public officials could buy on the official rate and sell through the 'kibanda' or black market. Despite the war, during this four-year period (1981–85) there were some gains. GDP grew by 5.5 per cent and inflation fell to about 20 per cent, while the current account was in surplus (Edmonds, 1998). Per capita incomes recovered from a low of US$136 per annum to US$187 per annum and the share of agriculture in GDP fell from 70.5 per cent in 1980 to 50.5 per cent in 1985. Yet this first attempt to stabilize and improve economic performance is largely remembered as a failure because of the continuing instability. Exports fell from US$415 million in 1980 to US$368 million in 1984 while the external debt rose from US$568 million to over US$1 billion in 1985. Inflation had initially been tamed by external aid and relief assistance, but shot from 47.4 to 156 per cent, between 1983 and 1985.

Economic recovery, 1986–2002

Obote's second government was toppled on 27 July1985, ironically by sections of his army. The bush war, which had started in 1981, also ended shortly on 25 January 1986 with victory for the NRM. Led by Yoweri Museveni, the NRM had begun its 'people's war' in 1981. In a 10-point programme, it declared that the people had a right to defend themselves against those who threatened the democratic order and human rights, and that no more would the state be used to violate the rights of the people. The NRM formed a broad-based government, with promise of elections after four years. The NRM-ruled government scheduled elections for 1989, but did not carry through, on the pretext that the new constitution was not ready. Over the next eight years an official commission produced a draft constitution, which was debated in a Constituent Assembly (partly an elected body) and promulgated in 1995. In the first election for president and members of parliament (1996), Yoweri Museveni was victorious. In a second, more bitterly contested election (2001), his margin was considerably reduced. The results were challenged in court but were upheld by a Supreme Court majority of three to two.

When the NRM government came to power in 1986, it deeply opposed IMF programmes. Instead, it favoured revaluing the Ugandan shilling, allocating commodities administratively, and in controlling prices and maintaining monopolies. Some NRM functionaries believed strongly in statist economic policies, and pointed to the rapid economic deterioration between 1981 and 1986 as a consequence of the first structural adjustment efforts. Faced with an-almost bankrupt treasury, however, the NRM was forced to abandon this 'go it alone' strategy. Inflation was running at 147 per cent between July and December 1986 and the effective exchange rate had increased by 128 per cent (World Bank, 1993a). In May 1987 the NRM government accepted an economic reform programme sponsored by the World Bank and supported by the IMF and agencies of the European Union (Brett, 1995).

The reforms involved orthodox adjustment measures – policies to liberalize and stabilize the economy. In Uganda's case, liberalization involved the removal of price controls, the institution of a free exchange-rate mechanism and allowing interest rates and foreign-exchange transactions be market-determined. Stabilization meant imposing a tight regime of fiscal and monetary management on public-sector borrowing and reforming the regulatory framework. The aim was to control macroeconomic indicators such as inflation so as to improve incentives to the private sector, and develop human capital through investment in education and health (Sejjaaka, 1996; World Bank, 1996).

The structural adjustment programme was implemented vigorously, albeit with mixed results. A currency-reform exercise involving a 30 per cent tax was implemented and the shilling was devalued from 14 to 60 to the US dollar. Yet there was no consistent direction or grasp for that matter of how economic fundamentals (fiscal deficit, exchange rates, inflation and exports) should be dealt with. Between 1987 and 1992, inflation fell from 200 to 48.5 per cent, but continuing drought, insurgencies and shortfalls in donor assistance forced the government to increase the money supply. Loose budget control also resulted in huge deficits. Macroeconomic stability was eventually restored through prudent budgeting as well as fiscal and monetary policy (Henstridge and Kasekende, 2001). Many civil servants were retrenched, while the government cut expenditures and curtailed public-sector borrowing. A 'cash flow' budget system was introduced to monitor resources and spending while ensuring that fiscal policy remained consistent with low inflation. In 1993, the dual foreign exchange rates were unified, by introducing inter-bank currency auctions. Also in 1993, the Uganda Revenue Authority was established, helping to improve tax revenue collection, and the Bank of Uganda was given autonomy in supervising commercial banks.

These measures restored the revenue-to-GDP ratio to 11.2 per cent, though this remains still very low compared to other Sub-Saharan countries.

As part of the liberalization programme, the Uganda government moved to eliminate tariff and non-tariff barriers, particularly for agricultural exports. Before 1987, exports of coffee, tea and cotton were managed through marketing monopolies. Trade in tea and cotton had declined drastically. Coffee exports persisted because coffee production required low inputs, and coffee as a product depreciated slowly and was easy to smuggle (Henstridge, 1995). The government switched from export to import taxes because the latter did not penalize exports. The liberalization of export crop marketing also involved elimination of the inefficient, state-run marketing boards. Despite depressed prices on the world market, farm-gate prices for coffee rose by as much as five times. Still, the coffee sector continues to suffer from the vicissitudes of the world market. Uganda also continues to suffer from an unfavourable balance of trade. Imports constitute 26 per cent of GDP, while exports are only 10 per cent. Moreover, 94 per cent of those exports are primary products with little added value.

To attract foreign investment, the Government of Uganda needed to restore its reliability. In 1991, it established an investment code and attempted to undo or at least mitigate the past expropriation of foreign investments. The confiscated properties of departed Asians were returned, and the provisions of the Preferential Trade Agreement, which had favoured firms with majority domestic ownership, were revoked (Collier and Reinikka, 2001). Between 1991 and 1999, many nationalized companies were returned to their owners or privatized. All these measures were intended to encourage and fast track foreign investment. The tax incentives provided under the 1991 investment code have since been abolished.

The government also instituted a programme in 1992 to reform and divest public enterprises (PEs). At this time there were 116 public enterprises, of which 60 were industrial (Livingstone, 1998). These enterprises were characterized by low productivity, endemic losses and huge indebtedness to government and the private sector. They received subsidies amounting to 50 per cent of public domestic revenue, despite contributing only a meagre 10 per cent to GDP, and they accounted for 18 per cent of total bank credit (Collier and Reinikka, 2001). They constituted an excessive administrative burden on public resources and needed to be offloaded. It was, however, politically difficult to privatize them. For years they had provided a safe haven for inept public officials, employed relatives of high-ranking government officials and were a cash source for predatory politicians. This strong constituency opposed and continues to oppose privatization. Nevertheless, 103 PEs were either sold off, restructured or liquidated by the end of 2002 – leading to increased output, higher tax payment and more meaningful job creation. Privatized companies have attracted significant new investment, at least where profiteers have not stripped the assets of the companies they·

purchased. The privatization programme succeeded, but not as well as it might have. A survey by Uganda Manufacturers Association Consultancy and Information Services found that the programme achieved its fiscal social, and economic objectives, but that the process was perceived to be corrupt (Collier and Reinikka, 2001, p. 38). Because of its inadequate legal and institutional framework and because responsibilities were ill defined, the privatization programme received severe criticism from parliament and was partly suspended.

Parliament suspended the privatization programme in part because it was lacking in transparency. Corruption has become a serious impediment to business in Uganda. It increases the costs of doing business because firms must pay bribes when dealing with public officials; the bribes are based on the issues at stake, and higher bribes do not necessarily result in more beneficial government favours to business (Svensson, 2001). Corruption is a tax, which reduces the return to private capital and slows growth, but even as a tax it does not end up as public revenue.

Conclusion

At the dawn of independence in 1962, Uganda's economic prospects seemed bright. It had very good social services, a buoyant economy and visions of emancipation. Not many could have foretold the capricious and degenerative path that Uganda took. Various writers (Kasozi, 1994; Collier and Reinikka, 2001) have attributed the destructive development path that Uganda took to a number of internal factors: Uganda's dependence on primary commodities; the slow growth of economic opportunity, as measured against the rapid growth of the population; ethnic intolerance and lack of democratic institutions; social inequality; and the absence of a property-owning class to counter the effects of social disorder. These factors have hardly been resolved and the state remains dysfunctional in several respects. Because Ugandan society was so fractionalized, the administrative structures inherited by the state at independence could not hold the centre, and the economy became weaker as a result of dependence upon primordial forms of economic production and declining world market prices. These vulnerabilities foster a kind of rent-seeking in the political and economic spheres of life, which operates to the detriment of lawful existence. Business enterprise, which is morally acceptable and upright, comes in a poor second for those who can appropriate wealth to themselves through corruption and violence.

Civil strife and political instability between 1966 and 1986 seriously eroded prospects for economic development. The nationalization of multinational businesses resulted in both mismanagement and the flight of capital. The expulsion of the Asian community destroyed the bulwark of commerce. The atrocious civil conflict and destruction of infrastructure also contributed to the degeneration. The collapse of farm-gate prices for primary products (coffee, cotton and tobacco) depressed the rural economy. All these factors combined to negate government capacity to raise taxes and develop adequate social and physical infrastructure. The ongoing AIDS crisis, and ethnic conflict in the north and southwest continue to hinder efforts to rebuild the Ugandan economy. As in the 1950s, Uganda's political and economic development remains fragile.

However, despite the recurring political crises, there has been increased political stability since 1987. The country has made some political progress during the 17 years of NRM rule. The press has a reasonable degree of independence, and the country has recovered some of its original international standing. Peace has been restored in most of the country, and a large part has remained relatively stable and amenable to the authority of the state, although insurgencies occur in the northern and south-western regions. Extra-judicial killings appear to be a thing of the past. The legislative and judicial branches of government continue to enjoy a reasonable degree of freedom from the executive branch. The political system since 1986 has been a 'Movement' system or non-party democracy. According to the 1995 Constitution, all Ugandans are members and free to vie for any elective post on the basis of 'individual merit'. In reality, factional candidates still seek elective office. The 2001 election marked the beginning of a legitimate and cohesive challenge to the authority of the NRM. Charges of corruption, intolerance and perceptions of social inequality have led to the NRM developing a siege mentality. Internal dissent or criticism is increasingly unwelcome. Consequently the broad-based and inclusive approach that had been championed in the early years is being steadily restricted (Kanyeihamba, 2002).

Since 1987, Uganda also has achieved a certain measure of economic stability, thanks to aid from international finance institutions and improved foreign investment. Key economic indicators for the period 1987–2001 show the overall impact of economic reform programmes as positive, with improvements in law and order, rehabilitation of the infrastructure and sustained GDP growth at about 5.6 per cent from 1986 to 2002. Inflation fell to below 5.8 per cent in 1999.

Yet problems persist. The Ugandan state is still fragile, and the economy is weak and dependent on the magnanimity of the lending and foreign policy prescriptions of donor countries. Since independence, Uganda has borrowed more than US$3.1 billion, and it is one of the most 'Highly Indebted Poor Countries' (HIPC) in the world. Aid flows peaked in fiscal year 1993–94 at fully two-thirds of public expenditure. From 1989 to 2001, these aid flows dropped to 51 per cent. Yet with donor input still running at over half of the budget, it remains to be seen how long Uganda can remain a successful case of adjustment, especially in the light of creeping donor fatigue. The current debt burden, according to the Uganda Debt Network, exceeded US$4 billion by June 2003 (Uganda Debt Network, 2003). The burdens imposed by this debt are worsening. As measured by the ratio of debt to exports and other relevant services, which in effect measures the amount of foreign exchange earnings foregone in servicing debt, this ratio increased from 16.2 per cent in 1989–99 to 20.4 per cent in 1999–2000.

As a result of these ambiguous trends and indicators, the challenges for international business remain enormous. The liberalized environment has encouraged the return and arrival of several multinational business corporations through an aggressive investment promotion programme. The challenge to the Ugandan government and guest multinationals is to reduce poverty while holding onto the gains recorded so far. Yet potent obstacles remain: disregard for constitutionalism, lack of democracy, intolerance and poverty all combine to make a powerful statement. Growth has not been evenly distributed, and in some respects poverty has been intensified by continued civil strife, especially in northern Uganda. It is in this environment that multinational corporations are required to invest and operate at world-class standards. Those multinationals that seek to honour the principles of good governance are on the receiving end of intractable pressures to appease diverse and often conflicting constituencies. Weak institutional environments, poor observance of human rights, low social capital and a poor policy environment create fickle business conditions. Still, the demands for social responsibility and good governance remain real. The case studies that follow will explore how several multinational firms have addressed these challenges.

References

Brett, E. A. (1995) *Structural Adjustment in Uganda: 1987–1994* (Copenhagen: Centre for Development Research).

Collier, P. and Pradham, S. (1998) 'Economic Aspects of the Transition from Civil War', in H. B. Hansen and M. Twaddle (eds), *Developing Uganda* (London/Ohio University Press, James Curry).

Collier, P. and Reinikka, R. (2001) 'Reconstruction and Liberalization: An Overview', in R. Reinikka and P. Collier (eds), *Uganda's Recovery: The Role of Farms, Firms and Government* (Kampala: Fountain Publishers).

Edmonds, K. (1998) 'Crisis Management: The Lessons for Africa from Obote's Second Term', in H. B. Hansen and M. Twaddle (eds), *Uganda Now: Between Decay and Development* (London/Ohio University Press, James Currey).

Henstridge, N. M. (1995) 'Coffee Money in Uganda: An Econometric Analysis', DPhil thesis (Oxford University).

Henstridge, N. M. and Kasekende, L. (2001) 'Exchange Reforms, Stabilization, and Fiscal Policy' in R. Reinikka and P. Collier (eds), *Uganda's Recovery: The Role of Farms, Firms and Government* (Kampala: Fountain Publishers).

Ibingira, G. S. (1980) *The Forging of an African Nation: The Political and Constitutional Evolution of Uganda from Colonial Rule to Independence, 1894–1962* (New York: Viking Press).

Kanyeihamba, G. W. 2002. '*Constitutional and Political History of Uganda from 1894 to the Present.*' Kampala: Century Publishing House.

Kasozi, A. B. K. (1994) *The Social Origins of Violence in Uganda* (Montreal: McGill-Queen's University Press).

Laleef, K. S. (1991) 'Structural Adjustment in Uganda: The Initial Experience', in H. B. Hansen and M. Twaddle (eds) *Changing Uganda* (London: James Curry).

Livingstone, I. (1998) 'Developing Industry in Uganda in the 1990s', in H. B. Hansen and M. Twaddle (eds), *Uganda Now: Between Decay and Development* (London/Ohio University Press, James Currey).

Obote, A. M. (1970) *Common Man's Charter* (Entebbe: Government Printer).

Sejjaaka, S. K. (1996) 'After Privatization: The Role of Government', *Makerere Business Journal*, vol. 1(1), January.

Svensson, J. (2001) 'The Cost of Doing Business: Firms' Experience With Corruption', in R. Reinikka and P. Collier (eds), *Uganda's Recovery: The Role of Farms, Firms and Government* (Kampala: Fountain Publishers).

Thompson, G. (2003) *Governing Uganda: British Colonial Rule and Its Legacy* (Kampala: Fountain Publishers).

Uganda Debt Network (2003) *Policy Review Newsletter*, vol. 3(1).

World Bank (1993a) *Uganda: Growing Out of Poverty* (Washington).

World Bank (1993b) *Uganda: The Challenge of Growth and Poverty Reduction* (Washington).

6
From Seed to Leaf: British American Tobacco and Supplier Relations in Uganda

Samuel Sejjaaka

Introduction

Tobacco is one of the most controversial agricultural products in the world because of the health risks it poses to producers and users. Despite this controversy, global tobacco consumption will increase from 1.1 billion 'sticks' or cigarettes per day in 2001 to 1.6 billion by the year 2025, according to the World Health Organization. Supply is expanding at a rate that has resulted in a worldwide glut and a corresponding decline in prices. Production grew by 59 per cent between 1975 and 1997, with most of this increase occurring in developing countries. Between 1960 and 1989, the world price for flue-cured tobacco declined in real terms by about 1.1 per cent to 1.7 per cent per year. Between 1985 and 2000 the price per ton fell 37 per cent from US$1950 to US$1221.[1]

Worldwide, tobacco is grown in more than 100 countries, but its production is mainly controlled by three multinational corporations: British American Tobacco (BAT), RJ Reynolds and Philip Morris (Hammond, 1998). In Uganda production is dominated by BAT, which controls 93 per cent of the market through its subsidiary BAT-Uganda (BATU). It is a formidable player in the Ugandan economy. By 2003 it was producing 1.7 billion sticks per year. It is also one of the largest companies in Uganda, with more than 2800 employees in 2003, of which 563 were permanent, 847 were contractual and 1452 were part-time employees. It exerts immense influence on the economy by purchasing tobacco from 65 000 contract farmers, other inputs from 200 more suppliers, paying taxes and selling tobacco locally and internationally (BATU, 2003). Over the years, especially with the demise of cotton-growing, tobacco has become one of Uganda's key exports. In 2000, 96 per cent of BATU's output was exported, earning US$35–40 million in hard currency. In the same period the company paid US$4.5 million in excise, value-added and income taxes. BATU is therefore a significant and important feature of Uganda's

"

economic landscape. It directly or indirectly affects the lives of over 600000 people, including employees, farmers, customers and suppliers. As a result it is critical to the development debate in Uganda.

While some may debate whether firms like BATU should be producing tobacco at all, this chapter focuses on the impact of this firm on the social economy of Uganda. After reviewing BATU's history, this chapter examines its operating philosophy and internal relations. Guided by initiatives from its global headquarters, BATU has made significant efforts to upgrade relations with employees and suppliers at its production and manufacturing sites. Next, I focus upon how BATU has managed its relationship with its largest group of stakeholders, the contract farmers. While BATU has attempted in several ways to become a socially responsible business with respect to its main operations, its impact on tobacco farmers remains open to severe criticism. BATU buys tobacco in a traditional way that leaves the farmers vulnerable and impoverished. Further, its relationship with its resource base is far from exemplary. The overall impact of BATU on Uganda therefore appears mixed. Can BATU operate any differently at the back end of its business, especially where it has to deal with vulnerable and less-empowered groups? What policies, if any, would help BATU achieve a more acceptable resolution of the negative externalities of its business? These questions can be answered only by observing actions, understanding their causes and exploring alternatives.

History, strategy and relation to business suppliers

The British American Tobacco Group was founded in 1902 and made its first foray into Uganda in 1927 by introducing commercial varieties of tobacco (BATU, 2002c). The next year it built a cigarette factory in Jinja, Uganda, for the East African Tobacco Company. In 1949 it acquired this company, and in 1965 formed BAT Uganda Limited. As a result of nationalization, BAT ceased operations in 1972. BAT returned to Uganda in 1984, and repossessed 70 per cent control of its Ugandan assets. In 1998 the company changed its corporate image and name to British American Tobacco Uganda (BATU). Two years later the government divested its 30 per cent, selling one-third of these shares through the Uganda Stock Exchange (USE). BATU remains a subsidiary of British American Tobacco (BAT) PLC of UK, which has effective control of 90 per cent of the authorized share capital: 70 per cent directly and 20 per cent through Precis BV, a subsidiary of BAT Investments Limited. Local Ugandan institutions and members of the public own the remaining 10 per cent of BATU.

BATU is classified as an operating company, which means that it is mainly a tobacco-growing and leaf-production site. Its activities are spread through four leaf-growing regions: West Nile, Bunyoro-Mubende, North Kigezi-Rukungiri and Lira/Middle North. The field survey for this study was carried out in the Masindi-Hoima area of the Bunyoro-Mubende region, where dark fire-cured and burley tobacco varieties[2] are grown. BATU also processes domestic green leaf at its major site in Kampala, the capital city. It both exports the leaf and engages in domestic manufacture of cigarettes at Jinja, which lies 80 kilometres to the east of Kampala. The key motive of BATU is to earn a fair return for its stockholders; this is a motive driven by self-interest and self-preservation on global stock exchanges. In pursuing this objective, BATU also has to satisfy the tax demands of a developing country government with a very small tax base. Uganda has one of the lowest ratios of taxes to gross domestic product in Sub-Saharan Africa (11.2 per cent). BATU has been paying 1.8 to 3.2 billion shillings (US$1.5 million to US$2.0 million) in taxes per year, according to its own financial statements (BATU, 2003).

As an operating company, BATU belongs to the BAT Eastern Africa Region, which includes BAT subsidiaries in 12 other countries. The chief executive officer of the Company is the managing director, who is assisted by a team responsible for all day-to-day decisions. BATU is nominally governed by an eight-member board consisting of three executive directors and five non-executive directors, including the chairman (BATU, 2002a). The local non-executive directors are chosen from the public. They are supposed to be persons of high standing because they are expected to boost the image of the company and also give the company a 'local face'. Currently, the chairman of board of BATU is the former chairman of the Uganda Manufacturers Association and a close confidant of Uganda's president. In another life he would be an anti-tobacco activist because of his puritanical lifestyle. The non-executive board also includes the president's media advisor (Karugaba, 2001). The elevation of these prominent citizens is clear evidence of how the company wishes to present itself to the body politic, even if it does not explicitly admit to this strategy. Still, effective control of the firm is in the hands of the executive directors, who are all expatriates chosen by the parent company in the United Kingdom. The non-executive directors attend the annual general meeting and quarterly reviews and are consulted regularly on locally sensitive issues, but do not participate actively in policy decisions.

BATU's stated mission is 'To lead and excel in everything we do, through our people, through our products, in support of the community whilst ensuring profitable growth' (BATU, 2002c). The company is expected to follow best global practices as defined by its parent company. BATU claims that it has a high level of integrity and zero tolerance for corruption. Its stated corporate policy is to be the employer of first choice, recruiting the best and providing competitive pay through continuous review of the company's remuneration policy. The company strives to empower its employees to be self-driven, to understand company strategy, to grow with suppliers, and to communicate with them regularly, individually and collectively. Since 1928, the company claims, it has maintained strong ties with the community in the belief that the development of its tobacco-growing activities will enable the communities where it operates to prosper. This has involved providing extension services and other amenities to contract farmers, which would make the farmers, model members of society, practising modern agronomy.

The current management philosophy can be traced to 1996, when BATU's parent company initiated a revolutionary way of looking at its business. It introduced fundamental changes in the way that it perceived itself and its business partners. Committees for the Removal of Antiquated Practices (CRAP) were introduced to eliminate archaic practices that added no value. It strived to create a new work culture by delayering itself, re-engineering its people processes and providing quality products. The programmes were aimed at creating a high-performance culture, breaking down barriers to communication and increasing efficiency. The boardroom was discarded in favour of 'meeting rooms', and employees were encouraged to dress down and to be on first-name terms. The arrangement of separate facilities for different cadres of employees was discouraged in favour of an 'open office' system. BATU introduced flat-team structures to balance the 'soft' human aspects of management with the 'hard' business aspects. The purpose of the less hierarchical structure of teams was to keep financial imperatives in sight when making business decisions. The success of this strategy is demonstrated by improvements in BATU's performance. Measured in the local currency terms, sales doubled between 1996 and 2002, from 66 to 136 billion shillings (US$60 million to US$78 million).

BATU believes that its success has been a result of continuous reinvention, particularly of its relationships with its suppliers. In 1996 it had more than 800 suppliers, and its relationships with them were complicated by its bureaucratic structure and its failure to focus on its core business. The company changed direction by centralizing its procurement function, contracting out all services not part of its core business, such as legal work, cleaning, canteen management, transportation and security. It also deliberately began to engage in 'relationship management' with suppliers. In the past, suppliers were selected through competitive bidding, but this resulted in counter-productive attrition as suppliers engaged in cut-throat competition. As larger contracts became available, competition became stiffer and the tendering process itself became more susceptible to corruption. Many suppliers were unreliable, erratic and financially weak. Today BATU focuses upon growing a relationship with its suppliers according to a set of stated principles and practices. It aims at a mix where 20 per cent of its suppliers provide 80 per cent of its needs, so as to cut down on time-wasting interactions. It has reduced the number of its suppliers to 200. The company maintains an interest in a proposed supplier's financial and logistical condition, in part through an exhaustively detailed questionnaire. It conducts workshops to educate suppliers about its needs and the performance appraisal benchmarks that it will use in appraising them. It tracks their performance on a half-yearly basis regarding cost and quality, and this assessment becomes part of the contract renegotiation process. It requires suppliers to supply the same services to each other that they supply to BATU. Such linkages generate synergy, and enhance BATU's value chain by standardizing inputs.

BATU's farmers: the most vulnerable end of the value chain

The modern management fad of 'growing' employees and suppliers has been instrumental in improving BATU's business by allowing for flexibility, efficiency and constructive partnership. The question, however, arises: how has this faddish innovation improved the condition of the contract farmer? The farmers are the most vital link in BATU's value chain; by growing tobacco, they are positioned at the dirtiest and riskiest end of the tobacco business. If growing tobacco is BATU's core business, then the contract farmers are the company's core suppliers, and the company's practices in relation to these farmers should be most instructive of its approaches to business and corporate social responsibility.

Until 1995, BATU bought tobacco through cooperatives because of legal requirements and statist policies. However, it viewed cooperatives and the unions that controlled them as bureaucratic, corrupt and inefficient. In 1995, for example, the company was able to purchase only 7000 metric tonnes of tobacco. The cooperative movement had suffered from incessant government interference, which had destroyed any business ethos it ever pretended to have, by installing civil service bureaucrats without a business history at its apex. Tobacco production had been declining seriously because the incentive regime was poorly managed by the unions. The unions paid farmers using promissory 'chits' instead of money. They had no direct interest in maintaining the quality of tobacco en route to BATU, because the union officials were not necessarily tobacco growers themselves. Furthermore, the unions did not provide extension services to farmers.

In 1995 BATU began to alter its relation with its contract farmers, in line with its philosophy of 'growing supplier partnerships' and donor-inspired liberalization policy reviews. In 1997 the company was authorized to deal directly with farmers as part of Uganda's economic liberalization programme, which began in 1987. These direct dealings reduced bureaucracy and ensured that farmers got paid. As a result, the productivity of the farmers increased, and their numbers as well. In 2001 the company purchased a total of 21 000 tonnes, or three times its purchases six years earlier. In 2002 the tonnage increased to 35 000 tonnes. BATU now keeps close tabs on the 65 000 farmers it contracts with. The farmers are issued a passbook that bears their photographs and a registration number; this passbook is used to record the amount of the inputs received and the amount of tobacco each farmer must supply to BATU. It facilitates their farming activities, including the provision of extension services and, *as the written contract*, it binds farmers to sell their tobacco to BATU. The contract also specifies conditions of supply of tobacco: BATU reserves the right not to buy poor-quality tobacco, and to buy only the weight of tobacco contracted. Farmers may not sell BATU any more tobacco than they have been contracted to grow (see also Muhereza, 1995).

Alur farmers and the receding forest: environmental and social degradation

There are two main ethnic groups of tobacco farmers in the Masindi-Hoima area, and their relations with BATU have been significantly different. The migratory Alur, who originate from north-western Uganda and the Democratic Republic of Congo, are squatters who have settled, with the permission of absentee landowners, at the edge of the forest as a kind of 'land-opening' force. They grow dark fire-cured tobacco, the most environmentally destructive of the three varieties of tobacco grown, because it requires large quantities of firewood to cure or dry the tobacco leaves. The landowners allocate these farmers a different forest plot each season, and they fell their firewood indiscriminately through slash-and-burn as they open up the land for tobacco growing. In the short run, this unwelcome development is beneficial to both sides. The farmers obtain access to land at no cost; they also save on fertilizer by opening up fresh land every year. The timber from the forests enables them to grow the dark fire-cured tobacco, which they prefer because of its robustness. The landowners, for their part, obtain labour to open their fields at no cost. They then plant these fields with sugarcane for sale to the nearby government-owned Kinyara Sugar Works. With the acquiescence of absentee landlords, these migratory Alur farmers have been responsible for much of the deforestation in the area. It is only natural that these farmers do not have a long-term interest in the planting of woodlots to replace trees felled for curing tobacco.

Tobacco growing is an energy-intensive business, especially at the curing stages. The use of wood has had a critical impact on the biodiversity in the tobacco-growing areas. Yet BATU has little effective little control over the destructive partnership of landowners and Alur farmers. In an interview, the BATU area leaf manager noted that it was inexplicably difficult to convince these migratory farmers to grow the burley variety of tobacco, which doesn't require curing by fire: '...They just won't change or listen'. The company does have a widely acclaimed reforestation programme. According to Karugaba (2001), BATU claims to have planted 23 million trees since 1997 in its tobacco-growing areas. Another estimate puts this figure at 29 million standing trees (BATU, 2002b). But even this programme has been vehemently criticized for replacing indigenous species like Shea butter and mahogany with eucalyptus, a species that is 'thirsty and anti-social...Their fast growth rate places great demand on soil water and nutrients while the shed leaves do not permit growth of any other vegetation. With loss of soil cover comes soil erosion (Karugaba, 2001). Instances of sheet erosion have also been reported in northern Uganda, where the topsoil has been washed away, leaving a hard pan on the surface (Ogen, 1993). And in the Hoima-Masindi area, there was no evidence of any reforestation by the migratory farmers despite BATU's efforts to encourage tree planting. The Alur were continuing to harvest naturally occurring wood lots to cure their tobacco because, according to them, these burn better and produce more smoke, which is crucial to good curing.

Environmental problems are compounded by social problems. The tobacco-growing areas are remote, since they lie at the edge of the receding forest line. The farmers live in poorly built temporary shelters and have no utilities. Their quality of life is incredibly poor. Many of the farmers, especially among the migratory Alur, live in the most inhuman conditions – illiterate and unkempt, despite the incomes they earn, and exposed to chemicals for nine months each year, from January to September, as they work to transform the tobacco seedlings into the cured leaf that will be bought by BATU. The back-breaking work is full-time, leaving virtually no time for other activities. The farmers hardly leave the field: they must open up the fields, tend nurseries, prepare and fertilize ridges for receiving the seedlings, nurture plants by cutting their tops and spraying them, harvest the yellow or ripening leaves, hang the harvest in barns, leaf by leaf, cure it using either smoke or sun, then grade the tobacco and take it to the buying centre. All this work is done manually and requires intensive labour input.

Concerns have arisen over the widespread use of child labour. BATU acknowledges the problem, but claims that it adheres to its Global Best Practices Programme in not buying tobacco from farmers who use child labour. This claim is at odds with realities on the ground. Women and children are the most vulnerable part of the tobacco-leaf supply chain, and the social dislocations caused by the labour-intensive nature of the crop involve not only child labour but also denial of education to children, family tensions and, in many cases, polygamous marriages – especially among the migratory farmers. Some farmers grow tobacco only to pay the dowry for a bride, and when it has been paid they will stop. Those who continue growing tobacco will usually marry another wife. Such farmers end up with two or more families, one in the town and another in the field. 'I have to live out here in the forest for nine months. My other wife won't leave our family home in Aru … surely I need a companion here … that helps make life a bit better,' said one migratory farmer. The 'farm' wife provides companionship in what are clearly harsh conditions; and over time, her children will more likely than not provide free labour for the farmer.

The issue of a farmer having both a 'farm' wife and a 'town' wife is not simply a matter of bigamy as it would be described from a Eurocentric point of view. Because tobacco is a labour-intensive crop, child labour is widely prevalent among the poorer farmers who cannot pay for hired labour. In order to be successful and earn a reasonable income, any rational farmer will have recourse to the most easily accessible labour: that provided by his 'farm' wife and her children. Moreover, many African societies have always been polygamous. Large families have greater access to labour and therefore are more likely to be successful. As for schooling, although primary education was made free in Uganda in 1997 and parents are not required to pay school fees, education is not a priority for people struggling to eke out a living. The children themselves eventually start their own families at an early age. As a result of the socialization process they undergo in the tobacco fields, these young farmers remain socially deprived and ignorant of the benefits of education. BATU acknowledges that the 'boys to men' phenomenon is deeply embedded in the culture and practices of the majority of its farmers; but the remoteness of the farming communities, the strategic benefit to farmers in using their children as labourers and BATU's lack of enforcement of its own stated position against child labour all combine to perpetuate this vicious cycle.

BATU claims that its effective control over the farmers ends with delivery of the crop to the buying centre. Still, the company has initiated a number of socially responsible programmes, such as the BAT scholarship scheme, health and education programmes, infrastructure rehabilitation and construction. While these programmes are welcome, they do not appear to alter the conditions of BATU's most important supplier in any fundamental way. The farmers remain mired in poverty, alcoholism and spousal abuse and they continue to deny their offspring the right to a better life through education. It is the lot of the farmer that BATU must improve in order to enhance social capital in the communities it operates. Yet BATU does not appear to have a long-term plan to improve their social conditions and awareness. If there were such a policy it would improve the productivity of the farmers and also make the growth of the tobacco more attractive.

The Banyoro and the Alur: constrained choices and unfair outcomes

The indigenous Banyoro, natives of the former Bunyoro-Kitara Kingdom, have permanent homesteads. They appear more prosperous and environmentally conscious than the Alur people. The smallest farm size is 0.4 hectare and a 'good' farmer can earn US$1200 per year, or about eight times the country's per capita income. In the 2001 season, it was evident from the field visits that some farmers have done well for themselves, especially the more settled Banyoro farmers who can contract external labour. Such farmers can earn as much as US$6000 per year.

It is popularly assumed that small-scale farmers benefit from tobacco, but this assumption appears to be at odds with reality (Ogen, 1993). On average,

BATU pays only about 15 per cent (16 billion shillings or roughly US$9.3 million) of its gross income for growing costs. This is equivalent to US$150 for each of its 65 000 farmers – well below Uganda's income of US$216 per capita in 2001 (Budget, 2002). Living standards have not risen enough to mitigate the externalities of tobacco growing. It is obvious, when the issue of fair pay to farmers is examined from the point of view of commutative justice, that exchanges between farmers and BATU are not on an equal footing. In most of the tobacco-growing areas, the standard of living is low and the priority is day-to-day survival – a fact acknowledged by BATU itself (BATU, 2002b). The sheer poverty of the growing areas raises the question: if many farmers are not really making any money from tobacco, why do they continue growing tobacco season after season? Is it due to unequal contracting powers? The evidence suggests that the contracting between not only the Alur, but even the relatively better-off Banyoro farmers and BATU fails to meet the standards of both commutative and distributive justice.

First, the farmers have certain advantages but lack meaningful choices, in making their contracts with BATU. Most of the farmers wish to have their earnings increased through other crops, but there are few alternatives. All able-bodied men have a duty to provide for their families, and tobacco-growing is effectively the only income-yielding activity. The tobacco-growing areas are remote, and the markets not only difficult to reach, but highly unfavourable. The farmers say they have tried alternative crops, but there are no buyers. Coffee, for example, has fallen to one-quarter of the world price paid in 1960, and now stagnates at the lowest price paid in 30 years, according to Oxfam International. In 2000–01, farmers in Uganda grew bumper crops of maize (corn), causing the price to plummet. As one interviewed farmer put it, 'Look at all that maize which I grew this season. When I planted, the price was 250 shillings (US$0.15) per kilo, now it is 20 shillings per kilo and I can't even find buyers. It is all going to rot in the barn.' BATU, in contrast, did purchase all the tobacco leaf it had contracted to grow. Ryan (2003) points out another advantage of having BATU buy the farmer's crop on the spot. As one farmer she quotes put it, '… The market is here (tobacco). If you grow good quality, you get good money. I have tried alternative crops on my farm. I had horticultural crops … I tried onions and tomatoes, I am 340 kilometres from Kampala, how do I bring these things to the market in Kampala? Then these middlemen try to screw you so bad, you will get nothing' (p. 15). On average, tobacco is the only realistic choice of cash crop for farmers. It is not perishable. The fact that the buyer is ever-present, with BATU's assurance that it will buy all the tobacco it has contracted farmers to grow, ensures some income for farmers. Yet by bringing the market to the farmer, as it were, BATU's passbook contract effectively gives the company exclusive access to the farmer's product because the farmer cannot acquire the needed inputs independently; once contracted, he must accept guidance from the assistant leaf technician in charge of his location. In this context, then, the farmer has ceded significant rights to the company.

Second, questions of fairness arise at the buying centres. There the tobacco is classified into 17 grades, depending on quality. The prices paid for these differing grades vary widely. The mean price paid for tobacco of good grade during the 2001 season was US$0.70 per kilogram, but prices range from a high of 1400 to as low as 350 shillings (from US$0.80 to US$0.20). Grading is done by BATU unilaterally and there is a strong perception that illiterate farmers are being cheated. As one stakeholder put it, these grades are 'assessed by mere human vision. Is this fair to farmers? Isn't this where BAT makes its profits?' (BATU, 2002b). The prices paid to farmers are determined solely by BAT, even though BAT claims that prices are agreed before the start of the season. Considering BATU's annual growing costs as a general indicator, farmers' earnings would appear to be below the national reported per capita income for Uganda of US$216 for 2001. If one takes into account that farmers also received inputs from BATU at the start of the season, their net earnings may have been considerably lower.

Third, the outcome for the farmers is not proportional to their contribution; the people at the dirtiest and riskiest end of the tobacco-growing business earn the least. The farmers take on great risk. Their earnings can be high and, in an environment of scarce opportunities very welcome for prudent farmers. Unfortunately, there are not many prudent farmers; BATU admits that only about 40 per cent of the farmers fall into the productive category (Ryan, 2003). BATU classifies farmers according to those who pay back the cost of inputs and those who do not – the company says it cannot afford to lose its capital input – but it does not reward its farmers proportionately. As noted above, BATU pays only about US$150 on average to each of its 65 000 farmers. In contrast, the company in 2001 paid some 573 million shillings or US$330 000 to the three executive directors (Annual Report, 2001, p. 10). Such a low percentage of its total turnover cannot make a lasting positive impact on the poverty of its 65 000 contracted farmers. It is further noted that net incomes of farmers are poor because of the production loans provided by BATU, the failure to factor in the cost of family labour and the fact that most of their tobacco is bought as low-grade – an issue that is also raised by stakeholders (BATU, 2002b).[3]

Fourth, the labour-intensive nature of tobacco farming imposes gross injustices on women. Traditionally, women are the main producers of food crops. However, when helping farm and cure tobacco they are forced to take on additional responsibilities, which reduce the time they can spend on domestic chores and producing other crops (Ogen, 1993). Less attention is paid to preparing proper meals. Time spent in the fields by women also reduces the level of care provided to children, including the likelihood of going to school. Women tobacco growers also lose out when rogue husbands confiscate their meagre earnings from tobacco leaf sales for purchase of alcohol.

Finally, as suggested above, the environment suffers injustice in the form of degradation through the use of fertilizers and pesticides in the propagation and growing of tobacco. BATU supplies non-organic fertilizers to its farmers, and these appear to degrade the soil, forcing farmers to extend tobacco growing to forests and other virgin lands. Because the fertilizers are expensive, farmers try to save on fertilizer cost by opening up virgin land. The effects of these fertilizers have not yet been properly documented in Uganda. BATU reports having instituted a programme balancing economically viable production of leaf with positive environmental management to farmers through a comprehensive extension service. The programme involves helping farmers choose the right seed, minimize reliance on agrochemicals, maintain soil fertility and water resources and reduce fuel consumption; it also provides them continuous training in all aspects of agronomy (BATU, 2002b).

BATU's conservationist approach is problematic in that it is anthropocentric, technologically optimistic and chiefly concerned with efficiency (Marcus, 1993). It ignores the linkages between human activities and environmental degradation, by proclaiming the superiority of technological solutions. BATU's vision of environmental protection is not supported by the facts on the ground. Every year more forest cover is destroyed, and farmers are entirely dependent upon BATU for all inputs, while remaining exposed to dangerous chemicals and smoke in the barns. At most risk are the women tobacco farmers, who spend entire working days hanging tobacco in poorly aerated barns, and are exposed to interminable streams of smoke. The men are also exposed to non-organic chemicals in the gardens. BATU's procedures for safeguarding farmers are weak. Farmers have no protective clothing whatsoever. In many cases, compliance with BATU's extension advice would mean increasing costs for inputs. Since the farmers are under contract to bring in the leaf, they have no alternative but to toil for long hours without adequate protection.

Conclusion

This study asks how a multinational corporation (MNC) in Uganda addresses issues of justice and good citizenship when balancing the competing needs of profit and social responsibility. In Chapter 2 Frederick Bird reviews three different strategies of engagement by MNCs in developing areas. One strategy consists primarily in the simple exploitation strictly for the advantage of the MNC. A second strategy focuses on reducing costs and achieving competitive advantage, through which the developing country also benefits by receiving wage-paying jobs, tax revenues, infrastructure development and technology transfers. By a third strategic orientation, firms intentionally work to add value to host countries by building capacity and developing assets. Overall, BATU seems to have adopted the second strategy. By providing jobs, paying taxes and exporting over 90 per cent of its leaf to earn much-needed foreign exchange, it seems to have been a good development partner in this limited sense. The company has higher-than-average wage levels, invests in the infrastructure of its business and builds local partnerships. Its intention to maintain a long-term presence is not in doubt. It has adopted global 'best practice' codes because its activities touch so many lives. It participates in as many socially responsible activities as it can possibly support. In the absence of an alternative, and unless one emphasizes negative long-run externalities such as deforestation, BATU's presence in Uganda is a positive development.

This chapter has also focused upon the practices and strategies of BATU with special emphasis on the contract farmers who are the core suppliers of the tobacco-growing business. The company's evident indifference to the social conditions of the farmers testifies to the difficulties multinational corporations face in balancing profits and benefits. BATU is answerable to a host of invisible investors who are several times removed from the grind of poverty in developing countries. These investors demand profit, and hence in the long run BATU has to show that profit. The question is where an acceptable balance might lie between the need to earn a profit and the need to benefit, in a more general way, the developing area in which it operates. Might BATU operate any differently from its traditional practices? If so, what policies might help the company achieve a more acceptable resolution of the negative externalities occasioned by its business?

The externalities at issue include deforestation, soil erosion, the use of child labour and the pollution caused by pesticides and other harmful inputs. To address these issues, BATU needs to resolve the conflict between ends and means – the desire to be profitable and how that profit is attained (Marcus, 1993). The route forward lies in increasing the social capital of the farmers. Ideally, BATU needs to make them understand that deforestation is counter-productive in the long run, that child labour is not socially desirable and that incomes from tobacco should be used to improve living conditions. But such initiatives by BATU would require a tremendous input of resources, which the company might not be able to provide. Between 1997 and 2002, BATU's after-tax profits dropped steadily from 12 billion to 4.8 billion shillings, or from US$11 million to US$2.7 million. The social burdens clearly lie way beyond business objectives as well; in this game there is a pecking order in which profit comes first, political agendas second and the community a distant third. It is difficult to see how BATU can operate differently from the way it does without conscious intervention and assistance from the Uganda government. BATU cannot be expected to create economic activity and also assume the responsibility of the state to improve social conditions. The development process needs to be seen as a satisficing process, in which we do not have the luxury of clear-cut standards for assessment.

Thus any improvement in social conditions occasioned by BATU will be a by-product of its core business – from seed to leaf.

Notes

1. The study draws upon two field surveys of BATU's activities in the Bunyoro-Mubende region and interviews with contract farmers and the company's field and leaf-production managers. These surveys involved 12 farmers, and 7 BATU managers (including the Eastern Africa Region Leaf Manager, Environment Manager and Corporate Affairs Manager) during the 2001 and 2002 growing seasons.
2. Air-cured tobacco (burley) is dried in the open air; dark-fire cured is dried by fire and smoke, while flue-cured tobacco is cured by heat through flue pipes.
3. Similar concerns about fairness have been raised by other observers. Muhereza (1995) argued that returns to farmers were poor because (1) BATU has a poor attitude to the welfare of farmers; (2) harvests are usually poor due to the vagaries of weather; and (3) the price paid to farmers is only 20 per cent of the world price (pp. 37–9).

References

BATU (2002a) *Annual Report 2001* (Kampala, Uganda).
BATU (2002b) *Report to Society 2002* (Kampala, Uganda).
BATU (2002c) *Mission Statement* (Kampala, Uganda).
BATU (2003) *Annual Report 2002* (Kampala, Uganda).
Hammond, R. (1998) *Addicted to Profit: Big Tobacco's Expanding Global Reach* (Washington: Essential Action).
Karugaba, P. (2001) 'Big Tobacco's Overseas Expansion: Focus on Uganda', The Environmental Action Network (TEAN). Paper presented to the San Francisco Tobacco Free Project, May.
Marcus, A. A. (1993) *Business and Society, Ethics, Government, and the World Economy* (Boston: Irwin).
Muhereza, F. M. (1995) *Agricultural Commercialization, Contract Farming and Tobacco: A Study of the Socio-Economic Effects of Tobacco Growing in Masindi District, Uganda.* Working Paper no. 48 (Kampala: Centre for Basic Research).
Ogen, K. A. (1993) *Paying the Price of Growing Tobacco: Environmental and Social-Economic Impact of Production in Arua District* (Kampala: Monitor Publications Limited).
Ryan, O. (2003) 'No Smoke Without Cash', *The Monitor* (Kampala, Uganda) 24 June, p. 15.

7
Seeking a Better Connection: Mobile Telecommunications Network and Social Responsibility in Uganda

Ida Mutoigo and Samuel Sejjaaka

Introduction

Mobile Telecommunications Network (MTN) is a global cellular provider headquartered in South Africa and owned almost completely by corporate investors outside Uganda. Its subsidiary MTN Uganda provides both mobile and fixed telephone services, and data and fax communications. The company prides itself on its technological innovation, dynamism and standards of excellence. Its goal is to be the leading telecommunications provider in Uganda by offering an affordable service to clients through a convergence of cellular, internet and satellite technology. It advertises that it offers a 'better connection', and that better connection is evident in several respects. MTN's strategy of making telephone services widely available to all, especially women, has significantly expanded and enhanced the quality and coverage of telecommunications in Uganda. MTN employs more than three hundred Ugandans directly, and several thousand indirectly, enabling them to improve their job skills. Their families and other social units have increased their incomes. MTN's investment has contributed significantly to the tax base of Uganda, which is one of the smallest in Sub-Saharan Africa. Its social interventions as a responsible corporate citizen have begun to improve the humanitarian conditions of some of the most disadvantaged sections of society. Overall, MTN Uganda has had an outstanding impact on Uganda's economy considering that it only commenced its operations in late 1998.

Yet in its quest for profit and economic development, MTN Uganda has missed several 'better connections' and has engendered some negative externalities. Its communications services are unaffordable for a large percentage of Ugandan women. Its human-resource practices offer glaringly preferential treatment to expatriates, generating considerable tension in the workplace.

Its governance practices exclude locals from meaningful participation. Its marketing practices encourage socially harmful consumption of scarce resources in the form of cell phone usage. Overall, MTN is well positioned to add much value to Uganda, but its 'better connection' has yet to be realized in full.

New markets for rapid growth, 1998–2002

As a result of botched government policies, shoddy infrastructure and corruption, the telecommunications sector in Africa has been largely stagnant in its growth. Infrastructure developed more as a monument to the African independence movement or because funding was made available by international finance institutions, rather than because it was driven by demand or users. In the past 10 years, technological developments and a liberalized economy fostered a quick jump from landline technologies to mobile communications. The landline system stagnated while mobile communications have grown rapidly (Ugandanetwork, 2002). Until 1995 there was only one licensed national operator; the government-owned Uganda Posts and Telecommunications Company Limited (UPTCL). Uganda currently has about 40 000 fixed lines in contrast to 500 000 mobile phones.

The quick jump to mobile communications presented challenges that MTN Uganda met with greater success than its competition. In the absence of appropriate regulatory frameworks in most African countries, the market does not immediately or inevitably deliver the best outcomes, and incoming investors or multinationals hold sway over the course of new developments in the private sector (Stiglitz, 2002). The first mobile telephone operator in Uganda was Celtel Cellular Limited, which started operations in 1995. Its name since has been changed to MSI-Cellular Limited. MSI-Cellular confined its services to the capital city of Kampala and its immediate environs. Thanks to monopoly clauses in its contracts, it priced most average users out of the market. Only with the arrival of MTN Uganda in 1998 did the industry begin to experience some competition. UPTCL was restructured into two companies and privatized; renamed Uganda Telecommunications Limited, it was designated as the first national operator. MTN Uganda secured the second such licence, which requires it to provide all types of telecommunications services including international gateways. MSI-Cellular did not acquire this licence. The Uganda Communications Commission (UCC) was also created in 1996 to oversee the operations of the three companies. Thus at the time MTN Uganda started its operations the market for telecommunications was still largely unexplored, and this has been the most critical factor in its rapid growth – making telephone services accessible to all and sundry.

MTN Uganda is now the fastest-growing company in the country. The company has cashed in on the popularity of its 'phones to the people' investment, as is reflected in the phenomenal growth in revenues over the last four years of its operations. Between 1999 and 2002, service revenues grew tenfold while the company's asset base grew fivefold, with an investment base over US$100 million. Over its short lifetime, it has become the largest telecommunications provider in Uganda, controlling about 65 per cent of the market and operating within over 80 towns and trading centres. The company has over 300 000 subscribers and 5000 fixed lines. MTN Publicom is a 45 per cent owned subsidiary of MTN Uganda and is responsible for providing payphone services or what it calls 'shared access services'.

Empowering women customers

'Maama, Taata, Nange' (Mother, Father and Me) is the nickname popular radio shows bestow upon MTN Uganda; it symbolizes how all three use the MTN network. This nickname reflects the powerful impact of MTN on Ugandan society. Its mobile telecom network services especially have enabled Ugandans to make 'better connections' by growing their businesses and to fulfil their familial responsibilities more effectively. MTN Uganda's telecommunication services have given Ugandans greater access to local and global markets, and have enabled some to invest in capital items such as vehicles, land and houses, to save on time and travel expenses. Especially noteworthy is the impact that this service has made in the lives of women, as learned in a survey conducted explicitly for this study.[1] Women in developing countries like Uganda tend to be the most vulnerable to exploitation. They have two viable avenues for enhancing their status in society: education and professional training on the one hand, and economic prosperity on the other (Abena, 1991). The combination of computer technology with telecommunications technology opens both avenues for Ugandan women, enabling many to use savings on business investments to improve their household management.

Rachel,[2] a 36-year-old widow from Luwero who has six children, provides one example of how access to markets through mobile phone services has become vital to her business:

> Before my husband died, we had started a baking and decorations business in 1996. I have been with MTN since 2000 and have noticed it has made my life so much easier for contacting customers. I would say I have been able to increase my income by about 30 per cent as a result of this. Even during financially difficult times, such as when I have to pay all the school fees for the children, I must have my service fee maintained so that I do not miss my business deals. Luwero is an up-country location that does not have landline service in the villages. Having the MTN network then gives me access to customers I would never have had access to. The only drawback is that when I travel very deep in the village while

doing my wedding decoration business, the network is poor, which makes it difficult for customers to reach me.

Mary, a Kampala businesswoman who has run a clothing materials and fashion business since 1998, is another MTN customer who has been able to access global markets since she began using a mobile phone in 2000.

> I use the mobile phone to contact suppliers in India, Bangkok, Thailand or Indonesia. I use it to ring a clearing agent, who then clears the goods. He can either ring me when the goods are cleared or can even bring the goods to my shop. I do know that I have been able to make more savings than before and now am able to take full responsibility for all of the home management and general family upkeep without really any help from my husband. Even more so, we are starting to build a house of our own.

Businesswomen have found that access to the reliable services of MTN generates savings in time and travel. Beatrice, a 30-year-old woman from Jinja, testified to a sudden increase in her monthly income after using MTN services for only about five months:

> I spend about 35,000 Uganda shillings on airtime and service fees, but the savings that I have been able to make as a result far outweigh the costs. Before I became a subscriber with MTN, I had to go shopping at least four times in a month and each trip would cost me 50,000 Uganda shillings. Now, all I have to do is ring my suppliers and they bring me the commodities I need. That means I now can save an extra 200,000 Uganda shillings (equivalent to US$111) each month. It feels great to be in control of the business I have with my husband. I know the future prospects are for our business to expand.

In Uganda, virtually all women work an average of 15 to 18 hours a day. Fully 25 per cent work 18 hours per day (Barton and Wamai, 1994). Any technology that saves time will be welcome, especially if it saves money as well. These time-savings were appreciated by 58.5 per cent of the 147 women interviewed in the survey.

Increased earnings translate into better 'home management'. This term includes the ability to purchase household items, daily consumables, furnishings, clothing and pay utility bills. In the survey mentioned above, 50 per cent of male and 39.5 per cent of female MTN users noted this as an important consequence of their subscription to MTN Uganda's services. The savings and profits that women achieve have enabled them eventually to purchase land or build a house. Olivia, for example, recently bought her own land after experiencing an 85 per cent increase in her income. She attributes this dramatic increase primarily to the improved connections

MTN Uganda provided to her customers in her hair salon business. Her achievement is all the greater considering the fact that only 7 per cent of women in Uganda own land (Barton and Wamai, 1994).

What can be learned from MTN Uganda's experience is that when international businesses operate in a developing country, they generate influences that can improve the lot of marginalized populations. In this regard, MTN Uganda's technology is exciting; it shows great potential to increase the social capital of disadvantaged groups in Uganda. Social capital refers to those valued social resources that assume the form of networks of social relations, the trust that facilitates social cooperation, as well as the commitments that lead people to volunteer time, goods, hospitality and forbearance to others. It has now become possible to maintain and develop social networks within the population that were previously very difficult or costly to sustain. For example, the greatest portion (at 49 per cent) of all female MTN users consists of young women from 20 to 30 years; they use this communication technology primarily for developing their social relationships. MTN Uganda's services also provide customers with better access to family and dependants, in the opinion of 65 per cent of the women and 60 per cent of the men who completed the survey. Such communication links have given women access to a 'safety net' that helps them live through difficult times and impoverished situations. Nina, a 26-year-old Sudanese refugee living with her aunt in Lubaga, Kampala, is a widow with one child. She feels the MTN Uganda service network is the lifeline that links her to relatives and friends abroad who 'send money for her to survive with her child'. It might not be an exaggeration to claim that MTN Uganda has in effect promoted a caring community in Uganda.

Yet MTN Uganda's management of social capital has experienced lost opportunities as well as 'better connections'. While its 'phones to the people' outlook shows much promise of an impact on those who have access to its services, that access has been more limited than it might have been for poorer people, the majority who are women. Although MTN Uganda should be congratulated on its ability to engage female customers, it faces a challenge of avoiding economic exploitation of a segment of the population that is typically more economically disadvantaged than the rest of MTN Uganda's subscribers.

While MTN Uganda promises to deliver a 'better connection' than any other mobile telecommunication company, its service still proves to be so expensive that large portions of the population, including women and rural areas, are effectively excluded. Until July 2003, a subscriber had to pay a service charge of US$5.60 per month to have access to the network. This figure has since been reduced to US$3 per month. The company argues that it has the lowest cost of penetration of any service provider in Uganda and that its charges are relatively low when seen in an international context. Still, the subscribers to MTN and other mobile phone company networks number only one woman to every three men, a ratio which is deeply unequal in a country where women compose 51 per cent of the population (Wasike, 2002). In spite of the positive contributions that MTN Uganda has made in the development of Ugandans, the more disadvantaged groups in society, largely women, continue to be excluded from the benefits of mobile telecommunications.

It should be noted that MTN Uganda customers also may contribute to the problem as a result of their service consumption habits. The company argues that the overall cost of usage of telephony services is aggravated by social calls, which divert resources without creating commensurate value in the lives of users. Beth, an MTN client who works as a public sector employee in Mbale, appears to agree: 'I think the MTN service is expensive. Being on the network is a source of disturbance. There is too much dependency on the phone, which results in impulse calling.' More than half of MTN Uganda's customers cope with the cost of service by using a strategy called 'beeping': they call someone and let the phone ring once or twice but then hang up in order to alert the other person to call them back. This is evidence that telephony service has become critical and that customers have access to the network services they paid for. Customers, for their part, charge that they bear the brunt of disruptions in service. One subscriber complained:

> On November 6, 2002, the MTN network was off in Gulu from 10:00 a.m. in the morning to 12:32 p.m. the next day. Could something be done about this? At least the public relations officer should inform subscribers what's happening. MTN should also subtract the days off (from the bill) when the network is poor. Subscribers prefer people who care about them not those who exploit.

Overall, MTN Uganda has succeeded in providing an effective telecommunications service at moderate cost within the context of a poor landline infrastructure. Yet developing an affirmative-action plan with reduced rates for the poor and higher-quality relay stations could enable MTN Uganda to achieve its promise to be a 'better connection' for all Ugandans. As Sethi (1993) has observed, foreign corporations could have more impact if they concentrate on areas where they have most direct control. He advocates more affirmative action related to improving the lot of marginalized groups.

Human resource practices

The impact of MTN Uganda on the labour market has been felt nationally. This is especially so when one takes into account that the company has been in operation for slightly less than five years. By July 2003 the company created over 310 new jobs for direct employees in an area riddled with unemployment. In addition, MTN Uganda provides employment for contractors, as it outsources work on information technology, switching systems and fibre optic cable installation in Kampala. Finally, over 6000 people are employed indirectly through its franchise system or as providers of ancillary services such as the sale of mobile phones and accessories, phone repairs, advertising and events promotions and many other less obvious businesses. MTN Uganda has opened more than 600 service outlets in the country. It can be said that of all foreign direct investment in Uganda the communications industry has become the most conspicuous.

At the onset of its operations in 1998, MTN Uganda's workforce consisted of approximately 80 direct employees, of whom 25 were expatriates. Over time, the labour force has changed. The number of expatriates has declined to nine, while its local staff increased to 310. MTN Uganda is one of the most sought after employers in the country for remuneration, given that the market is afflicted with high unemployment. In Uganda, the per capita income averages US$215 per year; MTN Uganda pays yearly salaries which range from US$5000 for support staff to more than US$25 000 for managers. This pay structure, coupled with the growing local significance of the company has attracted some of the best labour in Uganda.

However, this is not the whole picture. The company's reward system for expatriates is fundamentally different from that of locals, causing considerable tensions. To be sure, one local was hired at wages of about US$7000 per month, plus the benefits expatriates typically receive. Across the board however, expatriate staff receive preferential treatment. The average expatriate earns about US$15 000 per month. Although the number of expatriate staff has been reduced from 25 in 1998 to nine in July 2003, the total wage bill for these expatriates has not reduced proportionately. The 2002 wage bill for 14 expatriates was almost the same as that of the 240 locals! MTN Uganda managers argue that this fact misrepresents the situation. According to the marketing manager and de facto spokesman for MTN Uganda, 'The figure for expatriate wages includes "management fees" which are paid to the parent company in South Africa.' There appear to be at least two further explanations for this seemingly gross inequality: differences in skill and the 'risk factor' associated with living in Uganda. The marketing manager argued that expatriates have skills that locals do not have, and that there is a shortage of management skills in Uganda. 'Our expatriates are employable in any international company in the world. If you were asked to go and work in Cambodia, would you not demand higher pay? Would you let your kids study in local Cambodian schools?'

The expatriate problem is generic to most multinational corporations. Expatriates serve a particular function, which Bartlett and Goshal term 'socialization' in their recent study of Unilever (Bartlett and Goshal, 2002). Expatriate managers serve as the vanguard for international finance capital; they are custodians of the company's assets in a country that is perceived to have high economic and political risk. Their role is to provide confidence to shareholders with respect to their investments in developing areas. Yet while socialization may represent the 'company way' of doing things for multinationals, it is a two-edged sword. First of all, it reduces rather than increases shareholder value, due to the incredible cost of maintaining expatriate managers. The cost of maintaining an expatriate manager runs two to 10 times higher than maintaining a local manager in the same position (Bartlett and Goshal, 2002). Not only are expatriates paid excessively high salaries and pensions, but they also have tuition provided for their children in 'international' schools. Second, socialization creates distributive inequity and ensures that a large amount of host-country generated income, which would be more beneficial to local consumption, is appropriated in the form of expatriate wages. Third, it reinforces and confirms the stereotype of multinational corporations as exploitative and racist rather than developmental and egalitarian in their employment practices.

Like Unilever, MTN International relies on a select cadre of expatriates to transfer corporate knowledge and develop operations abroad in a manner consistent with its values and objectives. The problems that Bartlett and Goshal identified also afflict MTN's Uganda operation, where the arguments for using expatriates seem slender, at best. An MTN Uganda manager claimed that using expatriates increases the flexibility and ease of decision-making:

> Other international companies with which we have to deal are invariably run by expatriates. Local firms do not have access to credit, and it is difficult for us to have to pay up front for services all the time. Take the case of Plessey of South Africa … they can afford to give us six months credit; which local firm can do that? Inevitably we must deal with Plessey.

What this means is that the pattern of awarding contracts or promoting local activities inevitably favours other predominantly international or foreign-managed (preferably white-managed) businesses while excluding local businesses. MTN Uganda limits the involvement of local staff in certain key activities because of the 'absence of local capacity'; but the capacity seems clearly present. At the study site, we found some of the most sophisticated telecommunications technology in the world. With a few exceptions, local staff manages most of this equipment, including the switching systems. How then does MTN Uganda justify a costly complement of expatriate staff in other departments, like marketing and finance? One of the main reasons MSI-Cellular failed to match MTN's success was that its local top managers were given little or no authority to compete with MTN. It seems that MTN Uganda has fallen victim to a hiring mentality that perpetuates the 'glass-ceiling' effect – the belief that there are some jobs locals can do and others they cannot. Expatriate staff 'buy into' this mentality and keep alive the notion that there is a shortage of skilled staff, because this justifies their being rehired. Finally, the expatriate mentality also sees Uganda as a 'high-risk' area for which one must be rewarded handsomely to 'brave the dangers' of living in a 'Cambodia-like' environment. The truth is that the risk of living in Uganda is hardly greater than in South Africa, where a vicious official policy of inequality and deprivation bred so much insecurity.

The result of MTN's 'socialization' strategy is that racial tensions and workplace discontent are recurring themes at MTN Uganda. To be sure, cultural diversity in its workforce is an area of some concern to the company. Diversity is achieved largely by targeting certain ethnic groups to fill customer services jobs that require persons speaking a specific language. To foster a feeling of corporate family, social functions are organized regularly, and free SIM phone cards are provided for spouses. The company has attracted highly educated people for whom social distinctions are minimal and yet, as mentioned earlier, racial and ethnic tensions persist. Some have been fostered by preferential recruitment practices. MTN is also perceived as nepotistic in local hiring. Positions that fall vacant are either filled internally, or employees are asked to suggest replacements. Naturally most employees then tend to look to their relatives as potential employees. Said one manager:

> Imagine the level of unemployment in this country. If we were to advertise the job of a sales person, for instance, we would be flooded by applications. It is wiser to search for employees quietly rather than go through bureacratic procedures that waste valuable time.

But the most significant racial tensions are a result of an organizational culture that remains entrenched in the apartheid value system of the South African expatriate staff. Local employees see expatriates as a domineering force, protecting an investment in a risky area from corrupt locals, including politicians as well as employees. Staff meetings are rare, and are dominated by counter-accusations and workplace manoeuvring.

The telecommunications industry has become an important economic brand in Uganda, with a sizeable number of citizens deriving their livelihood from its activities. Most visible are the dealers. The distribution of MTN Uganda's services is franchised. The country is divided into 33 franchise regions. A dealer, who in turn appoints sub-dealers or agents, controls each franchise and is fully responsible for company activities in the area. According to the company, any business person who applies to MTN Uganda to be appointed a dealer for a given area must have a capital of about US$15 000 and must submit to a due-diligence test (the E-test), which is designed to determine whether the applicant is suited for a dealership. This test covers the past business experience, levels of commitment to other business and reliability of the prospective dealer, including credit references.

When MTN Uganda started operations, no such processes or procedures existed for the selection of dealers; dealers were chosen because the company managers knew them personally. Because many people are applying for dealerships today, the company has been forced to devise a system for awarding dealerships; however it is not clear how transparently this system works. Several dealers have substantial political connections or are politicians in their own right.

Overall, MTN Uganda's human-resource achievements, in terms of job creation and professional development of local staff, have fostered a 'better connection'. However, the company has lost the opportunity to enjoy 'better connections' with staff due to the disparities in its hiring practices. Its in-house hiring is definitely tainted by an unjust reward system. The gap in compensation packages between the local and expatriate employees accentuates racial tensions. If these wage disparities are creatively addressed and more genuine participation of local staff is encouraged, MTN Uganda will more effectively live up to its promise to be a 'better connection' – a caring organizational community. Considering the context of an increasing competition from Uganda Telecom Limited (UTL) in the telecommunication industry, MTN would ensure its corporate sustainability better by addressing these issues in more creative ways.

Governance practices

Governance concerns how transparently and effectively economic resources are managed. The Commonwealth Association for Corporate Governance (CACG, 2000) defines governance as

> the manner in which power is exercised in the management of economic and social resources for sustainable human development. It is now globally recognised that good governance is a vital ingredient in the dynamic balance between the need for order and equality in society, the efficient production and delivery of goods and services, accountability in the use of power, the protection of human rights and freedoms, and the maintenance of an organized corporate framework within which citizens can contribute fully towards finding innovative solutions to common problems.

Measured against this definition, MTN Uganda's systems of governance illustrate a mixture of achievements and challenges.

MTN Uganda is a subsidiary of the MTN Group (South Africa) and is effectively controlled through a series of external investment companies, which hold 97 per cent of its share capital. These companies are MTN International (Mauritius), Telia Overseas (Sweden) and Tristar Rwanda. As a result of this shareholding arrangement, the company is answerable primarily to an external constituency of shareholders. Governance is the preserve of a board made up of shareholders. They appear to have managed governance issues in an above-board manner. However, MTN Uganda faces a challenge in its effort to invest to the benefit of local economies because the board includes only one Ugandan, representing Invesco Uganda. Moreover, this shareholder appears to be no more than a go-between the company and other powerful interests in government, with a role mainly limited to handling politically sensitive issues and other public relations matters requiring a local face. As a result, there is essentially no local input in governance issues at the board level; no interests of the local community are presented in its strategy and policy.

MTN Uganda management counters that governance issues are the responsibility of every employee. All employees must be upright and desist from corrupt practices, honouring the strict conduct codes that the company has developed as part of the process of increasing its transparency. However, employees have no say at the board level, and it is difficult to see how their interests are protected. MTN Uganda therefore faces a dilemma. It wants to manage human resources in a way that respects and develops the capacities of its workers, and has set up mechanisms to do so; but these mechanisms are not working well, in the view of employees. Employee issues nominally are handled through the Employee Consultative Council but this body is 'barely active', according to interviewed employees. Employees are encouraged to contribute to policy-making through a 'letter to the CEO', and the company also has an 'open-door policy' through which employees can raise governance issues directly with senior management. Yet interviews revealed that management did not address many complaints raised by employees in the past via the 'letter to the CEO' and intranet. The last general staff meeting at the study site was held two years ago. As a result, employee input now is scant. Employees are characterized by creeping apathy and a 'culture of silence'. They have little or no belief in the capacity of such arrangements to address employee concerns. Interviewed managers claim that departmental meetings were taking place, and the Employee Consultative Council was functioning. One manager said:

> If employees are apathetic, that cannot be the problem of management. Channels exist for dialogue and everybody is free to use them. As far as we know, tension of some sort exists in most international companies, but MTN South Africa is predominantly black-owned and we are an equal-opportunity employer. International companies are basically run by highly skilled people who can obtain jobs anywhere; we are not just here to earn huge pay checks, but to add value.

What can be learned from MTN Uganda's experience in terms of its governance? The balancing of interests and concerns between shareholders largely outside Uganda and local staff and communities within Uganda is probably MTN's most significant challenge and opportunity in its governance. Does MTN Uganda genuinely intend to achieve its full potential for improving the lot of poorer marginalized communities in Uganda? If so, its objectives as outlined in Sethi's code, could include providing the local population with greater access to ownership and control of productive assets as well as encouraging their participation in top level decision-making (Sethi, 1993). At least three ways can be envisaged to accomplish this namely: increase the number of local shareholders, hold more regular staff meetings with one staff assigned to voice concerns at board level and continue replacing expatriate employees with local staff.

Corporate citizenship and social relations

In terms of prudently managing its monetary capital as an international business, MTN Uganda has the challenge of creating shareholder value while operating in a 'risky' developing country. In seeking to maximize shareholder value, the firm has worked diligently to expand the market and increase its competitive advantage. In doing so, MTN Uganda generally has met the formal legal and fiscal responsibilities spelled out for its operation in Uganda. It has met its obligation to comply with tax laws and government regulations. It has fulfilled the conditions and exceeded all the targets set forth in its Second National Operator (SNO) licence, as overseen by the UCC. As required by law, MTN Uganda contributes 1 per cent of gross revenue to the UCC Rural Communications Fund in order to help promote rural communications development. To date, MTN has exceeded all targets that were set in its SNO licence, as monitored by the UCC.

If we examine the total efforts and net resources that MTN Uganda has invested in the service of its shareholders, the overall bargain with Uganda appears skewed, in terms of justice. The company has been criticized publicly for breaching WTO rules regarding liberalization because its licence includes a provision that prevents the UCC from issuing further national operator licences for a period of five years. This provision effectively rules out competition that might serve to lower the costs of telephony services. Moreover, the net balance of financial benefit is tilted against Uganda. Because the country periodically experiences economic shocks, Ugandans are particularly sensitive to the fact that MTN repatriates large sums of money to its home country, South Africa. MTN Uganda is a net consumer of hard currency, and all its inputs are imported. The company has not transferred new technology to Uganda. It should be noted that the company responds that it has made a massive investment in infrastructure for which it cannot expect a return in the short term; that it is a user and not a producer of technology; and that it is transferring skills, a process that takes time. Still, MTN Uganda can accomplish more of its potential and promise for developing communities if it ensures a fair share of benefits to internal stakeholders, not just external shareholders.

In another dimension of corporate citizenship, MTN Uganda has made recognized contributions. The general public appreciates the company's support to non-government charitable organizations such as Habitat for Humanity. In 2002, MTN Uganda renewed its partnership with Habitat for Humanity with a US$83 000 grant over three years which would enable 60 homes to be built for needy families (Najumansi, 2002). MTN has also co-sponsored events like the Miss Uganda annual contest. It spent over US$47 222 for the construction of a modern vocational training centre in the Apac District. It has supported street children, provided financial assistance for a secondary school in Ntungamo and sponsored sports teams in Kampala Kids League (Nsambu, 2002). As a result, MTN Uganda appears to have a positive corporate image. However, if net profits of the company over the past two years are compared with its community contributions through charitable organizations, it appears that these contributions are geared more towards promoting good public relations than to foster genuine community development. To realize its promise to be a 'better connection', MTN Uganda needs to move away from a posture that is philanthropic and paternalistic, and instead to consider ongoing support to community development programmes that have a significant impact on society through holistic and sustainable development. Although international businesses cannot be expected to take primary responsibility for the alleviation of poverty, they have opportunities to add to the economy and value to society. MTN Uganda has a unique opportunity and challenge to use its profits to make its mobile phone technology more accessible and affordable to wider segments of the population, as well as other creative social investments. Such initiatives will enable it to live up to its promise to be a better connection.

Conclusion

This case study has focused upon MTN Uganda's relation with stakeholders most vulnerable to exploitation: employees, women subscribers and franchisees. The aim is to inform the company's leadership as to what can be done to make 'better connections', as it has promised – and what similar international businesses can do to achieve the common good in their societies. While MTN has added value to Ugandan society, it also has imposed costs, in terms of missed opportunities. Its positive contributions to Uganda's economic and social development include creating many jobs, developing the competence of its staff, providing communication services that foster personal and business development, paying taxes and fostering community welfare. As an international business, its orientation has remained commercial, but it has not neglected its social responsibilities nor, of course, its responsibilities to its shareholders.

Still, MTN Uganda needs to take into account the opportunities and connections it has missed in its management of human resources, in its relations to society and in its overall governance. These 'missed connections' include the special treatment of expatriates, which inadvertently raises organizational tensions; the high cost of cell phone subscriptions that exclude marginalized populations; the nepotistic approach to hiring, which often excludes more qualified people in the community; the expatriation of profits; and its paternalistic approach to community welfare. The balancing of interests and concerns between shareholders, who are largely outside Uganda, with those local staff and communities within Uganda is probably MTN Uganda's most significant challenge. These opportunities appear to have been missed largely because of differences in cultural values, and because of the high level of control that expatriate senior executives and owners use in their attempts to manage in Uganda as a risky environment. These factors affect MTN Uganda's vision, its human resource management, societal relations and governance. It is not enough to simply maximize profits for shareholders; MTN Uganda must find creative and imaginative ways to be a true partner for development with its host country.

There are several options for MTN Uganda to consider in turning its missed opportunities into opportunities for growth, for converting missed connections into better connections. In human resources, the company should build on its strengths in the areas of job creation and staff professional development. It should use innovative ways of addressing the gap in local and expatriate compensation; here it would help to open a forum of dialogue between its local and expatriate staff, who then could develop a package both sides would consider fair. They could also emulate promising practices of multinationals like Unilever, which provides housing, education and pensions in the home country for its local managers.

MTN Uganda should manage its relations with the local society better by making its communications services available at a much lower cost, with the intent of gaining many more subscribers. As the number of customers increases, the costs of services are likely to decrease. An expanding customer base would enable the company to expand its infrastructure into areas and populations currently on the margins of this technology and all its potential benefits for their development. MTN Uganda might establish collaborative relationships with non-governmental organizations (NGOs), which could promote the distribution of services in return for rebates. Through other unique collaborations with NGOs, the company could foster community welfare and development. Instead of donating towards projects that are likely to create dependencies, MTN Uganda could support NGO programmes that have a proven ability to achieve sustainable, holistic development. Ideally, these would include integrated programmes, matching-fund programmes and programmes where MTN staff would volunteer time to coach young entrepreneurs or small enterprise groups in the surrounding community.

To improve its governance, MTN Uganda might consider increasing the number of local shareholders on its board, replacing yet more expatriate staff with local staff and holding regular forums for staff to voice their concerns and suggestions for achieving the company's vision and values.

As this chapter has shown, investment by multinational corporations (MNCs) directly and indirectly adds to the stock of physical and financial capital in a society. It also improves social capital by transferring skills. Lastly, we recognize that MTN, like other MNCs, finds it difficult to achieve commutative justice and distributive justice in its management of human, monetary and social capital. Between internationally connected businesses and developing areas, this is especially true because the exchange process and the resource base are often unequal. However, there should be no excuse for abuse and exploitation. MTN Uganda holds great promise, with the resources it has, for improving life for people in Uganda. What remains to be seen is what steps it will take to achieve its promise to be the 'better connection'.

Notes

1. This study was carried out between April 2001 and June 2003. It involved meetings with six MTN managers, and a 2002 survey of 475 MTN service users in the major towns of Uganda.
2. Names of all service users mentioned or quoted in this chapter are pseudonyms.

References

Abena, D. F. (1991) *The Emancipation of Women: An African Perspective* (Accra: Ghana Universities Press).

Bartlett, C. A. and Ghoshal, S. (2002) *Managing Across Borders: The Transnational Solution*, 2nd edn (Boston: Harvard Business School Press).

Barton, T. and Wamai, G. (1994) 'Study of Women and Credit in Uganda', in *Equity and Vulnerability: A Situation Analysis of Women, Adolescents and Children in Uganda* (Kampala: UNICEF-Uganda National Council for Children), p. 114.

CACG (2000): The Commonwealth Association for Corporate Governance *Principles of Corporate Governance in Kenya* (Private Sector Corporate Governance Trust, Kenya).

Najumansi, L. (2002) 'MTN Renews Habitat Deal' in *The New Vision*, 27 September (Kampala, Uganda).

Nsambu, J. (2002) 'MTN Fourth Anniversary: A Fast Growing Network' in *The New Vision*, 23 October (Kampala, Uganda), p. 19.

Sethi, S. P. (1993) 'Operational Modes for Multinational Corporations in Post-Apartheid South Africa: A Proposal for a Code of Affirmative Action in the Marketplace', *Journal of Business Ethics* (January), vol. 12(1), pp. 1–12.

Stiglitz, J. E. (2002) *Globalization and its Discontents* (London: W.W. Norton).

Ugandanetwork (2002): The UK Uganda Network, 'Telephone Communications in Uganda', *Ugandanetwork* [website] (updated 7 May 2002) http://www. Ugandanetwork. org.uk./network/phone.htm, accessed 15 September 2002.

Wasike, A. (2002) 'Baganda Get Fewest Kids' in *The New Vision*, 6 October (Kampala, Uganda), p. 1.

8
A Short Economic History of Vietnam, 1945–1986

Stewart W. Herman

Introduction: reducing poverty through social-capital formation

Measured by modern economic standards, Vietnam has been very poor throughout its history. Its largely agrarian economy did not permit the accumulation of surpluses which would have fuelled economic development. While handicrafts and small-scale industry certainly did thrive, economic development in the Western sense began only after the mid-nineteenth century, under the impetus of French colonialism. Subjected to colonial exploitation, and then Soviet-style socialist development, Vietnam achieved a per capita income of only US$94 in 1981. This figure rose to US$138 by 1991, by which point some 70 per cent of its population still fell under the poverty line. Another decade later, however, its per capita income climbed to more than US$400, and the Vietnamese government claims that the percentage of people beneath the poverty line was halved, to 32 per cent.[1]

Not coincidentally, Vietnam in 1986 began turning to the market system as a means to accelerate economic growth and reduce poverty. The policy worked and continues to work, at least in broad macroeconomic terms. Growth has averaged 6 per cent or better per year for more than a decade. An important component of this policy has been to secure foreign direct investment (FDI), which contributed 22 to 25 per cent of the annual economic growth in 1998–2000, and somewhat less thereafter (World Bank, 2002, p. 8). The pragmatic question is: what can international firms most effectively contribute to economic development in Vietnam? The answer appears to be complex.

On the one hand, FDI may have only a limited, localized role in reducing poverty. In Vietnam, poverty is an overwhelmingly rural phenomenon tied to inefficient agriculture. Foreign industrial projects tend to cluster in export-processing zones or other areas close to cities. The largest percentage of these projects lie in broad belts around Ho Chi Minh City, where they benefit an urbanized or semi-urban workforce which already has escaped the worst poverty. As such, foreign investment is likely to have localized effects, which may not reach to the deepest pockets of poverty. For example, enormous garment-manufacturing plants draw in thousands of economic immigrants from rural areas. South Korean contractors employ some 46 000 workers in five plants to produce more than 10 per cent of Nike's worldwide output of sports shoes (Duc, 2001). But according to official estimates, while there are some 2.8 million households (17 per cent of the total) with incomes below the poverty line, only 183 000 of them are located in the Ho Chi Minh City region, where unemployment currently runs only 6 per cent (SRVN, 2002, pp. 18, 21). Indeed, government officials and observers have become alarmed at the widening income gaps between urban and rural dwellers. Foreign companies generate employment, products and services primarily for the rising middle class. The largest challenge in reducing poverty may simply lie beyond the direct reach of foreign corporations.

On the other hand, international firms might have an important if indirect role through building domestic capacity for economic growth. It seems clear from government policy and current trends that the domestic private sector is the major – if still underdeveloped – engine for poverty reduction. In 2002 the government adopted a poverty-reduction strategy, which singles out small- and medium-sized enterprises (SMEs) for 'encouragement'. Today, the most familiar rural economic institutions are the local market and small household enterprises. But from this base of millions of small entrepreneurial ventures, the private sector now is growing in business-unit size. Undoubtedly, wealth will be generated as household enterprises and other tiny ventures grow and morph or coalesce into more formally organized businesses. SMEs, in particular, number far fewer than they did during the heyday of the Vietnam War 30 years ago. But they now are being formed at the rate of 1600 per month, and seem to have an enormous potential to transform the economic landscape of Vietnam. Indeed, the entire Vietnamese private sector contributed almost 20 per cent of the nation's annual economic growth in 2002 – up from only 7.5 per cent four years earlier (World Bank, 2002, p. 8).

In order to increase its contribution to the economy, the private sector in Vietnam needs access to five kinds of capital. Most obviously, it needs financial capital generated through credit and revenues, and natural capital in the form of resource inputs and output for its production. In addition, Vietnamese are keenly interested in gaining productive capital in the form of technology and know-how, and human capital as workers and managers empower themselves through acquired skills. But perhaps most important of all in the context of Vietnam's turbulent history, the private sector needs a supportive atmosphere in which to develop, and broad, resilient networks of trust and cooperation. It needs 'social' capital, to use a term coined by sociologists.

Social capital refers to the institutional arrangements and the informal networks of 'generalized reciprocity', which enable individuals and organizations to pursue their ends efficiently (Putnam, 2000, pp. 19–22). Following a helpful distinction offered by Ismail Serageldin and Christiaan Grootaert of the World Bank, I will suggest that two levels of social capital formation are particularly important in Vietnam (Serageldin and Grootaert, 2000). At the 'macro' level, social capital takes the form of institutionalized permissions, encouragements and protections of the legal system and governmental policy: the rule of law, transparency and the other institutions of good governmental policy and regulation. All these conditions can be intentionally structured into an economy in order to facilitate individuals and firms in pursuing their projects. At the 'micro' level, social capital is evident where relationships are characterized by constructive reciprocity and spontaneous gestures of good will: where people and organizations develop habits of action which others can rely upon. Where such habits and expectations are absent, social relations express generalized mistrust. Like human capital, social capital increases with use, and it atrophies through disuse; as such, it is simultaneously a renewable and a depletable resource.

The challenge of generating and sustaining social capital is daunting in any society, but especially so in Vietnam. In the lyrics of one famous songwriter, Vietnam suffered 1000 years of Chinese domination, 100 years of Western colonialism and 30 years of civil war – followed by a decade of centralized planning. In the West, the work of nourishing social capital traditionally has fallen upon a host of independent associations. The growth of independent associations was effectively stunted in Vietnam. Vietnamese may belong to more groups, say, than Chinese, Japanese or Filipinos, but these groups are organized predominantly by the state (Dalton *et al.*, 2003). Currently, the major type of institution receiving authorization to be organized independently of the state is the private business enterprise – whether foreign companies, domestic household enterprises or the budding private sector of business corporations. Such enterprises must be registered, and are closely watched. But they are increasingly free to function as business enterprises: purchasing inputs and generating wealth for their owners, employment for their workers and products for their customers in Vietnam and abroad.

Consider the various dimensions of social capital needed by Vietnamese private-sector entrepreneurs. They need an atmosphere characterized by a broad social trust of market institutions, and they need to help establish the networks of reliability that will generate such legitimacy. Vietnamese enterprises need, at the macro level, a firm rule of law in commercial relations, both to provide permission for and set boundaries upon their activities. In addition, entrepreneurs need both to draw upon and to create social capital at the micro level. It is here that a distinction offered by sociologist Robert Putnam illuminates the basic problem (Putnam, 2000, pp. 22–4). Vietnam already generates much 'bonding' social capital, the kind produced by kinship and other groups based on identity (Dalton *et al.*, 2003). The economic payoff of this social capital is to be seen in the millions of 'household enterprises', which are organized along lines of kinship and other proximate loyalties. Such a superabundance of bonding capital is hardly surprising, given that social relationships revolve more closely around family in Vietnam than in other Asian countries (Dalton *et al.*, 2003). What Vietnam needs is 'bridging' social capital, particularly at the micro level of particular organizations and transactions, for its emerging private sector to grow and function effectively. This form of social capital is woefully underdeveloped. It is here that the contribution of international business may be most significant in the long run.

This study proceeds in three steps. This chapter reviews the economic history of Vietnam, in order to understand why forming human and social capital is such a pressing challenge to Vietnam's economic growth. In essence, a long legacy of colonial exploitation and post-colonial struggle reduced the private sector of Vietnam to small enterprises eking out an uncertain existence on the basis of face-to-face relations in the shadow of a suspicious colonial or socialist-governing authority. The private sector was reduced to myriad tiny networks of 'bonding' social capital at the micro level – necessary for economic survival, but hardly sufficient to foster major economic growth.

Second, Chapter 9 takes up the question of how 'bridging' social capital is being generated in small, largely indigenous international businesses in Vietnam. During the past 15 years, the private sector has begun a revival in which SMEs have been recognized to be significant engines of growth. From three case studies of small international business (Nhat Ban, Duc Khoa, /eMilton), this study isolates a sampling of strategies through which Vietnamese entrepreneurs build their enterprises as terrains of cooperation across kinship, community and other lines. This discussion provides a point of departure for comparison with large international businesses.

Finally, Chapter 10 takes up the question of how large international businesses can and might contribute to the formation of human and social capital in Vietnam. First, it suggests that foreign corporations might helpfully contribute at the macro level, by enlarging and levelling the playing field for the private sector. Second, it presents an extended case study ('Vietsani', a joint venture controlled by a US giant) to argue that there can be a benign relation between imported productive capital and human and social capital formation, but that it remains unclear whether a more distinctively Vietnamese patrimonial style might not be the preferred method of generating trust and reliability in such large enterprises as they become 'Vietnamized'.

An economic history of Vietnam: the legacies of French colonialism and East–West rivalry

There appear to be no direct sociological indices of social-capital formation specific to Vietnam's culture.[2] The best way to explain why Vietnam is short of social capital is to start is where a Vietnamese might begin, by explaining historically why economic development has been so difficult. Vietnamese often describe this history as tragic and unhappy: characterized by struggles against domination from without, and marked by political fractiousness and disunity within. Indeed, the country's experience of global economic relations has not been happy. During the past 150 years, Vietnam has experienced colonialism, wartime capitalism (in the South, 1945–75) and monopolistic state socialism (in the North, 1945–86, and the South, 1975–86). These experiences involved shortages of financial and productive capital, and retarded the growth of the macro and 'bridging' micro social capital needed for a market system to operate effectively.

Until the nineteenth century, Vietnam's trade with nations outside the Asian orbit was minor, and in any case fell far short of the level to spark industrialization. Vietnam's major model and market was China, which indeed had occupied Vietnam for a 1000 years. Then, after almost two millennia of largely agrarian isolation and self-sufficiency within an economic orbit defined by China, Vietnam was drawn forcibly into the colonial orbit of France. This unwelcome entry into global economic relations lasted from the mid-nineteenth century through the Second World War, when Vietnam was occupied briefly by Japan. To be sure, nineteenth-century colonialism brought some meaningful development of physical infrastructure. The French built a road and rail network – the best in Southeast Asia at the time, according to one historian (Duiker, 1995, p. 131). They introduced rubber cultivation and expanded rice production in the South, and organized coal mining on an industrial scale in the North.

These tangents of activity contributed in a significant way to the development of Vietnam's productive capital. But the aim of French economic policy was to repatriate wealth to France, not to develop Vietnam. The human capital of Vietnam languished, as the French pursued policies of exceedingly selective development. They opened up higher education only to a very few, concentrated agriculture for greater efficiency (and human misery) and stifled the independent development of business and industry (Duiker, 1995, pp. 31–6, 130–3). Whatever the merits of individual French administrators and firms, the net effect was to reinforce the deep suspicion of foreign intervention, which the Vietnamese carried over from their millennium of occupation by China. Perhaps the most significant 'development' Vietnam achieved was survival through resilient, small-scale enterprise. Colonial efforts to control the local economy by displacing local producers with imports from the West were foiled by the vigorous activity of petty enterprises. The value of these enterprises for the survival of Vietnamese economy under Western colonial oppression was considerable. But the 'bonding' capital these enterprises generated within themselves fell short of the 'bridging' capital needed to support an open market economy.

Northern Vietnam: the Soviet strategy

After 1945 the northern and southern halves of Vietnam pursued different pathways of economic development. In the North, Ho Chi Minh's armies liberated the Northern part from French colonial rule after a nine-year struggle that ended in 1954. The North embraced communism not only to declare independence from colonialism but also to create national wealth as a way to escape from widespread agrarian poverty. The new, avowedly Communist regime gradually but forcefully pursued socialist economic development of industry and agriculture, striving to build up productive capital on as massive a scale as possible. The North borrowed and adapted the characteristically centralized Soviet model of economic development: state or collective ownership of productive capital, with centralized planning to administer the capital for the good of the whole. This model succeeded at first, in macroeconomic terms. The GDP of Northern Vietnam rose for 10 years, albeit at considerable human cost. The government succeeded in bringing more than 90 per cent of the industrial and agricultural capacity under state or collective control by 1965 (Duiker, 1995, pp. 135–9).

The Soviet-style strategy was undermined both by war and by a resilient petty capitalism, which survived in the cracks of official economic policy. On the one hand, the burdens of the escalating war rendered the economy dependent upon foreign assistance from the Soviet Union and China (Duiker, 1995, pp. 138–9). 'Poverty reduction' was effectively put on hold as the war called forth enormous national sacrifice. Foreign assistance not investment was the material lifeline of the Northern Vietnamese economy, which was bombed back to an even more desperate poverty than it had experienced in 1945. On the other hand, the private sector never disappeared in the North. The state's five-year plans left trade and much manufacturing in private hands, and petty enterprise continued to thrive (Duiker, 1995, p. 135; Tran and Smith, 1997, pp. 61–2). In fact, the informal private sector continued to provide far more jobs than state enterprises (MPDF, 1999, p. 9). This 'capitalism in the cracks' literally provided the seeds for the later turn towards a market economy, even though its contribution to economic development was not recognized and incorporated into national economic strategy until 1987.

Southern Vietnam: embryonic capitalism

In the southern part of Vietnam, a very different trajectory of frustrated development occurred. After 1945 the imperial government, long co-opted by the French, was restored to power. For the next 30 years, the South enjoyed a political atmosphere permissive of capitalist development, as its political institutions underwent a forced evolution. An international diplomatic summit in 1954 prescribed a transition to democratic governance. The last emperor abdicated in 1958 but it effectively took 20 years to install the institutions of representative government (Duiker, 1995, pp. 92–4). Similarly, the war years were as unproductive for development in the South as in the North. The intensifying war discouraged foreign investment; yet indigenous enterprise boomed, on a small scale. While the South long had enjoyed the reputation of being more congenial to the entrepreneurial spirit than the more traditional and abstemious North, the Southern market organization that flourished best was petty enterprise and the small industrial firm. Only a tiny industrial base was planted in the outer suburbs of Saigon and in other cities. Such projects – sugar refineries, cement works, plants for producing textiles, drugs, food and paper products – were too few and too small to provide much in the way of human or productive capital. The Southern economy took on an air of artificiality, as massive doses of foreign aid financed the import of consumer commodities. The services sector grew to 60 per cent of the Southern economy, and by 1975 the miniscule industry's share of the Southern GDP fell to half its 1965 level of 13 per cent (MPDF, 1999, p. 10). Thousands of Vietnamese gained some exposure to Western styles of organization by working for US contractors or agencies. Vietnam thereby gained human capital of a sort, but this capital would only be persecuted and driven underground or abroad after 1975.

Vietnam unified: towards an uneasy mix of state socialism and market capitalism

During the 1945–75 wars of liberation, both halves of Vietnam received massive aid from both the Eastern and Western blocs, but such aid produced no meaningful growth in wealth. Indeed, both the northern and the southern portions of Vietnam suffered the postponement of development as their economies for a similar reason: both had become hooked on foreign aid, then lost it after the civil war ended in 1975. In the South, the foreign agencies, contractors and other companies linked with the US war effort departed abruptly; they took their productive capital with them, while the cream of Southern Vietnam's human capital fled by boat over the next 10 years. In the North, foreign aid dropped once the war was over (Duiker, 1995, p. 144). The Vietnamese learned once again that the flow of resources from outside is not reliable; that foreign expertise can be withdrawn; that foreign organizations often serve to manipulate or exploit Vietnam to their own ends – lessons hardly conducive to the formation of social capital. Vietnam retrenched in suspicion of foreign investment, and effectively banned inflows from non-socialist countries.

Resources were particularly meagre, therefore, to address the difficult question of how to reunite the two halves of the country. The civil war had reinforced significant cleavages in Vietnamese society reaching back to the colonial era: between North and South, urban and rural, those who aspired to become rich and those stuck with being poor, communists and capitalists, those who cooperated with foreigners and those who resisted. The Hanoi authorities were inspired by the Soviet model of communist development to transcend these social divisions by imposing a monolithic, party-centred conception of social governance upon the populace. All educational, social and economic organizations were to be subordinated to an overarching strategy of state-led development. Central to this strategy was the absorption of the private sector, and in 1976 a plan was unveiled to convert the entrepreneurial economy of the South to state ownership. As in 1954, the economic revolution from the top began cautiously. In 1978 some 30 000 private firms were effectively abolished, while the old Southern currency was replaced in a way that effectively stripped owners of their wealth (Duiker, 1995, p. 146). This revolution failed to kindle the loyal energies of the people in the South, in part because it simply failed to move Vietnam out of poverty. After 1975, the agricultural output of Vietnam climbed less than 2 per cent per year, less than enough to accommodate the greater than 2 per cent annual growth in population (MPDF, 1999, p. 11). Malnutrition and even famine appeared. Industrial output stagnated, as factories operated at only 40–50 per cent of capacity (Tran and Smith, 1997, p. 65).

Despite these depressing economic indicators, private enterprise was never crushed in post-war Vietnam. The Vietnamese were thrown back on their own resources. What they lacked in productive capital they made up in 'bonding' social capital. To this point, the most resilient and durable forms of economic organization in Vietnam had been (a) petty enterprise – the aggregation of many sellers in local markets, individual streetside entrepreneurs; and (b) household ventures in commerce, handicraft production and light industry. These petty enterprises had defeated the French effort to colonize and control the Vietnamese economy; they endured the transition to centralized collectivism in the North; they flourished during the American interim in the South; and now they kept the Vietnamese economy afloat during the difficult decade which followed the unification in 1975. Trade, for example, sprang up quickly and vigorously between the South and the North right after the end of the war, impoverished as the North was by decades of war. Such unofficial petty capitalism was messy; the black markets and corruption resulting from unofficial enterprise were not only offensive to the austere official morality of the state, but also undermined centralized control of economic development. Yet it was this informal system that kept the Vietnamese economy from collapse during the dark times of the early and mid-1980s (Freeman, 1996).

As economic stagnation spread, the state began accommodating private enterprise, in a recurring cycle of permission and control. It permitted some market activity to ignite spontaneously – at least enough to revive the economy. Then it pulled out the fire extinguisher in order to dampen the inequities, corruption and chaos that resulted from unregulated market activity. Through this dialectic of permission and control, it began to recognize, by fits and starts, the legitimacy of free-market exchange. As early as 1979 collective farms were permitted to experiment with contracting. In 1981–82, the state permitted the formation of import–export companies, but then disbanded them immediately when this relaxing of controls on imports generated short-term profits and sparked inflation (Tran and Smith, 1997, pp. 67–8). But overall, this strategy could not rescue the economy; state deficits grew and inflation skyrocketed.

Doi moi, or the 'renovation' of state socialism through capitalism

In 1986, the party at its sixth national congress took three steps (collectively dubbed 'doi moi', or 'renovation') to restore the Vietnamese economy. First, it legalized the coexistence of private markets with centralized planning. Second, it decided to delay the transition to socialism; and third, it decided to integrate its hybrid economy with the world economy (Tran and Smith, 1997, pp. 69–71). Each of these reforms had different implications for capital formation. Under 'doi moi' (pronounced dough-ee muh-ee), farmland reverted to the functional equivalent of private ownership,[3] cooperatives withered and the privatization of agriculture gained steam. In effect, human capital was freed to develop in a market system, as it drained out of the state system. Employment in cooperatives dropped from 20 million in 1990 to little over 100 000 between 1990 and 1998, while employment in the 'non-state' sector (chiefly agriculture) climbed from 6.5 million to 34 million in the same interval. Most of this startling increase is accounted for by the privatization of farmland. On the industrial side, private handicraft and light industrial enterprises were broken out from collective and state-owned organizations.

The legalization of private enterprise only served to ratify the fact that the Vietnamese economy already was in transition. At the time 'doi moi' was adopted, according to one view, 'more than half of the economy was market-oriented, and most commercial exchange took place according to market mechanisms' (Tran and Smith, 1997, p. 71). But in another sense, official reform was crucial, because it provided the first basic step in building social capital at the macro level. Until 1986, the regulatory apparatus of the state existed more to crush than foster the development of private commercial relations. Private enterprise had no institutional framework of protections, permissions and support; it suffered a dearth of social capital at the macro level. 'Doi moi' was the first meaningful step towards building the framework of legal and regulatory permissions that would enable economic actors to pursue their projects.

The resurgence of household enterprise: 'bonding' social capital at the micro level

Despite gradually expanding governmental permissions, the enterprise that sprang into vigorous activity after 1986 was the kind least dependent upon state toleration or favour. 'Household enterprises' are small firms which are informally financed, and often staffed, from within extended families. In 1997, the average household enterprise had six working individuals; but half of these or fewer are paid employees (Ronnas and Ramamurthy, 2001, p. 145). As such, they are independent of capital markets and tend to lack a wage structure. With minimal requirements for financial, productive or human capital, they provide a ready vehicle for economic development. And in Vietnam, once they were given a degree of recognition by the state in 1986, they multiplied rapidly. By 1994 household enterprises employed some 6 million people (out of a total labour force of 40 million); 3.3 million of those jobs were created since 1986 (Levine, 1998). According to another measure, there were some 800 000 of these enterprises by 1995, with half of them engaged in food processing, and the other half in small manufacture (MPDF, 1997, pp. 12–13).

The sudden flourishing of household enterprises after 1986 is entirely consistent with Vietnam's often-interrupted market development. Several historical factors – a colonial policy of accentuating social and class divisions, the deep cleavages produced by two generations of civil war, and then a socialist policy of discouraging private business and repressing independent associations – had served to stifle the networks of 'bridging' social capital that enable a free-market system to develop. Vietnamese entrepreneurs therefore coped with risk by turning to social capital in its most durable 'bonding' form, by drawing upon networks of kin and friends to staff their enterprises. In the absence of 'bridging' capital, bonding capital became the primary glue of enterprise.

Household enterprises are valuable because they drew upon, and reinforced, innumerable, loosely connected networks of bonding capital: tiny puddles of mutual trustworthiness, circumscribed by family and neighbourhood loyalties. But a market system cannot rely on bonding capital alone. Household enterprises are not stable. One study found that between 1991 and 1997, half the surveyed enterprises either declined or went out of business, while about one-third grew at a rate of over 10 per cent per year.[4] As these enterprises grow, their founding entrepreneurs cannot avoid the necessity of finding 'bridging' social capital – or generating some of their own. Networks of reliability have to extend farther, develop larger networks of supply and distribution and achieve economies of scale. Enterprises need to be able to tap cooperation and trust across lines of kinship, community, region and the other potential lines of fracture.

Consider one recent illustration, from a tightly knit Catholic community in Ho Chi Minh City. Mistrusted by the government, this community has turned to the only resource it has, its own 'bonding' social capital, for economic self-support. Since the mid-1990s, 10 to 15 households have divided up the work of producing cheap shirts for export to Russia. A Vietnamese contact in Russia places an order; a local coordinator buys cloth on credit

(20 per cent down, for a loan of three to six months' duration); the families make the shirts and send them off in bales. If all goes well, each family receives approximately US$200 for five months of work per year in producing 200 to 300 bales; this return is pitiful compared with wages in the more organized private sector. And the system is vulnerable to abuse. The enterprise is policed internally by a stern and demanding mutual trust among the families. But if the contact in Russia fails to remit the proceeds, there is no legal remedy; the cloth-buyer is arrested for defaulting on the credit, and the families are left short.

The tendrils of commercial trustworthiness need to grow beyond the bonds that hold small, cohesive household enterprises together. For this, 'bridging' capital is needed: those patterns of reliable transactions, mutual trustworthiness, generalized goodwill which enable economic activity among strangers to grow and flourish. But the work of extending social capital beyond the bonds of kinship and neighbourhood is laborious. For example, one problem that plagues Vietnamese entrepreneurs is the recurring failure of customers to pay for products or services received. Stanford researcher John McMillan has discovered that these entrepreneurs typically resort to non-coercive means of recovering their money: cultivating a friendly relationship with the buyer in arrears, coaxing partial payments and so forth (McMillan and Woodruff, 1999). Rather than add to a climate of mistrust by resorting to law or thuggery, they patiently cultivate the kind of trusting relationships that will, one day, result in at least partial recovery from their losses. In effect, these sellers take the laborious route of generating social capital to protect their interests. This strategy suggests a certain kind of forbearing wisdom. The entrepreneurs apparently realize that if they were to resort to the (ineffective) law, or effective but crude thuggery to recover their money, they likely would fail, and certainly would inflame the resistance of their debtors. In the absence of a firm legal environment where contracts can be enforced, the ingenuity, patience and forbearance of sellers in generating ad hoc social capital becomes crucial to remaining afloat.

Conclusion

The challenge that Vietnam shares with all developing countries is how to increase wealth within the constraints and promises afforded by its own history and culture. In the case of Vietnam, the kind of social capital necessary for a prosperous market economy historically has been in short supply. To be sure, Vietnam, like other Asian nations, is rich in the 'bonding' social capital at the micro level, a form of social capital which ties kin and identity-based communities together in tiny household and other enterprises. Yet decades of colonial exploitation, civil war, ideology-driven conflict and economic reorganization have done little to develop two kinds of social capital needed to make a market economy work: the macro capital of legal permissions and governmental encouragement, and the 'bridging' micro capital of generalized reciprocity which undergirds networks of contractual relations. The problem of forming social capital appears especially acute for Vietnam because it has had to rebuild the private sector of its economy virtually from scratch since the mid-1980s.

Notes

1. See SRVN (2002), pp. 16–17 and IMF/IDA (2002), p. 27. The 'total poverty line' includes people whose income fell below 1.79 million Vietnamese dong per year, or approximately US$130 in 1998, at US$1 = VND13 500. The material consequences of this widening prosperity are visible: by 1994, 64 per cent of households owned bicycles, 21 per cent owned an electronic appliance and 10 per cent owned motorbikes (Tran and Smith, 1997, p. 82). Still, a third of Vietnamese children remain malnourished, infant mortality runs 37 out of 1000 and disease remains widespread (World Bank, 2001, p. 67).
2. Methodological humility is also called for, since social capital is perhaps the most difficult dimension of Vietnam's development for outsiders to understand. It is formed through informal patterns of reciprocity, which of course take on distinctive contours in each culture, and appear particularly reticent in Vietnam. Some initial forays have been made in understanding how social capital is generated and sustained in Vietnam (see Dalton *et al.*, 2003). Much more work is needed, in that the study of social capital calls for a qualitative appraisal to enrich the quantifiable indicators of patterns of participation in social networks and memberships, the frequency of social contacts and attitudes towards family.
3. In Vietnam the state owns all property, but farmers, for example, can deed their properties to their children, as well as use it as collateral or sell it to others (interview with Truong Trong Nghia, Vice-President, Foreign Trade and Investment Development Center, 30 March 2000).
4. That is, some 32 to 37 per cent (Ronnas and Ramamurthy, 2001, p. 198). The study included some 339 household enterprises in 1991, and 326 in 1997 (pp. 4, 21, 25).

References

Dalton, J. R., Pham Minh Hac, Pham Than Nghi and Nhu-Ngoc T. Ong (2003) 'Social Relations and Social Capital in Vietnam: The 2001 World Values Survey', *Comparative Sociology*, vol. 1(2) January.

Duc, H. (2001) 'US Pact Prompts Nike to Expand Local Shoe Output', *Vietnam Investment Review*, 3 December.

Duiker, W. J. (1995) *Vietnam: Revolution in Transition*, 2nd edn (Boulder, CO: Westview).

Freeman, D. B. (1996) 'Doi Moi Policy and the Small-Enterprise Boom in Ho Chi Minh City, Vietnam', *The Geographical Review*, vol. 86(2) April, pp. 178–97.

IMF/IDA (2002): International Monetary Fund/International Development Association, 'Vietnam: Joint Staff Assessment of the Poverty Reduction Strategy', 6 June [online document] http://www.imf.org/external/np/jsa/2001/vnm/eng/032201.pdf, accessed 30 September 2003.

Levine, J. J. (1998) 'Untapped Potential', *Vietnam Business Journal* (January/February) http://www.viam.com/april98/coverstory.html

McMillan, J. and Woodruff, C. (1999) 'Dispute Resolution with Courts in Vietnam', *Journal of Law, Economics and Organization*, vol. 15 (October), pp. 637–58.

MPDF (1997): Mekong Project Development Facility, *The Emerging Private Sector and the Industrialization of Vietnam, Private Sector Discussions*, Number 1 (Hanoi).

MPDF (1999): Mekong Project Development Facility, *Vietnam's Undersized Engine: A Survey of 95 Larger Private Manufacturers, Private Sector Discussions*, Number 8 (Hanoi).

Putnam, R. D. (2000) *Bowling Alone: the Collapse and Revival of American Community* (New York: Simon & Schuster).

Ronnas, P. and Ramamurthy, B. (eds) (2001) *Entrepreneurship in Vietnam: Transformation and Dynamics* (Copenhagen: NIAS Publishing).

Seragelden, I. and Grootaert, C. (2000) 'Defining Social Capital: An Integrating View', in P. Dasgupta and I. Serageldin (eds), *Social Capital: A Multifaceted Perspective* (Washington, DC: World Bank), pp. 43–65.

SRVN (2002): Socialist Republic of Vietnam, 'The Comprehensive Poverty Reduction and Growth Strategy (CPRGS)' (Hanoi, May 2002) *International Monetary Fund* [website] (n.d.) http://www.internationalmonetaryfund.com:80/external/np/prsp/2002/vnm/01/index.htm, accessed 30 September 2003.

Tran, A. N. and Smith, D. (1997) 'Cautious Reformers and Fence-breakers: Vietnam's Economic Transition in Comparative Perspective', *Humboldt Journal of Social Relations*, vol. 24, pp. 51–100.

Truong, T. N. (2000) Trong Nghia, Vice President, Foreign Trade and Investment Center, Interview, 30 March.

World Bank (2001) *Pillars of Development: Vietnam 2010: Vietnam Development Report 2001* (Hanoi: Vietnam Development Information Center).

World Bank (2002) 'Vietnam: Delivering on Its Promise: Development Report 2003', Report 25050-VN by the Poverty Reduction and Economic Management Unit, East Asia and Pacific Region, *World Bank* [website] (updated 21 April 2003) http://www.worldbank.org.vn/topic/vdr2003.htm, accessed 29 September 2003.

9
Forming Social Capital from the Bottom Up: The Emergent Private Sector in Vietnam, 1986–2002

Stewart W. Herman

Distinct from the household and petty-enterprise sector of the Vietnamese economy is what the government officially terms the 'private' sector – that is, the private *corporate* sector. After 1986, this sector began from much smaller numbers than the household-enterprise sector, but it has grown exponentially in the last decade. In 1988 the state formally declared the private sector to have 'long-term importance' for the economy. The right to private property came four years later, with a new constitution in 1992 (MPDF, 1997, p. 16; 1999a, p. 11). The constitution also affirmed personal freedoms, which were further specified in a 1995 Civil Code. The Commercial Law of 1998 specifically affirmed private ownership and fair treatment in commercial matters. The Enterprise Law of 2000 reduced the imposing array of regulations which effectively discouraged private initiative, while an administrative court, established in 1996, provided redress against governmental heavy-handedness (Truong, 2000, pp. 134–9).

As the government gradually built up a legal hedge to protect the market economy, the number of private companies began to grow. In 1988 there were only some 318 registered private companies; by the next year, 1284 (Tran and Smith, 1997, p. 91). The number continued to grow as a series of reforms reduced official barriers and other obstacles facing private enterprise. In 1989, the fixed price system was abolished; Vietnam reportedly was the first planned economy to set prices fully free (McMillan, 1999, p. 93). In 1991, regulations were set forth for forming and operating private ventures. By 1993, the number of private enterprises registered with the government had climbed to 11738 (Hoang and Nguyen, 1995, p. 28). By 1998, some 26000 private companies had registered. This number is impressive because it took considerable entrepreneurial verve to establish companies in the face of the baleful and unreliable eye of the state. In the past few years, however, the Vietnamese state has stepped up the grudging pace of reform and has moved an enormous distance. After the Enterprise Law came into effect in

2000, the number of new registrations skyrocketed to some 1600 per month, reaching a total of 50 000 by the end of 2002, with an estimated capitalization of US$2.7 billion (World Bank, 2002, p. 8).

These new registrations suggest that the law has created considerable social capital at the macro level. When viewed over a span of decades, the transformation has been considerable. From a standing start – with negative social capital, in the form of state harassment of the private sector, it has taken not much more than 10 years for the Vietnamese government to institute enough reliability in its oversight to open the floodgates of private initiative. Moreover, clear signals from the top indicate the intention of Vietnam to achieve growth without inequity or injustice. A 'Comprehensive Poverty Reduction and Growth Strategy' adopted in 2002 commits the government to economic growth with equitable treatment for international businesses, 'encouragement' for small- and medium-sized enterprises (SMEs), active engagement with the global economy, continuing reform of administrative regulation and a solid safety net for the poor and disadvantaged.[1] Indeed, Vietnam's growth through the 1990s was achieved without increasing inequality – no mean achievement (World Bank, 2002, p. ii). Still, a substantial residue of mistrust and caution will remain as long as the state sees the private sector as subordinate and instrumental to the ultimate socialist transformation of the economy. A policy of forming social capital at the macro level requires a sustained, visible commitment to both non-interference and constructive support for the private sector.

Social capital appears to be in much shorter supply than the torrid tango of governmental reform and new-company registration would suggest – and for two reasons having to do with entrepreneurs themselves, rather than government policy. First, entrepreneurs grow their companies apparently by drawing most of their financial capital from bonding rather than bridging networks. Many of the new companies have evolved from household enterprises. Legally, household enterprises must grow into one of three forms recognized by the state. The most popular form by far is the 'sole proprietorship', where ownership is vested in one person. Of the 26 000 private companies registered by 2000, some 18 750 fit this category. Next in popularity was the partnership, with 7100 registrations (MPDF, 1999a, p. 13). Since both sole proprietorships and partnerships tend to be shell structures for keeping ownership concentrated within a family, they rely primarily upon the bonding social capital provided by networks of kinship. And since it is difficult for private-sector operations to obtain loans from banks, even nominally commercial banks, most entrepreneurs draw upon the personal savings of themselves or kin (Ronnas and Ramamurthy, 2001, p. 73). Portfolio investment plays only a minor role in funding Vietnamese ventures. As of 2000, only 171 companies were funded by stockholders. A stock market was opened in July 2000, but is closely controlled by the government. As of 2003, only 21 domestic companies were listed, and foreign investment is limited to a 20 per cent in any given firm (Vietnam Panorama, 2003).

Second, entrepreneurs are widely regarded with mistrust. According to a 1999 survey, 'The public tends to view the entrepreneurs who establish and manage private companies as generally unskilled and highly opportunistic individuals – people willing to exploit others to seize short-term gains' (MPDF, 1999b, p. 8). Respondents tagged private companies with a list of unsavoury attributes compiled by the researchers: unstable, exploitative, dishonest, opportunistic and uncaring about their employees. And the respondents also depicted entrepreneurs as individuals in similarly grim terms: authoritarian, greedy, untrustworthy, corrupt, inexperienced and deficient in understanding (MPDF, 1999b, p. 7). In effect, the public sees entrepreneurs engaged in consuming, rather than creating, social capital. A 1995 article by two Vietnamese economists offers one explanation of why and how this destruction of social capital occurs: they claim that Vietnamese entrepreneurs operate according to an exceedingly short-sighted logic of investment. The entrepreneurs gravitate to the service and trading sectors, where they can invest a small amount of capital, recoup it quickly, then dissolve the enterprise before being snagged by changes in governmental regulation. The entrepreneurs further reduce their risk by turning to blood ties or friendships for staffing, rather than looking for talent from outside their immediate circles (Hoang and Nguyen, 1995).

While it is easy to deplore such patterns as evidence of short-sighted greed, as suspicious Vietnamese are wont to do, these investment practices and patterns also suggest a rational response to unpleasant realities: fear of capricious governmental regulation, reinforced by a concern that capital tied too long in one place will be stolen or simply lost, due to the unreliable partners and employees. Recent data bear out these concerns: companies tend to appear and disappear quickly. One large-scale survey was unable to find a third or more of its sample firms after an interval of six years (Ronnas and Ramamurthy, 2001, pp. 192–3). And of the 26 000 companies registered by 1998, almost half were engaged in trading and more than 3000 of the rest in processing food – lines of business where initial investments need not be high. Only some 2000 were engaged in more capital-intensive manufacture (MPDF, 1999a, pp. 14–15). To whatever extent the greed of entrepreneurs is to blame, the 'bridging' social capital, which they appear to be depleting with their short-sighted strategies of investment, may indeed simply not be available to begin with.

Despite the evident lack of bridging capital, the Vietnamese private sector is growing in a direction which can only require more. Between 1991 and 1997, as noted above, one-third of surveyed companies were growing, and they were growing remarkably fast. And new start-up firms during the 1990s tended to be larger in all respects than the firms that had been started during the 1980s (Ronnas and Ramamurthy, 2001, p. 198). The question, then, is: how can these firms generate the 'bridging' social capital they require to operate? How can they extend trust and cooperation beyond the limits of what bonding social capital can achieve?

Three small international businesses in Vietnam: producers of human and 'bridging' social capital

Three small Vietnamese-owned international businesses – producers and exporters of handicrafts, plastic bags and software to overseas markets – were surveyed in order to learn how entrepreneurs generate social capital through distinctively Vietnamese methods for opening up terrains of cooperation and inculcating habits of mutual reliability with their employees, customers and suppliers.[2] It should be noted that the lead entrepreneur in each is a 'Viet Kieu'. The term, usually translated as 'overseas Vietnamese', refers mainly to those expatriates who left Vietnam during the enormous exodus following 1975 and established themselves in a diaspora that spans Australia, Europe and North America. Viet Kieu are significant actors in the development of Vietnam's private sector, mainly because of the sheer volume of financial capital they provide.[3] Because they are politically suspect – apparently forever – they receive close scrutiny, and so may feel pressure to prove that they are contributing productive, human and social capital to Vietnam's growth as well as financial capital.

The enterprises surveyed here fit the government's strategy of growth, technological development and job-creation through a closely monitored private sector. These companies invest transparently through the market, rather than rely upon kinship bonds. Moreover, these enterprises are not, strictly speaking, traditional: they are not based upon a simple inherited technology, minimal capital investment and limited to a single identifiable community. Rather, their enterprises are SMEs, which pursue innovation and growth. None has more than 70 personnel; most appear to have fewer than 40. The entrepreneurs contribute productive and human capital by introducing technologies and managerial methods from their years of education and experience overseas. Yet each enterprise is very Vietnamese: it is small enough that it is constructed of face-to-face relations between the entrepreneur who puts a patrimonial stamp of authority on the employee relationship. In effect, these SMEs constitute a transitional form between household enterprise and the international corporation. These three companies represent efforts to make Western technology and business practices compatible with Vietnamese sensibilities.

Nhat Ban Company: dispersed handicraft production for the demanding Japanese market

Nhat Ban's founder Huynh does not consider himself an entrepreneur. He left Vietnam in 1967 and spent more than thirty years absorbing Japanese methods of business organization.[4] On vacations to Vietnam, he began to organize handicraft production. He began with artificial flowers and embroidery, and expanded to bamboo and other local materials – all for export to markets he personally cultivated in Japan. One large room in his plant is filled with a stunning array of handicrafts. They are not only charmingly designed, but flawlessly executed, as demanded by Japanese customers' exacting tastes. Strict quality control is needed; to this end, Huynh has his engineers design each product to precise specifications. Actual production is farmed out to off-site workshops, where his engineers closely monitor the output.

The work of engineering the handicrafts is performed at his central facility, an airy whitewashed building of 6000 square metres. This plant occupies one side of a spacious campus behind a high wall down a long unpaved alley. No large sign announces the nature of the facility. The generous proportions and spotless appearance suggest a haven in the midst of crowded, dirty Ho Chi Minh City – and indeed, such appearances appear central to Huynh's strategy. He maintains a spotlessly clean building in order to keep his workers focused on flawless production.

When establishing the enterprise, Huynh faced a major challenge in training his workers. They lacked a commitment to cleanliness, precision and teamwork. Huynh wanted them to develop a sense of joint responsibility, pride and ownership – social capital in the form of commitments that would conduce to work of high quality. For this, he needed a dramatic illustration of common purpose. The first step was to persuade them to shed the slovenly and unhygienic personal habits they brought into the plant. Because of cultural sensibilities, he could not confront them directly with criticism of their personal appearance and habits. Instead, he captured instances of deplorable behaviour on tape, gathered the workers together in a party setting and showed the video to all assembled. The Hollywood format enabled them to laugh at themselves and at each other without feeling humiliated.

While this 'education' may seem mundane, it had a considerable impact on the ethos of the plant. Vietnamese normally engage in close observation of each other in groups. He in effect converted this 'mutual surveillance' into electronic entertainment, all the while lightening the considerable moral pressure that such surveillance generates. Mutual surveillance can be a powerful tool, as it stokes peer pressure. For example, many Vietnamese are smokers. After seeing themselves smoke on tape, Huynh's workers agreed on their own that in-plant smoking should be banned, with infractions subject to stiff fines. He notes with satisfaction that hardly any fines have been collected; simple peer pressure has eliminated the habit.

Huynh measures a sense of common purpose in his plant by the flow of spontaneously contributed labour. Workers have volunteered to bring in trees and embellish the large grounds which surround the plant. In a culture marred by littered public spaces, only two paid employees are needed to keep the entire plant building spotless; the workers spontaneously keep it from getting dirty. By Huynh's decree, workers sit at the cafeteria in tables of six, rotating the volunteered work of serving and bussing. At work, the 20-odd uniformed employees in their air-conditioned, spotless room radiate focused attention to their work and playful merriment at the same time.

Duc Khoa Company: a 'Swiss factory' for a reliable export market in Europe

Ngoc spent more than 15 years as a refugee in Germany before returning to Vietnam. While in Germany, he studied engineering and learned the plastics industry. He accumulated many contacts and much experience, including that of running a (German) company on his own.[5] In the early 1990s, he returned to Vietnam with the aim of manufacturing plastic bags – a high-volume consumer product. The company, with US$6 million in annual sales, has five vice-directors, but obviously bears the stamp of its founding entrepreneur. The model Ngoc consciously drew upon was that of a small, idealized Swiss factory, built and operated by an intellectual who ventures out into the wider world to help out his impoverished home village.

Like Huynh's plant, the factory is simple and tidy in appearance, occupying one corner of a spacious campus that is planted with a variety of ornamental shrubs and trees. The walled compound is set back from the road. Ngoc explained that it is wise for him to maintain a low profile. Visibility attracts attention; attention attracts problems, whether with local governmental authorities or freelance troublemakers. His relations with local party and governmental bodies are cool and distant. Occasionally he is tripped up by red tape, but has found that sheer stubborn persistence can serve to overturn onerous requirements. He says that it is not wise to consult lower-level officials, who tend to be hostile to Viet Kieu such as himself. Instead, he deals only with senior officials.

As with Huynh, Ngoc's principal challenges concerned the attitudes and habits of employees. Perhaps the most basic aspect of the social capital which undergirds the plant's harmonious operation involves uplifting employee expectations of themselves and each other. Ngoc says he devotes endless attention to issues of motivation and habit, as a means of orienting employees to the rhythms of the factory and the demands of imported machinery. Like Huynh, he faced challenges early on having to do with basic cleanliness. Located on the sprawling edge of Saigon, the factory suffers from the engrained dirt that tends to seep into the pores of cement buildings in the tropics, unless they are faced with shiny tile. The eating area looks particularly grubby. Still, it once was much worse. The workers, who come from poor families, used to throw food scraps on the floor, and didn't clean up after themselves in the toilets. General morale suffered as a result. Ngoc struggled to instil better habits, and eventually succeeded, particularly after one worker visited Germany and reported that the toilets there were spotless. Workers gradually came to realize the common benefit they would derive from a clean workplace; now they take turns with cleaning chores.

A second ingredient in the social capital which undergirds the plant's operation is impartially fair treatment, supported by an exchange which both sides regard as satisfactory. Finding workers is not difficult; more applications are received than positions available. The challenge is to retain them, because as they gain skill, they become more marketable. Ngoc hires and promotes according skill and seniority. Four employees, in separate and apparently unmonitored interviews, confirmed that there was no discrimination in hiring, whether by gender or region.[6] Also vital were transparency and fairness in wages, inasmuch as Vietnamese closely observe all details of the exchange relation. The wages Ngoc offers to workers appear low and turnover is high, but he succeeds in drawing applicants even from distant provinces. A chief attraction appears to be a salary structure that rewards length of service with steady increments in wages, and offers workers the opportunity to reduce their living expenses to near zero. New hires are paid only 14 000 dong (about US\$1 in 2000) per day, or less than the minimum wage. This wage rises to US\$1.25 after training, and potentially higher with evaluations at four-month intervals. There is a ceiling of 30 000 dong (about US\$2 per day or US\$48 per month, assuming six-day work weeks) or 45 000 dong (US\$3.50 or US\$84 per month) for the heaviest labour. These wages are supplemented with health insurance, which is required by law. The low wages are sweetened further with a free lunch daily (of solid and tasty fare). If workers agree to a 12-hour shift, they receive a second free meal on that day. Further, a majority of the workers live rent-free in a nearby company-owned dorm, five to a room that measures 3 by 4 metres (10 by 13 feet). These spare arrangements seem to suit many of the workers, who want to save most of their wages or remit them home.

But even such fairness is not sufficient to establish trust within the plant. Both the workers and Ngoc expect more, in an arrangement that might be termed 'patrimonial benevolence' initiated by the entrepreneur. Ngoc feels it necessary to look after his workers. 'In the Asian mentality, it is very important to bring gifts', he says. He distributes trinkets from his frequent business trips abroad, and asks workers out to dinner. Two or three times a year, he closes the factory and organizes a sports festival or a music festival, or takes them to the seaside. At the same time, Ngoc exercises gentle discipline. Minor infractions bring a warning; for more serious infractions, workers must write an essay explaining what they did wrong. And even such gentle discipline becomes impossible further up the ranks. For example, Ngoc is frustrated by the fact that Vietnamese mechanics tend to run machines into the ground, then patch them back together in ingenious ways. Four technicians maintain the machinery. Because their skill made them exceedingly marketable, he could not afford to browbeat them;

instead, he could only recruit their cooperation and teach them. It was a long struggle to persuade them to adopt exacting German habits of exercising preventive maintenance and repairing broken machinery by the book.

/eMilton: an American information-technology subsidiary

/eMilton is a Minneapolis-based dot.com founded in 1996.[7] It develops web pages and offers e-business services in cooperation with a network of partner firms. Its connection with Vietnam began when its vice-president, an American Viet Kieu, recruited five other American Viet Kieu engineers to develop software. They rapidly became the best team of software writers for the American company, and the vice-president resolved to establish a 100 per cent-owned subsidiary in Vietnam to write software for export to the United States. /eMilton Vietnam is growing fast, according to its deputy general director, Chau. By April 2000 it had seven engineers at work. By 2001, it had more, and occupied the whole floor of a high-rise in the heart of Ho Chi Minh City. Furnished only with desks and chairs, this workplace exuded an atmosphere of nerdy preoccupation with glowing monitors.

Despite its high technology, the fledgling company relies heavily on social capital of the 'bonding' kind – a network that extends at least beyond kinship. In 2001, all but one of its employees came from the province of Phan Rang, and the clubby atmosphere was thickened further by a protective, even paternalistic family-style of management. For example, as the software market heated up, Chau felt the need to 'protect' his employees from being poached by other firms. /eMilton's wages are generous, relative to more traditional industries: the company programmers, all university graduates, are paid US$60 per month at the entry level, and can expect to reach US$300 after five years. But the industry, as of 2001, was in a turmoil, which threatened to push these wages much higher. Between 2000 and 2001 the number of software companies zoomed from 10 to 40. The new companies offered enormous salaries in order to recruit software engineers quickly. In defence, Chau joined with seven other companies in a trade group, which commissioned a salary survey. Once Chau learned what the market was offering, he established a common salary range within the company to keep employees from being distracted – or lured away – by inflated expectations about compensation.

The trade group also offers Chau a platform for wrestling constructively with the Vietnamese government. The government's goal is to bring in foreign exchange. Its Ministry of Science, Technology and Environment is particularly anxious to develop information technology (IT) because this hot new industry has the potential of adding enormous value to Vietnam's exports. In 1999, the whole IT industry had sales of just US$9 million, but was growing rapidly (Liebhold, 2000). Because /eMilton intended to export more than 80 per cent of its production, it received a licence to operate in four weeks, rather than the customary 12 months. It also received a four-year tax holiday. Having enjoyed these breaks, Chau now energetically lobbies for further breaks, even to the point of getting involved in squabbles among governmental ministries. For example, Chau and his trade group in 2001 were chafing under a marginal personal income-tax rate, which is so punitive that it had become cheaper to hire foreign expatriates than to hire Vietnamese, at salaries above US$700 per month. The Ministry of Finance decided to give software development engineers the same preferential treatment as expats, but Chau and his trade group joined forces with the Ministry of Science, Technology and Environment to extend the privilege to all employees. Despite such boldness, the company restricts its lobbying to resisting governmental policies it disagrees with, rather than proposing new permissions or exemptions. 'Our rule of thumb is, never ask the government something that it knows nothing about', says Chau, because the government typically responds by clamping down.

Still, /eMilton relishes developing a closer relationship with the government in the future. It wants the government to require companies to register their software; it also wants the government to keep track of /eMilton's exports and revenue, even though it currently pays no taxes. /eMilton hopes to develop partnerships with local university programmes and even anticipates forming a joint venture with some state-owned enterprise five years down the road – once government-owned ventures have developed sufficient quality in their high-tech work. In short, /eMilton wants to deepen its cooperative relations with the government, proactively to create social capital at the macro level.

Four markers of social capital formation in small Vietnamese companies

The three Viet Kieu ventures suggest that small-scale enterprise can serve to create islands of reliability in the turbulent ocean of Vietnamese business. Their entrepreneurs have established work cultures which reflect some patterns of traditional enterprise, but which grow social capital of a 'bridging' kind. Four interrelated factors appear important. First, the enterprises all operate on a *small scale* which permits, second, a distinctively Vietnamese *patrimonial relationship* to develop between entrepreneur and employees. The small size enables the forceful founding spirits of these companies to develop and communicate stringent expectations regarding a variety of behaviours: regarding design and production, collective hygiene, maintenance and repair of machinery and so forth. All the entrepreneurs have designed their organizations to be vehicles for training and socializing workers to the particular kinds of loyalty and discipline needed for corporate business undertakings. Yet the small size of these three firms enables their founders to make use of personalized relationships in moulding the behaviour of subordinates, rather than the distanced impersonality of rule-driven bureaucracies. Very few layers in status separate those at the top from those at the bottom. The entrepreneurs take a personal interest in how well their employees adjust and perform. Such patrimonial management, at its best, creates social capital in the form of a working space where the parties can develop reliable expectations of each other, expectations crafted largely by the entrepreneur.

Third and fourth, these enterprises operate at what are for Vietnamese manageable terms: where *mutually satisfactory exchanges* can be crafted and where *mutual surveillance* might be effectively practiced. The entrepreneurs pay close attention to keeping their employees happy. Close attention is needed because employees themselves exercise what here will be termed mutual surveillance. They are adept at comparing rewards and expectations, and have a keen sense of justice. They keep close tabs on each other and on management, and so foster 'transparency' at the micro level. As a result, these entrepreneurs felt compelled to enforce strict equality of opportunity in their workplaces: to hire without regard to male or female, Northerner or Southerner; to establish wage ladders with public criteria for promotion and regular performance review. Owners set wages with close attention to what is seen by their employees as fair. Ngoc, for example, started his factory workers at US$1 per day, with compensation reviews every four months and relatively predictable promotions up to US$1.25. The wages involved are not great; but such regularity and fairness of procedure are very important. By closely observing what owners and managers do, employees effectively encourage them to be reliable. Employees thus foster a kind of trustworthiness, sustained by vigilant watchfulness, increasing the stock of social capital within their companies.

Mutual surveillance is also a tool for management. It can be used to encourage workers to change unhygienic habits through peer pressure – as did Huynh in his Nhat Ban Company. It can be used to enforce strict fairness in the distribution of rewards and punishments. It also can be used by management to promote and enforce a sense of thrift. Vietnamese have learned habits of economizing and making do which put even the most conscientious green recycler to shame. It is all too easy for Westerners to overwhelm this sense of thrift by lavishing resources on a problem; instead, it is important to listen in on how Vietnamese observe each other in using organizational resources, and to encourage the social disapproval of wastefulness. The thrift sometimes has to be redirected; Ngoc, after all, had to train his technicians to engage in what they saw as extravagant preventive maintenance, rather than deploy traditional Vietnamese thrift and run machines into the ground.

In all these ways, mutual surveillance forms social capital by rendering owners and employees transparent and reliable to each other. Mutual surveillance enables all sides to monitor and exert pressure upon each other, and it is that constant pressure that is the medium through which mutual trust is sustained. Such trust is fragile; networks of trust are torn apart when either side finds the leverage to render its own actions non-transparent and beyond the influence of the other party. Networks of social capital are therefore subject to sudden and catastrophic tearing. As will be seen, what foreign companies might provide are relatively more stable environments than the more turbulent Vietnamese private sector can provide for supporting such fragile networks of mutual reliability.

Notes

1. Its 'major objectives' (abbreviated for relevance to this study) are to:

   (a) 'Promote rapid and sustainable economic growth coupled with attainment of social progress and equity…At the same time, concentrate on developing agriculture and rural areas…reduce the development gap between regions…

   (b) 'Create an equal business environment for all types of enterprises from all economic sectors, including enterprises with foreign direct investment (FDI)…and encourage the development of small and medium-sized enterprises.

   (c) 'Continue with structural reforms to bring about a transformation of the nation's economic structure; reorganize, renovate and improve the efficiency of state-owned enterprises (SOEs); restructure the state budget; reform the commercial banking system, reorganize and strengthen the health of financial and credit organizations; continue with trade liberalization…

   (d) 'Encourage human development and reduce inequality…

   (e) 'Develop and expand social protection and safety nets for the poor…

   (f) 'Undertake public administration reform…Implement fully the Decree on Democracy at the Grassroots Level to improve citizens' participation in the planning and implementation of community socio-economic development…

   (g) 'Establish a system of qualitative and quantitative socio-economic development and poverty reduction indicators…' (SRVN, 2002, pp. 3–4).

2. Informal, unstructured interviews were conducted in March 2000; follow-up interviews were conducted with two in May 2001. Names and identities have been disguised, by agreement with the interviewees. The sample is small and therefore intended only to provide a few brush strokes rather than an entire picture.

3. The position of Viet Kieu business people is anomalous. They are seen as politically unreliable, but a source of sorely needed capital. Viet Kieu were granted permission in 1987 to send money home to Vietnam, and to return to invest. Even so, their capital largely escapes government control. Between US$600 million and US$1.2 billion is remitted to Vietnam annually, according to official tabulation; perhaps twice as much flows in unofficially. Of the money that Viet Kieu invest, 70 per cent comes through families and only 30 per cent through market channels (interview with Co Minh Duc, Director of the Viet Kieu Association, 5 April 2000). The Vietnamese government would like to see more channelled through the market, for it prefers private, non-kinship firms to household enterprises based on family capital.

4. Interview with 'Huynh', 5 April 2000.

5. Original interviews with 'Ngoc' and a sample of workers on 28 March 2000; follow-up interview with Ngoc in May, 2001. Unless indicated otherwise, all interviews were conducted on-site and in-person.

6. Relations are strained between Southerners and Northerners, not only because of subtle cultural differences but also because of bitter feelings engendered by the imposition of Northern hegemony upon the South after 1975.
7. Interview with 'Chau' on 4 April 2000; follow-up interview on 18 May 2001.

References

Hoang, K. G. and Nguyen, D. T. (1995) 'A Profile of Vietnamese Owners of Private Enterprises', *Vietnam Economic Review*, vol. 4 (December), pp. 27–32.

Liebhold, D. (2000) 'Software For Hard Times', *Time*, 2 October, *CNN* [website] http://www.cnn.com/ASIANOW/time/magazine/2000/1002/vietnam_it.html

McMillan, J. and Woodruff, C. (1999) 'Dispute Resolution with Courts in Vietnam', *Journal of Law, Economics, and Organization*, vol. 15 (October), pp. 637–58.

MPDF (1997): Mekong Project Development Facility, *The Emerging Private Sector and the Industrialization of Vietnam*, Private Sector Discussions, Number 1 (Hanoi).

MPDF (1999a): Mekong Project Development Facility, *Vietnam's Undersized Engine: A Survey of 95 Larger Private Manufacturers*, Private Sector Discussions, Number 8 (Hanoi).

MPDF (1999b): Mekong Project Development Facility, *Private Companies in Vietnam: A Survey of Public Opinions*, Private Sector Discussions, Number 9, (Hanoi).

Ronnas, P. and Ramamurthy, B. (eds) (2001) *Entrepreneurship in Vietnam: Transformation and Dynamics* (Copenhagen: NIAS Publishing).

SRVN (2002): Socialist Republic of Vietnam, 'The Comprehensive Poverty Reduction and Growth Strategy (CPRGS)', Hanoi, May, *International Monetary Fund* [website] (n.d.) http://www.internationalmonetaryfund.com:80/external/np/prsp/2002/vnm/01/index.htm, accessed 30 September 2003.

Tran, A. N. and Smith, D. (1997) 'Cautious Reformers and Fence-breakers: Vietnam's Economic Transition in Comparative Perspective', *Humboldt Journal of Social Relations*, vol. 24, pp. 51–100.

Truong T. N. (2000) 'The Rule of Law in Vietnam: Theory and Practice', in *The Rule of Law: Perspectives from the Pacific Rim, Mansfield Center for Pacific Affairs* [website] (updated 12 March 2003) http://www.mcpa.org/rol/perspectives.htm

Vietnam Panorama (2003) 'Government Delays Raising Foreign Investor Shareholding Cap', *Vietnam Panorama* [website] (n.d.) http://www.vietnampanorama.com/stk/stockmarket.html, accessed June 2003.

World Bank (2002) 'Vietnam: Delivering on Its Promise: Development Report 2003' Report 25050-VN by the Poverty Reduction and Economic Management Unit, East Asia and Pacific Region, *World Bank* [website] (n.d.) http://www.worldbank.org.vn/topic/vdr2003.htm, accessed June 2003.

10
Developing Social Capital through Human Resources: 'Vietsani' and the Future of Western Management

Stewart W. Herman

The previous two chapters have suggested that Vietnam needs to cultivate social capital of the sort necessary for a market economy, and that small Vietnamese enterprises have their own way of generating such capital. The thesis of this chapter is that international corporations can foster social capital at two levels, and so contribute indirectly to the reduction of poverty. This chapter first reviews recent history and explores how these businesses might contribute at the 'macro' level of rendering Vietnamese governmental institutions more responsive and transparent. Then an extended case study shows how companies might contribute at the 'micro' level through human-resource practices that encourage managers and workers to develop 'bridging' networks of collaboration and mutual reliability.

History since 1986: foreign direct investment (FDI) and social capital at the macro level

The macroeconomic goals adopted by the Vietnamese Communist Party in 1986 were to generate economic growth and reduce poverty. To this end, Vietnamese authorities decided not only to permit the growth of a market economy under state control, but – as a key strategy – to open the door to the global market economy. International firms were invited to provide not only financial capital but also productive capital in the sense of advanced technology and managerial techniques (Permanent Mission, 2003). Vietnam certainly was starved for such capital. After 1945 in Northern Vietnam, and after 1975 in Southern Vietnam, foreign capital had arrived mainly in the form of grants and loans from Eastern Bloc nations, particularly the Soviet Union. By the 1980s, this flow was diminishing.

The response of international business after 1986 was slow at first, but it escalated into a frenzy in the mid-1990s, providing a major boost to the economy. Investors were attracted by an untapped market of more than

70 million people and a workforce with a strong work ethos and adequate education – but low wage levels. In 1994, the US lifted its twenty-year-old trade embargo; full diplomatic recognition soon followed. In 1995, Vietnam joined the Association of South East Asian Nations (ASEAN). By 2000, a total of US$36 billion was committed by outside investors to almost 3000 projects. The major fraction – some US$27 billion – was committed to industrial, hotel and other construction ventures (US Commercial Service, 2002, ch. 7). With growth rates often climbing above 7 per cent during the early and mid-1990s, Vietnam's GDP climbed from US$9 billion in 1992 to US$35 billion by 2002 (World Bank, 2003).[1] Foreign direct investment was a significant fraction of this growth. But the roller coaster could go down as well as up. In the mid-1990s, the annual rate of new foreign investment dropped precipitously and the amount actually disbursed also tumbled. By 2000, less than half the US$36 billion committed by foreign companies was actually spent. Disbursements peaked at US$2–3 billion per year between 1995 and 1997, fell in half by 1999, and dropped to perhaps US$0.5 billion in 2000 – for a total of US$14 billion (USCS, 2002, ch. 7; see also World Bank, 2001, p. 5).[2] The results of this falling investment were publicly visible. Hotel projects, for example, accounted for US$8 billion of the licensed capital, but by 2000 several constructions, even in the heart of Ho Chi Minh City, were shelved or shuttered. The in-country offices of foreign multinationals cut staff and hunkered down to weather the doldrums.

The drop could be blamed only partially on the Asian crisis of 1997. If the foreign business press is to be believed, the loss of momentum during the later 1990s was due to a severe shortage of social capital at the macro level. Euphoria yielded to disillusionment as foreign observers laid long list of endemic difficulties at the doorstep of the Vietnamese government: a lack of transparency in governmental operations and oversight, resulting in arbitrary demands and requirements (Stier, 1997; *The Economist*, 2000); a government schizophrenic in its approach to foreign capital – divided between welcoming receptivity and suspicious obstructionism (Chanda, 2000); graft and corruption in licensing and regulation the absence of a firm rule of law, particularly to enforce contracts; nepotism and cronyism in hiring; and predatory practices by Joint Venture (JV) partners (Frank, 2000). These problems are summed up in the term 'reliability' – shorthand for the macro social capital that makes it possible to do business. According to a US consulate official in 2001, US firms will not see Vietnam as comfortably 'reliable' until they see its infrastructure and regulatory practice aligned with what they have come to expect from other nations.

Both foreign governments and businesses have taken on the role of improving Vietnam's macro social capital by vigorously protesting the legal gaps and dysfunctional practices which reduce such 'reliability'. In response, the Vietnamese government steadily has increased its transparency and reduced burdensome licensing and the (non) rule of law. For example, in early 2000, the Prime Minister abolished, by fiat, more than 80 licenses. He also told the various government ministries to cut back on their interminable licensing requirements (as many as 200 were being required of some businesses). In a related step, governmental agencies were newly required to publish all formalities and rules right on their office doors, so that requirements can be known in advance of alleged infractions. Newly promulgated laws and administrative rules now had to clearly define what was prohibited and delineate any limitations on what is permitted. Otherwise, activities not explicitly prohibited or qualified were fully permitted – breaking with the past judicial assumption that activities were prohibited unless explicitly permitted (Truong, 2000). Macro social capital is being generated as formal irritants are slowly squeezed out of the relationship between foreign corporations and Vietnamese officialdom.

The payoff has come for Vietnam as new agreements commit the nation and its trading partners to reliable mutual expectations. In 2002, a bilateral trade agreement (BTA) was signed and ratified with the United States. The agreement reduced tariff barriers on both sides. Vietnam was enabled by reduced tariffs to expand its range of exports – particularly garments. US firms gained greater access to participate in hitherto-protected industries, such as banking; property-rights protections were strengthened as well. In aggregate, the distance the Vietnamese government has moved between 1986 and 2003 is nothing short of remarkable for a state still committed to socialist development. Yet the list of irritants to a workable business environment remains long. According to one close observer, it includes 'poor physical infrastructure, weak banking and financial markets, privileges still enjoyed by state-owned firms, inadequate service providers, poor and/or expensive communications, high land costs, corruption, high tax rates, poor protection of intellectual property rights, currency controls…' (Freeman, 2002). Philippe Auffret of the World Bank notes that Vietnam's bid to join the World Trade Organization is stalled because Vietnam is offering fewer concessions than it did under BTA (Auffret, 2003). Clearly there is a role for large international businesses in forming social capital at the macro level in Vietnam. With their vast economic clout, they can continue to influence the government to improve the reasonableness, reliability and predictability of public regulation.

'Vietsani'

The following case explores the viability of one foreign-controlled international business to incubate social capital at both the macro and micro levels.[3] 'Vietsani' (a pseudonym) appears to be a solid corporate citizen in the newly emerging entrepreneurial capitalism of Vietnam. It has provided employees with human capital in the form of portable experience and skills. Yet despite the valuable learning experiences, generous remuneration and admirable working conditions offered by Vietsani, its Vietnamese employees retain a preference for patrimonial management, where the relationship between manager and employee is cemented by personal loyalty, rather than the Western business practices of functional linkage and impersonal procedure. The question raised by this case is whether durable social capital of the 'bridging' sort requires a distinctively Vietnamese patrimonial style of management.

Vietsani is a joint venture, 85 per cent owned by the giant US-based 'Goodproducts' (also a pseudonym), a major manufacturer of products for residential construction. Its sole plant, located near Ho Chi Minh City, manufactures a humble product of indispensable social usefulness from raw materials that are abundant in Vietnam. A key factor in its success appears to be the productive technology it imported: its Vietnamese managers are gaining experience in the exacting discipline of disinterested management centred on the value of efficiency in production. This productive capital is of no small benefit in a country which historically has suffered from corrupt and sclerotic state-owned companies and a huge and burdensome bureaucracy.

By its own account, Vietsani management has developed fair relations with employees, cooperative relations with its (socialist) host government and a minimally destructive impact upon its physical environment. The major issue that arose during May 2001, on-site interviews concerned the company's management style – more as a question of cultural sensitivity than injustice. From an outside perspective, Vietsani offers a reassuring example of classic American enterprise and managerial practice. From a more local point of view, however, this managerial style is less than satisfying to Vietnamese managers. Yet overall, Vietsani appears to be playing a constructive role in Vietnam's belated entry into the world economy not only by putting Vietnam's productive capital to good use, but by increasing its human and social capital as well.

History and market strategy

The short history of Vietsani began with the 1994 resumption of trading relations between Vietnam and the United States. The Vietnamese government required foreign firms to form joint ventures with state-owned enterprises. In searching for a partner and a location, the US-based Goodproducts was steered by a venture capitalist to the 'People's Committee' which governs Dong Nai Province, which lies just outside Ho Chi Minh City. This province already was receptive to foreign investment from Asian countries such as Taiwan. Goodproducts was paired with a province-owned export-import company to form Vietsani, with an initial capital investment of US$16.5 million. Thanks to its close connection with the provincial administration, the new venture secured a business license within a few months in 1994, and began construction the next year, on five hectares carved out of a former US military base. The company's single plant, which cost

US$23 million to build, has operated since 1997. The 15 000 square-metre facility is located no more than 15 miles from the centre of sprawling Ho Chi Minh City, in a spacious industrial park dotted with giant Asian garment plants. The plant was built with the capacity to produce 400 000 units per year, but by 1999 was running at only 65 per cent of capacity. Thanks to a rebounding Vietnamese economy, the plant ramped up to full throttle by the end of 2001, and in the middle of 2002 celebrated its first six months of running in the black.

Vietsani's output is sold mostly within Vietnam, where it has four major competitors: two state-owned companies, and private companies from Taiwan and Japan. The nationwide sales volume of 1.2–1.5 million units runs well below the 2.1 million-unit capacity of all producers. Capitalizing on its well-known American brand name, Vietsani has targeted the high-end of this market, which it dominates. Competition is intense; by 2002, the market price of its best products had dropped in half, relative to the price of products it imported in 1995. Vietnamese customers are demanding, and the quality of Vietsani's local product is identical to that sold in the United States. According to Vietsani's general director, Stan Potts, the two Vietnamese competitors have tried unsuccessfully to tap the high end by copying Vietsani's and other designs, misrepresenting lower-grade products as of the highest quality or presenting them as imported. One of these firms was sued successfully by the Taiwanese competitor. Still, legal recourse is of little help; the fine for such infringement runs only to US$600 and enforcement is lax.

For its main defence, therefore, Vietsani counts on finicky Vietnamese consumers to shop for quality. 'A brand is like gold', Potts said in 2002. To support its brand's reputation, Vietsani relies on quality assurance and efficiency in production. All the producers use the same basic technology; Vietsani has differentiated itself by devoting unflagging attention to increasing the efficiency of its production process through incremental improvements. In 1998, only 75 per cent of the products made it through the production process; 25 per cent had to be scrapped. By 2002, the success rate had climbed to 92 per cent. 'We are performance driven', said Potts. 'It's hard to say our competitors are as driven.' Further improvements are anticipated.

Managers

Newly hired Vietnamese managers are attracted to Vietsani because they can develop their human capital more fully in a foreign company than in a Vietnamese company: the wages are better, they receive training and there is the possibility of travel outside Vietnam. One manager, for example, has been sent three times in five years to the Philippines for advanced training. The four interviewed managers all had advanced technical or university-level educations, and years of relevant experience before being hired by Vietsani. The infrastructure of educational institutions is poorly matched to the kinds of skills they want to gain. They value Vietsani for the opportunity to gain further skills on the job – usually in supervision, as they move up the ranks. The managers evaluate their jobs according to their potential for learning and promotion.

Keeping his managers happy is a significant challenge for Potts, because the market for well-trained managers is hotly competitive. Opportunities are opening up for those who have both training and experience. Five years ago, managers (9 in 2001, 12 in 2002) were entering their first jobs with foreign firms; now they can 'shop' their newly gained experience around for jobs with more potential for advancement. As a result, Vietsani is beginning to have a problem retaining its managers, and has to be sensitive to their wishes. Potts seeks to anticipate how they evaluate working at Vietsani. 'Do they feel good about their contribution? Do people in the company care about their future? They like to know they are heard and that their contributions are appreciated.' In 2001, their salaries ranged from US$150 (supervisors) to US$250 (engineers) per month; Potts had to raise their salaries in 2002. Other expectations also are rising. For example, the rural location of the plant forces all employees to commute. All employees above the level of supervisor expect free transportation to the factory. And Vietsani supports the enrolment of its managers in business-degree and other advanced programmes to gain further credentials.

Some conditions of employment are fixed; others are not. The work week is fixed at six days or 48 hours. The managers – unlike workers at the plant – appear to enjoy significant latitude to reshape the processes they are responsible for. One engineer reported performing a time study to reconfigure work tasks for greater efficiency. Another manager with responsibility for three sub-teams consisting of 78 employees reported that he meets daily, sometimes hourly, with the sub-team leaders, to impart instructions. Supervisory skills have far outstripped in importance the technical skills he had learned in university, and he feels driven to gain more skill in leadership. In essence, the division of labour in the plant encourages managers not only to exercise considerable latitude in their assigned tasks, but imposes upon them new skills to learn, thus creating a beneficial loop of reinforcement between task and enlarged skills. It appears that the managers have ample scope to enrich their human capital.

The managers have regular access to the general director through Monday-morning staff meetings. One manager reported making a suggestion to reduce production costs, which was accepted; two other suggestions (to reduce fuel consumption and to screen for defective products) were under consideration. For all, language and culture present a barrier. Since the general manager does not speak much Vietnamese, the managers must communicate in English. Beyond the language barrier, they seemed frustrated by the fact that the imported US managerial style encourages written communication of complaints. The Vietnamese reported preferring face-to-face conversation. In a Vietnamese context, direct conversation enables subordinates to read unspoken signals, to communicate their own feelings and to gain a sense of what the other party really feels. None of these needs would be well served by a suggestion box or other formal procedures for communicating dissatisfaction. In 2001, Potts took steps to enlarge the circle of face-to-face communication to include unofficial channels, the 'dotted lines on organizational charts. Such channels are good; they force you to talk to people.' It is during such informal conversations that he hears important if uncomfortable feedback: 'I gave you an idea; what happened to it?'

Corporate culture: from process to function – and a wistful longing for patrimonial management

Vietsani seems to provide a rich soil for developing the human capital of its managers. They can see themselves as engaged in a common, intensely collaborative enterprise where they gain valuable skills and the sense of being heard and valued in their distinctive roles. Such functional cooperation builds social capital as well – the good will and trust that enable managers to get ahead individually by developing horizontal networks of cooperation. Process management effectively formed social capital by developing the human capital of managers within a fundamentally horizontal network of 'teams'. In process management, the goal is continuous incremental improvement in quality; the corresponding strategy is to emphasize that all employees have a stake, and a competence, in improving the production process. Process management brashly de-emphasizes hierarchy in a society where generations of Chinese- and French-influenced administration have embedded a reverence for vertical differentiation in bureaucratic status. Facing these ingrained ideas in his Vietnamese managers and employees, Potts took pains to educate them to think of themselves as contributing to a horizontal process flow, through their teams. As recently as 2001, the Vietsani organization had only three layers: the general director; 9 to12 subordinate managers, and approximately 260 other employees. All were Vietnamese except Potts, who had served as general director since the beginning of the venture in 1995.

A year later, however, the process-team approach is being eclipsed by a different paradigm. In 2001 Goodproducts began centralizing its corporate structure. Newly appointed senior executives decided to integrate the far-flung and loosely linked worldwide branches of the corporation into a single, cohesive, tightly run operation. Vietsani was encouraged to replace its process-team structure with a more traditional functional structure, with more levels and a wider range of job descriptions. The Vietnamese managers, never entirely comfortable with the way the process organization flattened differences in status, were pleased by the innovation; now they have more titles to aspire to, more steps on the ladder of advancement.

When interviewed in 2001, the Vietnamese managers expressed an ambivalent feeling about process management. They enjoyed the pragmatic American atmosphere, where technical knowledge counts, particularly in service of achieving goals. They appreciated the emphasis on empowerment. They strongly endorsed the value of efficiency, and the spirit of teamwork it requires. They appreciated the open environment of communication, and direct access to the general director. They appreciated human-resource practices that emphasized impartial, merit-based treatment. They welcomed, for example, the egalitarian collegiality of the Monday-morning strategy meeting, in which each participant – no matter what rank – contributes a 10-minute update to the assembled staff, and solutions to problems are hammered out together. In short, they appreciated the 'bridging' social capital of horizontal, functional networking that process management fosters.

Yet the Vietnamese managers reported that they missed the traditional Vietnamese flavour of social capital: patrimonial loyalty. They longed for the 'feeling' of being treated as family, where the lofty chief takes the time to visit their homes at crucial rites of passage, whether to participate in weddings, or to present gifts at funerals. In their eyes, good Vietnamese managers are careful to observe tradition cultivating the loyalty of subordinates by demonstrating a commitment to them as persons. Subordinates expect managers to be visible, to walk around, to be accessible to casual conversation and face-to-face meetings. Their loyal energies were not being sparked by the more cold and distant media of emails, reports and suggestion boxes.

It is unclear whether an American general director might be able to elicit and channel such patrimonial loyalty. With seven years of experience in Vietnam, Potts saw himself as approachable, congenial and interested in Vietnamese culture: 'I go to weddings and funerals, and I laugh and cry with them as much as I can.' In this respect, he stands out among other expatriates who rotate in for one or two years and view Vietnam as a necessary evil on the ladder of advancement. But he acknowledged that there remains a significant obstacle. He lacks fluency in the Vietnamese language. He couldn't achieve the verbal and non-verbal flow which is important to generating the kind of personal loyalty Vietnamese like to cultivate towards their bosses. In a US facility oriented to sustaining the routines of efficient production, the social capital of patrimonial loyalty may not be necessary. In a Vietnamese organization, it still might not be necessary, but its absence likely will be keenly felt.

Workers

According to Potts, Vietsani provides an encouraging environment for workers (who numbered 305 in 2002) to develop their human capital. He asserted that workers might become managers – in principle. Indeed, skilled workers have been promoted to supervisors. In a recent 'Six Sigma' programme for quality analysis and improvement, three lower-level employees, two men and one woman, were recruited to study the manufacturing process closely. They demonstrated such an instinctive aptitude for statistical analysis that Potts promoted them to management. 'Their ideas are going to save a lot of money', he said. Vietsani encourages the workers who want to upgrade their skills by offering training that leads to professional certification in their technical specialties. Still, opportunities to move up the ranks appeared limited. Most workers have only a high-school education, so they are not often eligible for promotion.

Workers have some opportunities to learn skills. Shop-floor employees receive copious amounts of training specific to their jobs, and they can be rotated among two or three jobs. Nevertheless, for most employees, work at Vietsani means following rather than innovating. They are expected to comply with explicit procedures and instructions, and they are held responsible for results. According to one manager, the system is not tyrannical because it is impersonal and ordered to the goal of efficiency. Workers never reject the directions they are given; they are responsible to a process, not to the whims of their supervisors. When failures occur, it is assumed that the worker simply failed to understand the instructions given. 'So we just need to explain', said one manager. Employees are invited to make recommendations about improving processes. But participation in broader corporate governance is all but non-existent. While management encourages employees to submit suggestions, rarely do employees respond.

Other leverage of the employees appears limited. First, in compensation, there appears to be only a modest degree of individual bargaining, largely because the wages already are generous by Vietnamese standards. Production workers start at US$70–80 per month during a probationary period, and their wages rise to US$100, for a six-day, 48-hour week. It should be noted that such pay exceeds the US$35-per-month minimum wage by a factor of two or three, and amounts to four times the US$25 which employees receive at large shoe factories. Interestingly enough, the clerical workers at Vietsani start at US$120, reflecting the greater status Vietnamese place upon office work. Their salaries range up to US$1000. When being hired, applicants are invited to state what wages they expect, and sometimes the standard range is stretched to accommodate their expectations. The employees have a keen sense of fairness, and are quick to resent injustice – as when, for example, overtime is required. Salary schedules therefore are checked against country-wide surveys, and adjusted to keep pace. But once hired, employees enjoy only limited bargaining power. They may petition for raises by requesting a performance review, or by approaching the human-resources manager directly. With the recently more competitive employment environment, such requests are approved more frequently.

Second, the workers at Vietsani have no effective means of collective bargaining. Vietnamese law requires them to be organized in labour unions, but the Vietsani union meets once a year and it is active mainly in off-site social activities: sponsoring picnics, helping sick members, and the like. It raises money by selling scrap from the plant, with the permission of management. In the absence of a strong union, employees are encouraged to approach their supervisors directly. But the supervisor can be the source of the problem. A recurring problem is the hot tempers of some supervisors, which contrasts jarringly against Vietnamese expectations that they will be treated in a familial way.

Relations with government

Vietsani operates under one of the very few self-declared socialist regimes in the world. Back in 1995, Goodproducts had little choice but to set up a joint venture with a state-owned enterprise (SOE). Some joint ventures have became 'forced marriages' from which the foreign partner sought to escape, and the Vietnamese government in 1999 gave foreign partners the right to exit those unhappy ventures. But Vietsani has proven a viable partnership; Goodproducts has no desire to go it alone, by converting Vietsani into a wholly owned subsidiary. Having a well-connected Vietnamese partner has given Goodproducts two advantages: access to land in a country where all land is owned by the government, and easier resolution of the issues which inevitably arise under a system where corporate behaviour is closely and often suspiciously regulated.

Potts expects to continue to gain benefits from the relationship, as Vietsani expands. The responsibility for securing the needed permits falls to Nguyen Nam, the deputy general director, who formally represents the province of Dong Nai's minority stake in the enterprise. Nam was assigned to Vietsani after more than 10 years of experience in the export/import business. As second only to Potts in organizational hierarchy, he has the portfolio of promoting the interests of both Vietsani and the province's import/export company – sometimes against the interests of his province. For example, when the Dong Nai authorities imposed excessive import duties, he went to Hanoi and secured a judgement that restored more than US$70000 to Vietsani. In a tax case, he saved Vietsani another US$7000. While serving as an advocate for Vietsani, Nam also is charged with maximizing revenue for Dong Nai. For several years, the local authorities received only taxes, and rent for the land that Vietsani occupies. But since Vietsani posted its first profit in 2002, Dong Nai stands to gain eventually a percentage correlating to its 15 per cent stake.

Human and social capital formation at Vietsani

Vietsani makes its most direct contribution to reducing poverty in Vietnam largely by the generous conditions of employment it offers to its 305 managers and workers, and of course the wider circles of economic activity to which it contributes through relations with buyers and sellers. So far, its contribution can be quantified – and is probably not very different from other foreign ventures in Vietnam. The more intriguing question is how and to what extent its operations are helping build Vietnam's capacity to thrive with a market economy. Vietsani appears to have contributed in at least three ways. First, it has helped advance the rule of law by holding the Vietnamese government accountable to its own rules; in so doing, it has cultivated a measure of social capital, however incremental, at the macro level. Second, and also at the macro level, it has helped firm up expectations of trustworthiness between itself and its joint-venture partner. In many interviews, government officials and private-sector managers emphasized that a viable business relationship must benefit both parties. Vietsani appears to have modelled a cooperative, mutually beneficial relationship with the import–export SOE of Dong Nai; this achievement is a welcome counterpoint to Vietnam's long history of exploitation by foreigners.

Third, and perhaps most interesting, Vietsani has used its imported productive capital – 'process'-centred management – to form human and social capital within its organization. The venture operates in a cultural environment scarred by mutual envy and suspicion among Vietnamese. Vietsani appears to have finessed such tendencies by the structure it has developed. The single-minded focus on lean, process management has created a cohesive set of values centring on efficiency over hierarchy, and has enabled Vietnamese managers and workers a means to develop a reservoir of trustworthiness among themselves. Even while the Vietnamese managers long for the personal loyalties cultivated within traditional Vietnamese organization, they recognize the value of disinterested, impersonal management technique, and welcome it. Managers have an excellent environment for increasing their human capital; a similar benefit extends to at least some employees. The emphasis on efficiency has opened up moral space for employees to participate as respected contributors to the productive process, to be rewarded according to the merits of their contributions and to trust each other as colleagues on the same trajectory of efficient production – no small feat in a culture vulnerable to the worst excesses of stagnant, inefficient and capricious patrimonial organization.

Looking ahead at Vietsani

When the Vietsani plant was running at 65 per cent of capacity in 2001, Potts had hopes of exporting to the United States. Such a strategy now appears unlikely. The domestic market for Vietsani's product is robust. Indeed, as Vietsani pays down its debt, it appears to have considerable potential to return a profit. Vietsani has staked out the high end of the market; its product sells in Vietnam far more than in the United States; its plant is producing at a rate that is over capacity; its aggressive cost-cutting drive is yielding significant improvements; and at least some employees and managers are stretching to meet the continuing challenge of increasing its efficiency.

At some point, employees – with their exacting Vietnamese sense of justice – may wonder how large that profit is becoming, and whether it ought not be redistributed. A generation of egalitarian socialist teaching likely will find some expression. Of course, that day may be deferred, perhaps indefinitely. Potts expects that Vietsani will encounter stiff competition. By 2006, currently stiff import taxes for competitive products that now shield the market from most outsiders will be reduced to near zero per cent. In 2004, a formidable Japanese competitor will begin producing in Vietnam for the high end of the market. To prepare for these moments, Potts emphasizes to his staff the need for continued improvement. For a factory organized primarily around improving the efficiency of its production process, such competition may be more of a blessing than a burden. Competition from outside underlines the need for employees to collaborate; it calls attention to and glorifies the human capital that employees develop on the job; and it provides a clear rationale for deciding who should be promoted. As long as this lean, competition-driven focus can be maintained – and as long as the need for efficiency keeps Vietsani management listening to its employees – Vietsani may have an internally acceptable substitute for patrimonial management.

Vietsani has created, in effect, a small bubble of social capital in a wider cultural ocean where such networks need to be linked to provide a viable environment for the private sector to flourish. While the paradigm works at Vietsani, its real value will be known only if it can be transplanted to enterprises in the embryonic Vietnamese private sector. At this point, the bubbles of social capital are few and far between. Potts signalled just how vulnerable is Vietsani's social capital when addressing the question of succession. As the sole foreigner in the operation, he anticipated that his successor very well might be a Vietnamese, and welcomes that prospect – in principle. In practice, he recognized that a Vietnamese general director would be subject to pressures for favouritism payoffs, nepotism and other common forms of corruption to which he, as a foreigner, is immune. Exactly when the reservoir of Vietnamese social capital will fill to the needed point, at both the micro and macro levels, is unclear. Until that point is reached, Potts' strategy is to hold on to the human and social capital of his Vietnamese managers. Ironically enough, the success of Vietsani at generating human and social capital is measured not only by its success in the market, but by the departures of its managers for yet more challenging and lucrative jobs elsewhere.

The future for Vietsani and other large international businesses

This study began with the broad question of how foreign investment might serve to reduce poverty in Vietnam. Vietnam presents a complex history of durable poverty, a poverty which has endured despite major shifts in macro-economic strategy, and only now seems to be yielding to a tentative blend of market capitalism and state socialism. While the past 15 years of impressive economic growth strongly suggest that market capitalism must and will be a central engine for lifting Vietnam from poverty, exactly how foreign investment, especially Western investment, might contribute most helpfully to this dynamic is unclear. Currently, investment by international business appears critical to Vietnam's development. By 2003, foreign inflows were accounting for 30 per cent of investment and 21 per cent of exports, and had generated some 300 000 jobs, according to one official count (Permanent Mission, 2003).

The challenge for foreign corporations in overcoming poverty is to generate wealth. Wealth – as capital – comes in a variety of forms. For Vietnam, the bottom line is whether foreign corporations are increasing the capacities of Vietnam to house, feed, educate and employ people who are now poor. There is no question that the foreign ventures observed and surveyed in Vietnam are putting financial capital to productive use. Interviews with Vietsani and two other firms (not reported here) suggest that these ventures minimize the use of expatriates, pay generous wages, expand their customer base and treat their customers and suppliers honestly.[4] As such, there is no question that they are contributing materially to the reduction of poverty. But an equally necessary and perhaps more challenging question is whether they are contributing to alleviate the critical shortage of a more elusive form of capital in Vietnam: social capital.

In Vietnam, social-capital formation is deeply intertwined with human-capital formation. Multinational firms appear uniquely positioned to foster the growth of social capital at the micro level, by extending and intensifying their normal practices of cultivating the human capital of their Vietnamese employees. These foreign ventures, to their credit, consider human capital formation an important part of their business in Vietnam. With their access to financial and productive capital from overseas, they import the sophisticated managerial techniques which will enable Vietnamese eventually to grow their own human capital. They have opened up almost all of their positions to Vietnamese applicants, trained these employees and even financed their further education. (Indeed, for Vietnamese governmental authorities and scholars, the benefits of foreign investment for the work force of Vietnam are a significant measure of the political acceptability of foreign multinational corporations.) The human capital these international businesses generate shades into social capital. The discrete skill sets of individuals require, as a background, the attitudes and motivations needed to support networks of generalized trust and cooperation.

Exactly how the investments made by large international businesses will play into Vietnam's future is a politically touchy question. Vietnamese historically have been sensitive to foreign domination, because conquest (or investment) has served to undermine Vietnamese institutions and destroy indigenous social capital. The most radical and least welcome possibility is that the advent of massive foreign investment will simply crush the embryonic sector of domestic private enterprise. For example, Coca-Cola has invested US$100 million and, together with Pepsi, effectively has destroyed the Vietnamese soft-drink industry. It is for this reason that Vietnamese continue to protect industries from international investment. A less extreme possibility is that the Vietnamese private sector will survive in niches ignored by larger foreign companies, and the household sector will simply adapt to new opportunities. In either outcome, large international companies might be seen as merely the latest instrument of Western domination. As such, they would destroy far more social capital than they could ever create, at both the macro and the micro levels.

There is a third possible outcome of foreign investment, confidently put forward by Vietnamese managers during interviews in 2000 and 2001: that foreign companies indeed will gain control over large portions of the Vietnamese economy, but that such control will be a passing phenomenon. Over time, Vietnamese will work from within to gain control of these ventures and so reclaim their economy. These energetic and optimistic managers are eager to learn foreign practices and are confident that they will rise through the executive ranks. As they gain control, they surely will adapt and domesticate Western corporate practices, just as Vietnamese have sought for two thousand years to adapt foreign influences (Chinese, French, American) in their body politic.

This optimistic scenario directs attention to the question of how foreign companies best might prepare for their eventual 'Vietnamization' – a topic that already concerns thoughtful expatriate managers. In what way can these foreign-controlled ventures contribute to the social capital needed for these enterprises to thrive in a specifically Vietnamese context? Here the insights of Chapter 9 may be of use. The Viet Kieu entrepreneurs directed attention to four features of authentically Vietnamese enterprise: small scale, patrimonial relationships, a mutually satisfactory exchange and mutual surveillance. In the future, large international businesses may incorporate some of these features. But as these enterprises are Vietnamized, they may simply prove unaffordable, and so be downsized into smaller, more distinctively Vietnamese enterprises. Consider how dramatically the scale of investment increases from the small- and medium-sized enterprises (SMEs) surveyed in the last section, to the joint ventures or wholly owned subsidiaries funded by foreign capital. Vietsani created some 300 jobs with an investment of US$23 million, or US$76 000 per job, while a survey found that household enterprises create jobs for US$2394 each, and other private Vietnamese companies for US$4423 to US$6107 each.[5] From a Vietnamese perspective, foreign ventures can be astonishingly profligate: the wage scale jumps, Western managerial methods are imposed from outside, and expectations about job performance and certification escalate. Foreign investment comes at a price which Vietnamese enterprises simply may not be able to afford in the future. The challenge for Vietnamese managers who have apprenticed at Western ventures may be how to enlarge the social capital of their firms while economizing on financial capital.

Summary and conclusion

Any strategy for generating social capital in Vietnam ought to draw from patterns of organization that already work in that cultural context. That is why Chapter 9 reports on strategies used by indigenous entrepreneurs to form 'bridging' capital at the micro level. The three short case studies of small ventures organized by Viet Kieu (returned overseas Vietnamese) discovered a total of four ingredients: small scale, mutually beneficial exchange, patrimonial leadership and mutual surveillance. These elements contribute to a distinctively Vietnamese form of 'bridging' social capital, based upon patrimonial relations of authority and loyalty. The question then arises whether this patrimonial strategy reflects, or ought to be reflected in the practices of larger international businesses.

This last chapter explores one major international business venture at some length. Vietsani, a joint venture controlled by a major US firm, focuses the collective attention of employees upon lean production, as necessitated by a competitive domestic market. The US director pushes managers and workers to collaborate on 'process' teams, teams which de-emphasize hierarchy in favour of close communication and coordination. The impersonal, efficiency-driven style seems to provide an especially reliable basis for employees to trust each other, and so to foster the growth of 'bridging' social capital. By learning to make this 'process management' work, the employees gain not only very marketable skills but also the habits and practices of mutual reliance and cooperation. Imported productive capital appears to be a major factor in generating not only human but social capital.

In short, the Western way of generating social capital within the enterprise appears to be working in Vietsani, in the sense that the enterprise is functioning efficiently and profitably. Still, it may make only a limited contribution to forming distinctively Vietnamese forms of bridging social capital. While the Vietsani managers firmly endorsed Western techniques, they long for the traditional patrimonial leadership as a way to build trusting, loyal relations with their superiors. It remains unclear, therefore, to what extent the Western strategy will take root in Vietnam, as international businesses become 'Vietnamized' over the course of time or experienced managers depart to head up their own Vietnamese companies.

This study begins with a 'macro' question of enormous scope – how to reduce poverty in Vietnam – and ends with a minute examination of managerial and human-resource practices. While this final focus may seem trivial, given the scope of the problem, it is actually central to a society's capacity to reduce poverty. Social capital is the catalyst that enables financial, productive and human capital to be utilized effectively, and it is accumulated only through the painfully incremental processes of increasing the values of trustworthiness, cooperativeness and sheer resilience in a society. At the micro level, this progress happens one organization at a time, as possibilities for generalized reciprocity are identified and reinforced, one transaction at a time.

Notes

1. By yet another count, total capital committed amounted to almost US$39 billion by April 2003, while disbursements totalled US$21 billion (USVTC, 2003).
2. US Commercial Service 2002, chapter 7; see also World Bank 2001, 5. By another, rosier, count, disbursements averaged US$2 billion per year from 1996 through 2001 (Freeman, 2002).
3. All names and places have been disguised. Interviews with 'Stan Potts,' general director, and four Vietsani managers were conducted on 16 and 21 May 2001, with a follow-up telephone interview in July 2002.
4. Interviews with the human resources director of a major agricultural products multinational and the director of a health/beauty care multinational, 17 May 2001.
5. See Ronnas and Ramamurthy (2001), p. 37, table 2.4, 'Assets/worker' entries, as divided by 11 700 – the approximate dollar value of the Vietnamese dong in 1997.

References

Auffret, P. (2003) 'Trade Reform in Vietnam: Opportunities With Emerging Challenges', World Bank Policy Research Working Paper 3076, June, *World Bank* [website] (updated 29 September 2003) http://econ.worldbank.org/view.php?topic=16&type=5&id=27368, accessed 29 September 2003.

Chanda, Nayan (2000) 'Blowing Hot and Cold', *Far Eastern Economic Review*, 30 November, *Thong Luan* [website] (updated 30 November 2000) http://www.thongluan.org/EN/Opinion/NayanChanda_BlowingHotAnhCold.html, accessed 30 September 2003.

The Economist (2000): 'Good Night, Vietnam', 8 January, pp. 65–6.

Frank, R. (2000) 'In Paddies of Vietnam, Americans Once Again Land in a Quagmire', *Wall Street Journal*, 21 April, A1.

Freeman, N. J. (2002) 'Foreign Direct Investment in Vietnam: An Overview', paper prepared for the DFID workshop on Globalization and Poverty in Vietnam, Hanoi, 23–24 September.

Permanent Mission (2003): Permanent Mission of the Socialist Republic of Vietnam to the United Nations, *Permanent Missions to the United Nations* [website] (updated 14 April 2003) http://www.un.int/vietnam/dev_bus/Foreign%20direct%20investment%20in%20Vietnam.htm, accessed 14 July 2003.

Ronnas, P. and Ramamurthy, B. (eds) (2001) *Entrepreneurship in Vietnam: Transformation and Dynamics* (Copenhagen: NIAS Publishing).

SRVN (2002): Socialist Republic of Vietnam, 'The Comprehensive Poverty Reduction and Growth Strategy (CPRGS)', Hanoi (May), *International Monetary Fund* [website] http://www.internationalmonetaryfund.com:80/external/np/prsp/2002/vnm/01/index.htm, accessed 30 September 2003.

Stier, K. (1997) 'In Search of Direction', *Asian Business* (December), pp. 31–4.

Truong, T. N. (2000) Truong Trong Nghia, Vice President, Foreign Trade and Investment Center, Interview, 30 March.

US Commercial Service (2002) 'Vietnam Country Commercial Guide 2002', *US Commercial Service* [website] (n. d.) http://www.usatrade.gov/Website/CCG.nsf/ShowCCG?OpenForm&Country=VIETNAM, accessed 29 September 2003.

USVTC (2003): US–Vietnam Trade Council, 'Foreign Direct Investment to Vietnam', *US Vietnam Trade Council* [website] (updated 14 September 2003) http://www. usvtc. org/Trade%20Statistics/foreign_direct_investment_to_vie.htm, accessed 30 September 2003.

World Bank (2001) *Pillars of Development: Vietnam 2010: Vietnam Development Report 2001* (Hanoi: Vietnam Development Information Center).

World Bank (2003) 'Vietnam at a Glance', 4 September 2003, *World Bank* [website] http://www.worldbank.org/data/countrydata/aag/vnm_aag.pdf, accessed 30 September 2003.

11
Forestry, Gold Mining and Amerindians: The Troubling Example of Samling in Guyana

Gail Whiteman

Introduction

While forestry, mining and other forms of natural resource development can provide developing countries with economic benefits, such projects can also carry significant social, environmental and economic costs to local indigenous peoples. This case study examines the direct and indirect impacts of the Barama Company Limited (a subsidiary of the Malaysian-based Samling Group) on local Amerindians in Guyana, South America, and explores what the company could have done differently in order to reduce negative outcomes for local Indigenous peoples. The case study followed an iterative research design (Hammersley and Atkinson, 1995) and includes qualitative field data from 2000 as well as extensive document analysis.[1]

Guyana is the only English-speaking country in South America. Its population of approximately 770000 is sharply differentiated along racial lines, and the country has what its national development strategy terms a 'race-based geography' (Government of Guyana, 1996b). The interior, densely covered with forests and savannah, is home to some 54000 Amerindians. While only 7 per cent of the whole population, they compose the majority group in a number of regions in the remote interior including Region 1, which is the focus of this study. Most tribes continue to practice traditional pursuits of hunting, fishing and subsistence agriculture. The remainder of the population is largely continental Indian (48 per cent) or African (33 per cent). About 90 per cent of this non-Amerindian population live along the narrow coast and are colloquially known as 'coastlanders'. While coastlanders inhabit only a small portion of the country, they wield tremendous power over the interior. Political parties tend to reflect racial lines, with either the Indian or Afro-Guyanese parties ruling the country. At the national level, Amerindian rights are not well recognized. Amerindians nominally secured land rights at the time of independence, but in practice these rights are partial and often questionable. Many Amerindian communities never received official recognition as 'Amerindians' and have no legal rights whatsoever to their traditional lands.

Guyana's road to economic and social development has been long and difficult. It achieved independence from the United Kingdom in 1966. At the time, Guyana had one of South America's highest per capita incomes. After many years of colonial rule (first by the Dutch, then the British), hopes were high that an independent Guyana would emerge as the 'jewel of the Caribbean' (Colchester, 1997, p. 2). Yet that dream did not transpire. The first president, Forbes Burnham, declared the country a 'Cooperative Republic' and nationalized foreign business. Government-controlled cooperatives were established but were plagued by corruption, inefficiency and cronyism. Burnham, affiliated with a political party led by Afro-Guyanese, the People's National Congress, has been criticized for relying upon fraudulent elections and for wielding ruthless dictatorial power. He ruled Guyana for nearly 30 years without popular support. The economy plummeted, and the living standards of the Guyanese deteriorated rapidly. By the early 1980s, Guyana's economy had collapsed and the government began to default on its debt payments.

In 1978 and 1979 Guyana turned to the International Monetary Fund (IMF) and the World Bank for help. Guyana was one of the first countries to request and receive structural adjustment lending from the World Bank. The Bank and the IMF pushed Guyana to accept greater foreign direct investment. In 1988 Guyana created a new foreign investment code, with little or no restriction on foreign ownership. This code continues to be 'regarded as one of the most liberal in South America' (Hogg, 1993). Cheddi Jagan (1918–97) of the opposition party, the People's Progressive Party, became President in 1992. Under Dr Jagan's leadership, Guyana actively sought foreign direct investment from other developing countries – in the South. Jagan had a pronounced distrust of foreign companies from the developed world and so actively pursued policies and promotional activities among Asian counterparts like the Samling Group, the focus of this study. However, some of these Asian companies had questionable reputations regarding political corruption, environmental protection and human rights performance.

Despite such bids for foreign investment, Guyana's economic situation remains poor. The World Bank classifies it as a 'lower-middle-income' country (World Bank, 2001a), but that seems optimistic. In 1999 Guyana's gross domestic product was only US$679 million (North–South Institute, 2002), or less than US$900 per capita (World Bank, 2001a). Guyana averaged US$70 million in annual foreign direct investment (FDI) inflows from 1990 to 1995, but that figure dropped to $56 million by 2001 (UNCTAD, 2002). Guyana remains highly indebted: its ratio of external debt to gross national income was 245.7 per cent in 1999 (The North–South Institute, 2002). In

2000, The World Bank Group and the IMF agreed to support a comprehensive debt reduction package for Guyana under the enhanced Heavily Indebted Poor Countries (HIPC) Initiative.

In 1999, Guyana ranked a dismal 83 on the Human Development Index (HDI) and an even more dismal 88 on the Gender Development Index (GDI) (UNDP, 2001). Approximately 35 per cent of Guyanese live in poverty – one of the highest rates in the Western Hemisphere (World Bank, 2001a). Extreme poverty follows ethnic heritage, Amerindians being by far the poorest; 88 per cent of Guyana's Amerindians live below the poverty line. In Region 1, the focus of this study, 95 per cent of local Amerindians live in extreme poverty (IMF, 2000). The majority of Amerindians are illiterate and have limited access to higher education (Government of Guyana, 1996b). Access to health care is also extremely limited in remote interior regions (Verbeeke, 1994). Amerindian women are particularly susceptible to the impacts of poverty. A report commissioned by the National Commission on Women in Guyana identified Amerindian women as one of the most economically, socially, politically and culturally marginalized groups in Guyana (National Commission on Women, 2001).

While Guyana is poor in terms of living standards, its interior regions contain a rich storehouse of natural resources: forests, and large deposits of bauxite and gold. Guyana has, by official count, 65 000 square miles or 16.8 million hectares of forest (Government of Guyana, 1996c). Since the late 1970s, the World Bank and IMF structural adjustment policies have pushed Guyana to open up its minerals and forestry resources to privatization and foreign multinational investment. By the mid-1990s, nearly nine million hectares of rainforest had already been claimed by foreign logging companies. In contrast, only 400 000 hectares have been set aside as communal Amerindian lands (Colchester, 1997).

This case study reviews the impact of one major logging company on the Amerindians of Region 1. In 1992 development rights to over 1.6 million hectares of Guyana's national forest were granted to the Barama Company Limited, a subsidiary of The Samling Group, a Malaysian corporation. Despite Samling's general claim that the result of logging has, directly and indirectly, improved the lives of interior people, this case study describes a less rosy picture (Samling, 2003a). In early 2002, Barama left Region 1 to pursue 'sustainable' forestry in another part of the country. It announced that it would pursue Forest Stewardship Council certification in order to address shifting customer demand. Meanwhile, international non-governmental organizations (NGOs) like the Forest Peoples Programme (FPP) and civil-society organizations in Guyana such as the Amerindian Peoples Association (APA) had long complained of Barama's performance in Region 1. Local Amerindians have been severely affected by the Barama forestry operation: both directly and indirectly. On the one hand, social and environmental impacts of its operations were aggravated by unresolved land claims and lack of consultation with the indigenous peoples affected. On the other hand, destructive mining development was encouraged by Barama's road construction. In ways that were forecast but may not have been fully anticipated by Barama, the forestry operations indirectly led to a dramatic increase in small- and medium-scale mining, often illegal, by people who were not residents of the region (typically coastlanders or Brazilians). This mining activity in turn gave rise to environmental, social and economic abuses.

The Samling Group: corporate policy or corporate citizenship?

The Samling Group (Samling Strategic Corporation Sdn. Bhd.) is a large, integrated multinational timber company based in Malaysia. Established as a small firm in 1963, Samling has grown tremendously but remains controlled by the father and son team of Datuk Yaw Teck Seng and Yaw Chee Ming. The Group's many companies operate in Malaysia, Japan, China, Taiwan, South Korea, the United States, Canada, Cambodia, Papua New Guinea, New Zealand and Guyana. While the Samling Group focuses on forest products, it also has investments in plantations, property development and oil and gas services. In the company's own words, 'Samling, in Chinese, means three forests. It is a symbol of our three founding companies and represents growth, vigour and partnership – an organization that is progressive yet cares for its environment and people' (Samling, 2003b). Indeed, in recent years Samling has voiced a growing commitment to sustainable forest management: 'Through years of research, Samling has devised a forest management programme that balances … economical viability, environmental compatibility and social acceptance of forest resource management' (Samling, 2003c). In 1996, Samling received an ISO 9001 certification in forest management. In 2001 Samling joined the Forest Stewardship Council (FSC), and receiving FSC certification for its operations has become a key strategic goal.

Samling states that it respects the traditions of indigenous peoples; 'instead of uprooting the traditional way of life', its corporate policy 'complements existing customs and traditions' (Samling, 2003a). Samling also states that it has a strong commitment to community development. Despite the heavy criticism that the forestry industry has faced in the past, Samling boldly claims that 'Over the years, the tangible benefits and improvement to life can already be seen. The result of logging has, directly and indirectly, improved the lives of the interior people.' While Samling acknowledges the bad reputation of forestry, it dismisses the reality of many negative impacts at the local level: 'Nowadays, logging has undeservedly earned a bad name. The word logging itself is now synonymous with the destruction of the environment. In actual fact, logging brings economic benefits to the surrounding areas that more than offset any minor disturbance to the environment … And contrary to popular misconceptions, Samling has a well-structured, organized programme that identifies and promotes the needs of the local community' (Samling, 2003a).

Nevertheless, Samling has had a history of conflictual relations with indigenous peoples in many parts of the world. In Malaysia, the nomadic Penan people in Sarawak blockaded Samling logging operations in 2002 because they claimed their land rights had been ignored by the company and the government, resulting in 'increasingly severe living conditions due to the depletion of forest and river resources and their livelihood' (Magin *et al.*, 2001; Jalong, 2002). Samling has also been criticized for illegal logging and political corruption in Cambodia and Papua New Guinea and has also faced civil society opposition in Brazil and Romania (Johnson, 1996; Global Witness, 1997; Loone, 2002).

Samling has operated in Guyana since 1992, when Barama Company Limited, a joint venture between Sunkyong Limited of Korea (20 per cent) and the Samling Group of Malaysia (80 per cent), was granted a 1.6-million-hectare tract in Guyana's interior forest. Barama has long been a company of choice for the Guyanese government. At the opening of Barama's plywood factory south of Georgetown, President Cheddi Jagan explained his position: 'It is good that [Samling and Sunkyong] have now decided to come here … because they are coming here, not only with capital, but with knowledge of Third World backward countries, kept backward because of colonialism and neo-colonialism. They have been able to forge ahead, applying science and technology, a disciplined workforce, and setting the pace, in the world today of growth and development' (Colchester, 1997, p. 143). Barama has maintained strong governmental ties over the years, including helping to arrange a Presidential tour to Asia.

In fact, Barama has contributed little to government coffers, given to its extremely favourable 1992 contract (Sizer, 1996a). The 25-year agreement between the Government of Guyana and Barama gave the company the rights to log almost 8 per cent of Guyana's land mass. According to the Guyana Forestry Commission, 'Barama's annual production of 200 000 cubic metres represents more than 40 per cent of the total national log harvest.' This agreement, however, included a five-year tax exemption (automatically renewable for an additional five years), as well as other financial incentives. In 1993 Barama paid royalties of US$70 000 on exports of US$3 million; in 1993, its exports rose to more than US$31 million, while its taxes increased only to US$99 000 (Sizer, 1996b). The royalties and other fees are paid in Guyanese dollars, with no provision for inflation adjustments (Sizer, 1996a). Clearly, the Guyanese government receives only nominal income from the Barama concession.

Amerindian land claims in Region 1

The forestry agreement Barama signed with the government was a key element of the government's strategy to develop the interior (the 'hinterland'). The agreement committed both sides to respect the interests of Amerindians, stating that 'the Government shall assist the Company in the establishment, development and continuation of good relations between the Company and the indigenous peoples living and working in the Concession Area. The Company will honour and respect all rights of indigenous people as required by the laws of Guyana' (Sizer, 1996a). In fact, however, neither side has protected the Amerindians from exploitation.

Region 1 is a rainforest ecosystem, which is home to three Amerindian tribes: the Lokono (Arawak), Carib and Warau (Verbeeke, 1994). The Amerindian communities rely upon subsistence farming and hunting, craft production and (to some degree) small-scale gold mining. Most of their villages are located along rivers throughout the region and remain isolated with a low level of integration. Until the early 1990s they were accessible primarily by airplane or boat. While remote, Region 1 has a long history of development and trade, reaching as far back as the Dutch colonial period. A major gold rush occurred during at the beginning of the twentieth century; it resulted in significant small- and medium-scale mining activity, particularly around the road that was established between Matthews Ridge and Arakaka. As a result, the impacts of natural resource development have been severe on local Amerindians, particularly Caribs.

> The Peberdy survey of 1949 found the Caribs to be suffering severely from the intrusion of miners into their area and recommended that an Amerindian 'reservation' be established to protect them from further problems…The Amerindian Lands Commission, which reported in 1969, also noted the severe situation of the Caribs. The Commission likewise recommended that an area be set aside for them. (APA and WRM, 1994, p. 4)

Nonetheless, the Amerindian Lands Act in 1976 did not recognize Amerindian claims in this area and local peoples were not granted land rights. In 1977, a reserve was established for the Carib, but it did not vest title in the communities or councils so these lands remained State lands and the protection afforded to the Amerindians was ambiguous or non-existent.[2] Of the 16.8 million hectares of forest in Guyana, 8.9 million hectares lie within State Forest boundaries, 'where practically all commercial timber exploitation occurs' (Government of Guyana, 1996c). Even today, only some 400 000 hectares (or 4.5 per cent) have been set aside as communal Amerindian lands. Guyana's Forests Act of 1953 includes a clause guaranteeing traditional Amerindian rights and freedoms, but in practice, such protections have not been implemented. The Act does not require consultation or community consent on development projects. It also does not explicitly require environmental and social impact assessments. As a result, Amerindians in Guyana remain marginalized from most natural resource decisions. According to the Guyanese Organization of

Indigenous Peoples (GOIP):

> There seems to be an inherited ideology in Guyana not to consult with the Amerindians when woods are cut through their lands, when mining, forestry and petroleum exploration concessions are negotiated with outsiders, for this trend continues unabated…Lately…it has become fashionable for the Government and international financial institutions including the World Bank, to talk of 'consulting' with Amerindians and 'to acknowledge the role of Amerindians in managing protected areas', but this is by no means a substitute for land ownership rights and self-determination of Indigenous Peoples. (IAIP, 1997)

Guyana's National Development Strategy (1996b) recommended that Amerindians receive royalties of one-half (0.5) per cent from development that occurs on their land; to date, however, the Amerindian Development Fund has not, been created and this recommendation has not been implemented. Currently, there is no Minister of the Environment and local Amerindians perceive the Minister of Amerindian Affairs to be a token position without real influence or representation. A 1995 World Bank study 'concluded that the Guyana Forestry Commission was a perfect example of the 'capture theory of regulation', whereby the regulatory body is controlled by the industry it is suppose to regulate' (Colchester, 1997, p. 102). The Guyanese government (1996c) has acknowledged this criticism publicly, but this has not resolved the issue for local Amerindians in Region 1.

None of the Amerindian communities were consulted on the proposed Barama operations, and many continue to have unsettled land claims. The Barama concession enclosed four Amerindian communities with land title and also overlapped with a Carib reserve established in 1997, but did not provide title. Numerous Amerindians live along the main rivers within the concession – the Kaituma, Barima, Barama and Cuyuni rivers – also without title to the land they occupy.

Barama's self-assessment

During the first several years of its operation in Region 1, Barama received increasing criticism from Amerindians and NGOs. In 1993, Barama hired the Edinburgh Centre for Tropical Forests (ECTF) consulting group, with a contract that ran until 2000 to conduct an independent and publicly available social and environmental impact assessment (SEIA) of Barama's operations in Region 1, and to develop and implement more sustainable forest practices (Colchester, 1997). The SEIA was conducted in early 1993 (Colchester, 1997, pp. 120–4). During its site visit, ECTF identified a key environmental risk: '... timber harvesting may not be biologically sustainable at planned extraction levels' (Sizer, 1996a). The ECTF study also indicated that some Amerindians were positive about potential employment opportunities, and also expected better schooling and health services as a result of the company's entry. However, ECTF reported that the local Amerindian population lacked information about Barama's proposed operations and in some cases had unrealistic expectations about potential benefits. And the study recognized that some of the Amerindians lived in areas not legally designated as Amerindian land within the Barama concession. The ECTF identified five potential negative impacts on Amerindians:

1. An increase in mining activity, due to the road network built by Barama to facilitate its logging operations.
2. Disruption of Amerindian traditional subsistence activities, due to the reduction or elimination of traditional food, shelter and other forest products used by the Amerindians, from environmental degradation from logging and mining, and from the anticipated increase in illegal wildlife hunting.
3. Negative cultural impacts as Amerindians shifted from traditional hunting and agricultural to employment at Barama, mining operations and other non-traditional activities.
4. Increased conflict with the growing numbers of non-Amerindians who were entering the region for work, and who had increased access to Region 1 due to new roads. Negative health impacts, as the migrants brought in diseases, including sexually transmitted diseases.
5. Culture shock, especially for those more remote Amerindians who had previously had little ongoing contact with outsiders.

ECTF recommended that Barama mitigate these impacts by hiring a community liaison officer; appointing an Amerindian as 'Amerindian Liaison Officer'; establishing a local committee to help advise on community issues within the concession; regulating the use of the roads; demarcating the boundaries of Amerindian land titles and identifying Amerindian areas on Barama maps; and improving community health care, education and local development. Few of these recommendations were implemented, and with little marginal benefit. For instance, Barama did hire a community liaison officer, who was also hired to be the Amerindian Liaison Officer. However, she did not gain widespread support from within the Amerindian community and was believed to be a 'sell-out', and there were many complaints about her behaviour from the community. Barama never established a local committee to help advise on community issues within the concession, nor did they attempt to regulate road access.[3] It is not clear how Barama attempted to improve local development, health care or education since the company has not published a report on these issues. Sizer (1996) suggests that Barama was incurring 'significant social costs of roughly an additional US$200 000 annually maintaining a hospital, school, and so on', although these programmes are not specifically targeted towards Amerindians. The company appears to have provided minor funding to help the Amerindian community at 4-Mile to construct a playing field for children (GINA, 2002b). In 2002 Barama donated a generator to help improve local power supply to Port Kaituma (GINA, 2002a).

In 1994 the APA and the World Rainforest Movement (WRM) conducted their own study. They found that while dozens of Amerindian communities lived within the Barama forest concession and continued to practice traditional ways of life, including hunting, fishing and farming mixed with small-scale mining, the majority of these communities were not officially recognized as 'Amerindian' and lacked land rights. Amerindian communities in the area also lacked school facilities and health care and were suffering a high prevalence of malaria. Many Amerindians in Region 1 still lacked land rights, a major contention for Amerindian groups.[4] In 1994, despite the ECTF study, many of the Amerindians interviewed had never heard of Barama (which had only recently started operations) and 'most were indignant to learn that they now [found] themselves within a forestry concession being exploited by a foreign logging company' (APA and WRM, 1994, p. 1).

For the Amerindians who had contact with Barama, negative impacts during this initial period were already evident by 1994. In addition to the direct deforestation due to logging, interviews done by the APA and the WRM confirmed that people were concerned about pollution due to forestry and the disruption caused to their traditional way of life as wildlife were affected. Incidents occurred, such as the desecration of an Amerindian graveyard and the forcible relocation of the community of Orenoque in order for Barama to build a log pond and office complex. The Amerindians who were relocated found that their new site at 1-Mile at the edge of Port Kaituma contained smaller lots that were inadequate for subsistence activities. Community members claimed they did not receive the size of land they had been promised nor did they receive compensation for the loss of fruit trees. Some Amerindians had received initial employment at Barama but complained about the low wages paid to Amerindians. Local Amerindians also complained about the poisoning of the Kaituma River since Barama was improperly debarking Aromata trees (*Clathrotopis spp.*, which contains poisonous bark) although Barama subsequently improved its process and corrected the problem.

Land ownership was, and remains, perhaps the most intractable issue. Barama, for its part, did not implement plans to help demarcate the boundaries of Amerindian land titles and to include Amerindian areas on Barama maps. ECTF had recommended that Barama follow up the original study with a detailed assessment of indigenous claims, settlements and populations in the concession area, but this important action was never undertaken. In the beginning, Amerindians protested directly to Barama, and had a number of meetings with the company. However, these discussions did not prove fruitful.[5] Following the 1994 study, the APA has protested to the government of Guyana and requested both a freeze on all logging concessions and a land-claims inquiry (Colchester, 1997). The APA threatened to launch an international boycott of Barama products and called upon the government to establish a Commission of Enquiry into Amerindian claims (APA, 1994). At the end of 1993, the Minister for Amerindian Affairs promised to set up a Commission of Enquiry to review Amerindian claims and the Barama contract. Despite governmental assurances, the Commission was never established. One international protest proved temporarily more successful. In 1994, NGO groups persuaded one of Barama's US customers, the Georgia-Pacific Corporation, to not buy timber from Barama. Company executives visited Region 1 and made some suggestions to Barama. It is not clear what actions were taken, but Georgia-Pacific began purchasing plywood from Barama again in 1995 (RAN, 1995).

The Amerindians have continued to protest their lack of land ownership, but to no avail. In 1997, 'the Carib people of Port Kaituma lodged a petition against the exploitation of their people by Barama to the country's president' (WRM/FM, 1998). In 1999 the first National Toushaos [Amerindian leaders] conference discussed the negative impacts of mining and logging on Amerindians throughout the forested regions of Guyana. Leaders from Region 1 told the conference:

> We need our land issue resolved as soon as possible. Foreign companies come into our lands looking for lumber and minerals and destroy it. They exploit the peoples' labour ...

> Our village does not have land title and these companies are exploiting our forest. What will be left for my grandchildren? ...

> The government refuses to listen to the people. (APA, 1999, pp. 8–9)

The Toushaos conference concluded with the statement:

> We demand that the Government stop granting concessions to mining and logging companies in and around Amerindian lands. And all mining and logging operations [including Barama] be suspended [*sic*] immediately, until all Amerindian land right [*sic*] issues are settled. (APA, 1999, p. 29)

Direct impacts of Barama

Interviews in 2000 by author indicate that the economic benefits for local Amerindians from large-scale forestry were not significant. While Barama used to be a key employer in the Port Kaituma area, local employment in general has diminished significantly by 2000. At its peak, the company hired some 1500 mostly non-Amerindian Guyanese, at facilities like its large plywood factory (Haden, 1999). Barama has also purchased logs from outside its concession area, which allowed one local Amerindian village to benefit financially. However, this economic success was short-lived and subsequently resulted in economic losses, cash-flow problems and greater economic instability among local Amerindians (Sizer, 1996). Local employment benefits for Amerindians were negligible and no Amerindians were currently working for the company. The entry of Barama into the area had already negatively affected traditional subsistence activities, and led to forced relocations. As one interviewee said, 'A...problem is forestry. Like the Barama Forestry Company [*sic*] came here. We have a species of wood that they want. Another three acres cut out of the [Amerindian] area again. That's what the government is doing. That's the impact' (See Note 1).

Moreover, despite community expectations of improved health care, as reported in the ECTF study, the health situation for Amerindians in Region 1 has remained problematic. Amerindians also continue to lack proper education facilities. While Port Kaituma did have a school and Amerindian teachers, they were poorly paid and under-utilized. Social problems related to the alleged sexual exploitation of young Amerindian girls by Barama employees also were reported in interviews:

'It happened in this community, not with mining but with the Barama Company. They take the young girls and stay over night and bring them back to school.'

'I heard that they take rude pictures...'

'It's true. It's the Malaysians [from Barama] that do these things...The young girls are kicked out of school...These Malaysians take these young Amerindian girls and leave them pregnant.'

Indirect impacts from small- and medium-scale mining

Perhaps the most far-reaching impact of Barama's activities was the influx of (often illegal) gold-miners – an influx which Barama made possible. The roads built by Barama for its logging operations provided easy and convenient access to the area and helped facilitate the large influx of small- and medium-scale mining. Interviews in 2000 confirmed that by not monitoring or regulating its concession road, Barama permitted open and uncontrolled access, contrary to the recommendations made by ECTF. On-site interviews indicate that there were now many small-medium scale gold mining operations in the area band much of it was illegal.

Amerindians interviewed in 2000 by this author reported that the key gold mining areas were 5-Star, Big Creek, Tassawini, Arakaka, 18 Miles,

White Creek, Baramita, Whana, Pipiani, Eyelash and the Upper Warapa. Barima River, 4-Mile and Kariao were also experiencing small gold rushes (or 'shouts'). The majority of miners were coastlanders, although increased numbers of illegal Brazilian immigrants were also reported to be operating in the area. Barama also developed the port at Port Kaituma. One shopkeeper in Port Kaituma even exclaimed, 'God bless the Barama Company [Samling] for opening up the area to gold mining!'

Gold prospecting and work in mining camps represents an alluring yet illusory alternative to traditional forms of employment such as farming and hunting. It is also a job alternative in the wage economy previously fuelled by Barama. 'Most of the people are depending upon mining because there's no other jobs for them to do. Very little farming here now. Before Barama you used to find a lot of farming but when Barama came they lured a lot of Amerindians so the people stopped depending upon farming.' Interviews confirmed that a few local Amerindian men participated in small-scale mining, either as 'pork-knockers' (unskilled labourers) or as part of crews for land dredges owned by coastlanders. Big Creek, for instance, had about 300 'pork-knockers', but only 30 were Amerindian.

Mining work among Amerindians in the Big Creek area is plagued with inequities and exploitation. Said one interviewee, 'Anytime the Amerindians find a place [with gold], they [the coastlanders] go and "brand" the place. They go and send in the application for the place [to the ministry of Mines and Geology].' There are also inequities in mine concession ownership. Rarely do Amerindians own mine concessions or operate land dredges because they cannot afford the investment capital. 'The Amerindians don't have the type of equipment to work [a land dredge]. But the coastlanders do.' Amerindian women are involved to a small degree in small-scale mining; but they too suffer from exploitation. As one interviewee explained,

> Right now there is a Carib woman that has a claim at Big Creek…She went into the Amerindian Minister [when her claim got stolen]. He told her that she had to put up another claim board. She had lived there for years and now they [the dredge owners on her concession] don't want to give her a percentage. She got left with nothing.

The increase in gold mining made possible by the road network has also harmed hunting and fishing by reducing game populations. Field research also indicated that there were strong ecological impacts of uncontrolled small- and medium-scale mining on fish, game and water quality. Interviewees complain, 'We can't get fish here right. You have to go far to get fish. You have to go miles. You used to walk through the forest and get fish and meat but not now.' Interviewees also report health impacts: since mining intensified in the 1990s, there has been a significant increase in malaria throughout the area, since the stagnant pools of water (a common by-product of dredging) are perfect breeding grounds for mosquitoes. Said one interviewee, 'There is a lot of malaria in the area … Because of the pollution, malaria is worse in the mining areas.'

Perhaps the most intractable impacts concern unrecognized land rights for local Amerindians. According to interviewees, when gold is discovered, miners moved in without any consultation with or compensation for the local Amerindians, who are forced to relocate. Consider Big Creek, in the Barima River area. The area had been traditionally occupied by Carib farmers, although there were reports that Amerindians had also mined in this area in the 1920s. In the 1990s, a significant number of families were still trying to pursue a traditional Amerindian lifestyle of hunting, fishing and farming, at least on a partial basis, but found it increasingly difficult. The Big Creek area now has 25 land dredges, indicative of medium-size gold mining. 'When a dredge comes in they put you off the place … After they see there's gold, they take over the area as a concession … I can't live in peace.' According to another interviewee,

> There are about five Carib families living here [in Big Creek], mostly on their own. They farm with manual labour using a spade and pickaxe … The area is now owned by a [gold mining] millionaire and the pork-knockers can only work in the swamp not on the hill. He put the rest [including the Amerindians] out.

While participation in small-and medium-scale mining has the potential to offer economic gains to Amerindians, potential benefits are limited by inadequate governance mechanisms, from the top of the government all the way down. An interviewee told the author:

> I think mining … has a heavy impact on Amerindian areas … It has robbed the Amerindians of their land … Let's say a multinational comes into the area and discovers gold and diamonds, the government will say, 'OK, Mr de Souza, the [previous] Minister of Amerindian Affairs, get [the local people] to sign.' Instead of having ten square miles this certificate has only six because in that other area they've discovered gold or diamonds.

As another Amerindian man explained, 'Now we can't even farm. Nobody really has land around here. You can't do nothing.'

Even when Amerindians have been able to establish mining claims of their own, interviews revealed that on many occasions they had their claims stolen, were tricked into divulging the location or were bullied into giving up their claims by coastlanders who have more experience with the administrative system of registering claims. Amerindian men who work as prospectors or on mining crews often have trouble getting paid for their work. The local police appear to be complicit in such situations, or at minimum, are not helpful to the Amerindians affected. The Amerindian Minister had also not helped rectify the situation. The police, the army (the Guyana Defence Force (GDF)) and mines officers were identified as other antagonists. 'If you go and prospect and if you find [gold] there, they'll [non-Amerindians] take the police in and put you out. They use that, bullying tactics.' A raid at a mining camp at Pipiana was brought up in a number of interviews:

> [There has been] a lot of wrong doings [*sic*] in mining. Recently, mines officers came down and raided the miners who had taken out a little bit of gold. It is very unfair when you find something … Just because we have nobody to represent us, to look after this. It's very hard.

Most of the Amerindians living in Region 1 do not have any legal title to their lands, and Barama did not press for ownership claims to be clarified. Consequently, there is no requirement for community consultation on any mining or forestry activity in the area. Interviewees perceived this to be an institutionalized form of discrimination: 'I would say the government does this because the Constitution says in the Amerindian Act that the government can take away Amerindian land without any compensation … that is discrimination.'

Lack of land title and lack of official leadership also compounded community in-fighting:

> In this area, everybody is pulling and tugging each other. There's no council so there's no one to go and talk it out with. There are about a hundred or so Amerindians here [at 4-Mile] but nobody to talk to when something goes wrong. We're just trying to live … People are fighting about mining, farmland … sometimes they're quarrelling over drinking water.

Local families did not complain since they did not feel there was anyone to complain to.

The shift from traditional subsistence activities to mining employment has resulted in a variety of negative impacts on social structure and traditional family life. Amerindian women have been particularly susceptible to the dislocating and alienating aspects of small- and medium-scale mining. They were left behind with the sole responsibility for the family and for maintaining farms. Said one interviewee:

> Mining on the whole makes the workers strangers to the family. It really affected a lot of homes. Because the gold is getting scarce or under concession, most of the pork-knockers are running bush and the family really feels the strain … When you have a gold claim you have taken

rations from the shop and then the gold pays the shop and your family's deep in debt and you start all over again unless you get a shout. Going after gold isn't easy, boy.

Interview data and participant observation suggested that the Big Creek area operates in a lawless manner. Local people repeatedly referred to the area as a 'cowboy town' where complaints were met with further violence and abuse. Alcohol and drug abuse are serious problems; in addition, a number of Amerindian women and girls have been sexually abused and exploited by the large numbers of transient male mining and forestry workers:

One of the biggest problems is that these [miners] take advantage of Amerindian girls. They drunk [*sic*] them. That's one of the regular things … I remember one night they stripped a girl naked on the road there [at Big Creek] and it's [*sic*] a nice lady. And the men lined up. She was drunk. These girls are young girls, 13 or 14. Young girls. They should be in school. They drunk the parents first. And nobody really looks into the matter.

It is very dangerous for women in the mining areas. The women are there because the husband is, but when they start to drink, it's all of them [on her]. I think they should get rid of the women from the claims and only have men there.

One time I had to save a girl who was 16. The Coastlanders raped her. She's a Carib in 5-Star. When they were almost finished with she [*sic*], a boy came to wake me up. They drunk her. They had her in one of those bush toilets, 16 or 17 men. She didn't complain to the police. Next day when I asked what happened to her, she said nothing. She didn't want to say.

The local word for that is 'they bank the girl or the woman …' 'Buck night'. They call these girls buck girls when they come out to party at these drinking places.

They [the miners in Big Creek] had two little girls, 16 and 17. They had them naked, maybe they put something in their drink. Me, I'm Amerindian and I can't let this happen and I told the boys to stop.

Despite expectations of improved educational services in Region 1, the reality has been that many Amerindian children lived at mining camps and received no schooling. 'Right now if you go to Eyelash, they're working their eight-, ten-year-olds. We need someone to look into that. They [the children] get no kind of education.'

Barama pulls out of Region 1

In 2002 Barama general manager Girwar Lalalram announced that the company would close down the Port Kaituma operation because its concession in this area 'had been logged out' (Stabroek News, 2002a). James Keylon, Barama's managing director, suggested that Barama might return to the area 'in another 20 years when the trees regenerate'. As Barama leaves the region, the company has opened its concession to large-scale mining exploration. As of 2002, although there were no large-scale mines in operation in that year, a joint venture formed by Golden Star Resources Limited (20 per cent) and BHP-Billiton (80 per cent) signed exploration deals for copper and gold with Barama. Under the terms of the agreement, Barama will receive US$65 000 for signing the agreement; US$10 000 for transferring its prospecting licenses; US$25 000 in royalties per year; US$250 000 for each mine site developed by the joint venture; 1 per cent of the development cost of each mine, once the mine begins operation; and a royalty of 5 per cent on the net profits (Golden Star, 2002). It is unclear whether these cash flows will in any way benefit the local Amerindians. The company press release offered no indication that local Amerindians had been consulted on the deal, nor is there any public discussion on possible compensation or bene-fit sharing with local Amerindians who might be deeply affected by future large-scale minerals development.

In 2002, Barama and the government of Guyana announced a new forestry project on the Essequibo Coast. Barama's strategy is to develop a new forest concession in an area of Guyana where it might meet the strict requirements for sustainable forestry set down by the Forest Stewardship Council (FSC). Barama claims to be the first company in South and Central America to embark on the two-stage certification programme, which is run by a Swiss-based certifying body. The first stage involves a structured audit-ing of forest management, while the second involves tracking timber and products from participating forests through processing to the retail market (Stabroek News, 2003b). The bid for certification is a strategic response to shifting market demand towards sustainable products.

> Noting that BCL accounts for more than 50 per cent of the value of for-est products exported from Guyana, [Luvendra Sukraj, Barama's forest management officer] said certification has become a major issue, 'a way of doing business', in the big markets. BCL exports its products to the UK, North America, the Caribbean and parts of South America. The loss of revenue for Barama without certification, he said could have a significant impact on the local economy. (Stabroek News, 2003b)

To obtain certification, Barama will have to be judged to have complied with requirements that are demonstrably rigorous in protecting the rights of indigenous peoples. FSC principle 2 states that 'Long-term tenure and use rights to the land and forest resources shall be clearly defined, documented and legally established.' According to principle 3, 'The legal and customary rights of indigenous peoples to own, use and manage their lands, territories and resources shall be recognized and respected.' And according to principle 4,

'Forest management operations shall maintain or enhance the long-term social and economic well-being of forest workers and local communities.' Each principle is spelled out with quite specific requirements (Colchester *et al.*, 2003; FSC, 2003). Who will judge? The FSC stipulates:

> Independent certification bodies, accredited by the FSC in the application of these standards, conduct impartial, detailed assessments of forest operations at the request of landowners. If the forest operations are found to be in conformance with FSC standards, a certificate is issued, enabling the landowner to bring product to market as 'certified wood', and to use FSC trademark logo. (FSC, 2003)

Barama claims that certification will move it into a position of world leadership in responsible forestry: 'Once Barama attains certification, its model can be used throughout the Guianas eco-region for all stakeholders in the forestry sector. ... [Barama's efforts] would place Guyana in the forefront of world forestry and sustainability practices' (Stabroek News, 2003a).

While the process may be designed to protect indigenous peoples, it apparently entails little direct involvement by Amerindians. In the case of Barama, the certification process will be carried out by the Sustainable Forests Project, an initiative of the French Environmental Fund (FFEM), the Dutch Environmental Fund (DGIS) and the World Wildlife Fund (WWF). These organizations will also fund the certification process, with a four-year grant of US\$5 million (Stabroek News, 2002b). The certification process will be overseen by a steering committee and a 'national coordinating committee', neither of which includes Amerindian representatives as official members. Existing Amerindian organizations are not official members of either committee nor have they even been invited to serve as observers.

Nor is it clear whether a detailed audit of Barama's operations in Region 1 will be included in the FSC certification process, now that Barama has left the area. Such an audit is important because there is no public record to suggest that Barama has developed a comprehensive exit strategy to address the social impacts of its past practices, or of its pending departure, upon local Amerindians and non-Amerindian residents. The net benefits for Amerindians when weighed against the wide-ranging negative impacts appear negligible at best. Barama's contract with ECTF was terminated in 2000 because Barama judged that ECTF was not able to help the company reach FSC certification. The company has donated a generator and a number of company buildings to the governmental regional administrator, who has asked local businessmen for proposals on how to use them (GINA, 2002a). To date, the company has not publicly acknowledged any corporate responsibility for its negative impacts on the local Amerindians in Region 1.

Although Barama had contracted ECTF to help it identify and mitigate such problems, the ECTF recommendations were of little help. Apparently the consulting firm did not conduct any follow-up assessments to monitor emerging social impacts on Amerindian communities. Instead, it focused later work on the ecological dimensions of the Barama project. According to the Forest Peoples Programme, 'ECTF had decided to limit their advice to Sustainable Forest Management which they claimed … did not include concern for sustainable livelihoods.'[6] Consequently, after their preliminary social impact assessment that identified a number of key concerns for Amerindians, the ECTF focused on the technical aspects of biodiversity, run-off and soil quality. While ECTF did suggest that the next phase of its contract would include 'advising on social and environmental impacts of the forest based activities of BCL and other operators from whom BCL may purchase timber', there are no indications that ECTF undertook additional Social Impact Assessments (SIAs) or that Barama implemented any additional social mitigation measures. And in 2000, ECTF's consultancy with Barama was suspended.

Conclusion

This case study demonstrates that despite Barama's policy commitment to sustainable forestry, the situation for local Amerindians in Region 1 has not improved since Barama entered the area 10 years ago. In fact, the local Amerindians face severe social and environmental impacts, both directly from Barama and indirectly through the subsequent influx of small- and medium-scale miners. These negative impacts include:

- Environmental damage: deforestation; ecological degradation; mercury contamination; water pollution; negative impact on fish and game populations.
- Health problems: malaria; health impacts from polluted drinking water; mercury contamination.
- Abuse of human/indigenous rights: forced relocation; unrecognized land rights and lack of consultation; violence and abuse.
- Socio-cultural impacts: loss of traditional lifestyles; perpetuating poverty and inequality; community in-fighting; alcohol and drug abuse; negative impacts on Amerindian women and children.
- Impacts on Amerindian women and girls: sexual abuse and exploitation; social and economic hardship.

Many of these problems were identified by the consulting firm ECTF hired by Barama in 1994. Despite knowing for almost ten years about the impacts of its activities on local Amerindians, Barama did not implement adequate mitigation plans. Time has proven the ECTF forecast of negative social impacts to have been regrettably accurate. Many of the social impacts in Region 1 arose directly as a result of Barama's large-scale forestry operations. Clearly, Barama is not directly responsible for all of these impacts. However, by developing roads that were open to public use, Barama's operations opened the region to an influx of outside workers and facilitated deep and chaotic exploitation of the region. Further, Barama has left the region without addressing this negative legacy, as it actively pursues FSC certification elsewhere. Moreover, its exit strategy includes large-scale minerals exploration, which may have additional negative impacts on local Amerindians. While Barama stands to gain financially from any future minerals development and from FSC certification, local Amerindians do not – particularly those who live in the concession and still have outstanding land claims.

It is a bitter irony that despite all these negative impacts, forestry has contributed relatively little to Guyana's national economic development. From January through June 2000, Guyana exported only US$15 million of forest products, down 28 per cent from the comparable period in 1999. The government received US$5.2 million in royalties for total forest exports between April and June. In contrast, the mining sector generated royalties of US$180.4 million already in 1994, and exports of minerals such as gold and diamonds accounted for 16.5 per cent of GDP in 1995 (Government of Guyana, 1996).

A central question raised by this case study is whether a transnational forestry corporation like the Samling Group, with its Barama joint venture, might have conducted business operations in such a way as to reduce the severe impact it has had on the local community. Given Barama's strategic interest in gaining FSC certification, might the company have achieved less disruptive outcomes? And might other actors, such as the national government of Guyana, have acted to mitigate the adverse consequences and corollaries of this forestry operation?

First, Barama could have implemented mitigation plans. The original ECTF report identified what needed to be done. Among the most important was regulating and/or restricting road access. While NGOs acknowledge that Barama made some improvements in environmental performance as an outcome of the ECTF study (WRM and Forests Monitor, 1998), they argue that many environmental and social problems – including unrecognized land rights – remain unresolved. Barama also could have implemented economic and social development plans for local Amerindians. In particular, Barama could have been more aware of, and monitored, the impacts on Amerindian women and girls.

Second, Barama could have offered legal assistance to Amerindians fighting outstanding land claims. Throughout its tenure in Region 1, Barama has made no effort to resolve outstanding Amerindian land claims within its concession. Barama could have recognized Amerindian rights more explicitly in Region 1, and worked to strengthen those rights. Under international law[7] and the Guyanese Mining Act, Amerindians have the right to meaningful consultation on, and participation in, natural resource development plans. Barama could have considered Amerindians to be 'rights-holders', a stronger position than 'stakeholders', within natural resource development plans.[8] Barama could have supported a concrete land claims settlement process (like the one requested by the APA, see APA, 1999) as part of its negotiations with the Guyanese government. Unfortunately, the company chose to do none of these things; in fact, it did not include Amerindians in its most recent negotiations with BHP-Billiton and Golden Star.

Third, Barama could have implemented effective community relations and community consultations. The outcomes in Region 1 might have been different if the Amerindians had had jurisdiction to exert some forms of effective governance over this area. They lack viable means for governing this territory, and so have no means for exerting any kind of countervailing power over/against large or even small business operations. They distrust national government officials. Weak governance structures in Guyana magnify the impacts by allowing the interior region to operate as a 'Wild West'. Barama failed to develop ongoing collaborative consultations and relations with the existing Amerindian groups, and it is this failure which in large measure lies behind other missed opportunities. Samling and Barama might object that governance is not their business. After all, what do their operations have to do with corrupt police, or weak institutions for mining, forestry and the environment? Nevertheless, when transnational companies enter into a region plagued with weak governance structures, they have an ethical obligation to address these governance gaps as a part of local community development. Such ethical considerations in developing countries like Guyana are critical business issues, which need to be meaningfully addressed.

In sum, Barama could have acted differently to reduce the negative outcomes in Region 1. What about the future?

Reform is needed, by both the Guyanese government and Barama. Like many developing countries, Guyana continues to be faced with a number of critical governance challenges in achieving voice for its citizens and accountability for its officials, in achieving governmental effectiveness and stability, the rule of law, regulatory quality and control of corruption (World Bank, 2001b). Certain reforms bear directly on Amerindians. First, since Amerindians live on much of the natural wealth of Guyana, the government must ensure the ongoing meaningful participation of Amerindians in natural resource development planning, including the FSC certification process. Second, the government must resolve outstanding Amerindian land claims with an established procedure and timeframe for resolution, similar to the approach used by Canada and recommended to the Guyanese government by the APA (1999). Guyana's national Forests Act has been under review since 1998. The new draft Forests Act is viewed as an improvement, in that it includes language that recognizes that lands that are occupied, or being used by Amerindians will be considered lawfully occupied and some concessions cannot be issued for such lands (similar to the language in the Mining Act). However, this Act has yet to be approved by cabinet, and this delay is a pressing concern.[9] Finally, more regulation is needed. Guyana's 1989 national Mining Act gives the state ownership over all mineral resources. The government has the right to issue mining permits on all land (including lands with Amerindian title). Regulations limit small- and medium-scale mining on land with Amerindian title, but in practice, illegal mining continues, often on Amerindian land.

Barama, for its part, must pursue FSC certification in good faith, and be held accountable for its past legacy of direct and indirect impacts in Region 1. It is ironic that Barama was seeking to be certified by the FSC as an environmentally responsible firm just at the same time that it was closing down its operations in Region 1. The FSC certification process can provide a useful means of alerting the company to unanticipated adverse consequences if it chooses some development alternatives rather than others. Once the process of certification starts, companies are independently assessed for their compliance with FSC principles, which clearly support indigenous peoples' rights. But the FSC certification process is vulnerable:

> The social acceptability of FSC certification depends on the quality of the participation that leads to decisions. Where participation is weak or absent, national standard setting, forest management and certification assessments are all likely to fail to meet FSC's high standards. (Colchester *et al.*, 2002, p. 152)

In Guyana, with its weak governance mechanisms and a poor track record in terms of settling land claims, fostering Amerindian participation in natural resource development is a central requirement for the FSC certification to adhere to its goals. But it also a requirement that Barama has found difficult to meet in the past.

Despite the vulnerability of the FSC certification process, business and government cannot simply 'wish away' the ethical consideration of indirect or unintended consequences of their actions. If the sustainable development of natural resources is a sincerely held goal, then the problems highlighted in this case study cannot be side-stepped. Sustainable forestry and FSC certification should not be granted until the 'cowboy towns' of Region 1 are improved, until the rights and livelihoods of local Amerindians are respected and until the sexual assault and economic exploitation of local indigenous peoples end. More than 35 multinational business corporations currently operate in Guyana. Future negotiations with these companies should include a legitimate governance process for settling outstanding land claims, one that ensures meaningful Amerindian consultation and prior informed consent. Development contracts should include compensation and mitigation plans for Amerindians – including women – who may be affected directly and indirectly by such projects.

Notes

1. Field research was conducted in December, 2000 and consisted of a field visit to Port Kaituma and Big Creek in Region 1 of Guyana, assisted by the Amerindian Peoples Association (APA). Ten interviews in total were conducted with local Amerindians, mostly at 4-Mile, within the village of Port Kaituma, and also at the mining camp at Big Creek. Excerpts from these interviews are cited in the text of this study; however, for reasons of confidentiality, the interviewees are not directly named. These research findings were summarized in a field report, which was incorporated into the final report of the APA and North–South Institute, entitled *Mining and Amerindians in Guyana* (Colchester *et al.*, 2002), funded by the International Development Research Council.
2. Personal communication, Dr M. Colchester, Forest Peoples Programme, 2003.
3. Personal communication, Dr M. Colchester, Forest Peoples Programme, 2003.
4. Ibid.
5. Ibid.
6. Ibid.
7. Under international law, Amerindians have the right to self-determination; development of their natural resources as they see fit; meaningful consultation and participation in natural-resource development decision-making and operations; prior informed consent to development projects; benefit-sharing from natural resource development; and basic human rights (FPP *et al.*, 2000; Whiteman and Mamen, 2002). Under the Beijing Platform, Amerindian women have the right to participate fully in natural resource decision-making and environmental management (Whiteman and Mamen, 2002).
8. Thanks to Dr M. Colchester for identifying this point.
9. The situation in Guyana might well be improved if the governments of developed countries like Canada, international financial institutions like the World Bank, and civil-society organizations worked in concert to support Guyana's forest law, emphasized the need to protect indigenous land rights and reinforced Guyana's compliance with its World Bank approved Poverty Reduction Strategy.

References

APA (1999): Amerindian Peoples Association, 'Report of the First National Toushaos Conference, 27–30 April', *Sustainable Development Networking Programme* [website] (updated 27 September 2003) http://www.sdnp.org.gy/apa/topic6.htm, accessed 27 September 2003.

APA and WRM (1994): Amerindian Peoples Association and the World Rainforest Movement, *Joint Survey of the Barama Company Limited Concession Area* (Georgetown: APA).

Colchester, M. (1997) *Guyana: Fragile Frontier* (Moreton-in-Marsh: WRM).

Colchester, M., La Rose, J and James, K. (2002) *Mining and Amerindians in Guyana* (Ottawa: The North–South Institute) http://www.nsi-ins.ca/ensi/pdf/guyana/guyana_final_report.pdf

Colchester, M., Sirait M. and Wijardjo, B. (2003) *The Application of FSC Principles 2 & 3 in Indonesia: Obstacles and Possibilities* (Moreton-in-Marsh: FPP).

Forests Act (Act No. 15 of 1953), Laws of Guyana Cap. 67:01 (Government of Guyana, Ministry of Legal Affairs).

FPP *et al.* (2000): Forest Peoples Programme, Philippine Indigenous Peoples Links and World Rainforest Movement, *Undermining the Forests: The Need to Control Transnational Mining Companies: A Canadian Case Study* (Moreton-in-Marsh, UK/Stanford-in-the-Vale, UK/Montevideo: FPP/PIPL/WRM), *World Rainforest Movement* [website] (n.d.) http://www.wrm.org.uy/publications/undermining.pdf, accessed 27 September 2003.

FSC (2003): Forest Stewardship Council Forest Stewardship Council (International Centre, Bonn, Germany), 'FSC Social Strategy: Building and Implementing a Social Agenda, Version 2.1', *Forest Stewardship Council* [website] (updated 24 September 2003) http://www.fscoax.org/principal.htm, accessed 27 September 2003.

GINA (2002a): Government Information Agency (Guyana), 'GINA Daily Bulletin: Port Kaituma Has Not Been Neglected' (3 August), *Sustainable Development Networking Programme* [website] (n.d.) http://www.sdnp.org.gy/mininfo/gina/daily/b020803.html, accessed 27 September 2003.

GINA (2002b): Government Information Agency (Guyana), 'GINA Daily Bulletin: Minister Nokta Praises Four Miles CDC for Constructing Playfield, Community Center' (26 August), *Sustainable Development Networking Programme* [website] (n.d.) http://www.sdnp.org.gy/mininfo/gina/daily/b020826.html, accessed 27 September 2003.

Global Witness (1997): Global Witness Limited, 'Just Deserts for Cambodia? Samling/SL International, a Case Study', *Global Witness* [website] (updated 19 September 2003) http://www.globalwitness.org/campaigns/forests/cambodia/deserts/samling.htm, accessed 27 September 2003.

Golden Star (2002): Golden Star Resources Limited, 'Press release: Golden Star and BHP Enter Into Joint Venture on the Cuyuni Property in Guyana' (25 April 2002), *Golden Star* [website] (n.d.) http://www.gsr.com/News/042502.htm, accessed 27 September 2003.

Government of Guyana (1996a): Guyana News and Information, 'National Development Strategy, Chapter 21: Women, Gender and Development', *Guyana* [website] http://www.guyana.org/NDS/chap21.htm, accessed 27 September 2003.

Government of Guyana (1996b): Guyana News and Information, 'National Development Strategy, Chapter 22: Amerindian Policies', *Guyana* [website] http://www.guyana.org/NDS/chap22.htm, accessed 27 September 2003.

Government of Guyana (1996c): Guyana News and Information, 'National Development Strategy, Chapter 30: Forest Management', *Guyana* [website] http://www.guyana.org/NDS/chap30.htm, accessed 27 September 2003.

Haden, P. (1999) *Forestry issues in the Guiana Shield region: A Perspective on Guyana and Suriname (European Union Tropical Forestry paper 3)* (London: ODI).

Hammersley, M. and Atkinson, P. (1995). *Ethnography: Principles in Practice*, 2nd edn (London: Routledge).

Hogg, D. (1993) 'The SAP in the Forest: The Environmental and Social Impacts of Structural Adjustment Programmes in the Philippines, Ghana and Guyana' (London: Friends of the Earth) in Colchester (1997), *supra*, p. 40ff.

IAIP (1997): International Alliance of Indigenous-Tribal Peoples of the Tropical Forests, 'Third Conference, Resolution of the Guyanese Organization of Indigenous Peoples in Support of the Indigenous Peoples of the Morvica Reservation in Guyana' (3–8 March 1997, Nagpur, India), *International Alliance of Indigenous-Tribal Peoples* [website] (n.d.) http://iaip.gn.apc.org/third/resolu~1.htm, accessed 27 September 2003.

IMF (2000): International Monetary Fund, 'Guyana Interim Poverty Reduction Strategy Paper Prepared by the Guyanese Authorities' (30 October), *International Monetary Fund* [website] (n.d.) http://www.imf.org/external/NP/prsp/2000/guy/01/103000.pdf, accessed 27 September 2003.

Jalong, T. (2002) Sahabat Alam Malaysia (Sarawak), 'Press statement: The Penan, Kayan and Kenyah Protest Against Logging and Sand Mining Activities on Native Lands', *Native Forest Network* [website] (n.d.) http://www.nfn.org.au/pressrel/alert25.html, accessed 27 September 2003.

Johnson, A. (1996) Metla, Finnish Forest Research Institute, 'Asian Loggers Latest Threat to Brazil's Rainforest' (3 September 1996), *Metla* [website] (updated 24 September 2003) http://www.metla.fi/archive/forest/1996/09/msg00020.html, accessed 27 September 2003.

Loone, S. (2002): Mkini Dotcom Sdn. Bhd., 'Malaysian Timber Consortium Accused of Illegal Logging in PNG' (9 May 2002), *Malaysiakini* [website] (updated 27 September 2003) http://www.malaysiakini.com/news/200205090015528.php, accessed 27 September 2003.

Magin, G., Marijnissen, C., Moniaga, S. and Meek, C. (2001) *Forests of Fear: The Abuse of Human Rights in Forest Conflicts* (ed) Jessica Wenban-Smith [online text] (Moreton-in-Marsh: Fern) http://www.fern.org/pubs/reports/fear.pdf

National Commission on Women (2001): 'Issues facing Indigenous women in Guyana', cited in *Gender Dialogues*, vol. 3. (April) http://www.eclacpos.org/gender/Apr2001/Indigenous%20Women1.htm

North–South Institute. (2002) *Canadian Development Report 2001/2.* (Ottawa: North–South Intitute).

RAN (1995): Rainforest Action Network, 'Worldwide Forest/Biodiversity Campaign News: Georgia Pacific of US Kisses Off Guyana's Forests' (12 September 1995), *Pandora* [website] http://pandora.nla.gov.au/parchive/2001/Z2001-Feb-28/forests.org/recent/1995/guykiss.htm, accessed 27 September 2003.

Samling (2003a): Samling Strategic Corporation Sdn. Bhd., 'Giving Back to the People', *Samling* [website] (updated 10 January 2003) http://www.samling.com.my/content/forestry/community.html, accessed 27 September 2003.

Samling (2003b): Samling Strategic Corporation Sdn. Bhd., 'The Samling Commitment', *Samling* [website] (n.d.) http://www.samling.com.my/content/corporate/index.html, accessed 27 September 2003.

Samling (2003c): Samling Strategic Corporation Sdn. Bhd., 'Responsible Forest Management', *Samling* [website] (n.d.) http://www.samling.com.my/content/forestry/forestmgmt.html, accessed 27 September 2003.

Sizer, N. (1996) *Profit Without Plunder: Reaping Revenue from Guyana's Forests without Destroying Them* (Washington: World Resources Institute) http://pubs.wri.org/pubs_ content.cfm?PubID=2730, accessed 27 September 2003.

Stabroek News (2002a): Stabroek News, 'Barama Granted Concessions for Essequibo Project' (30 June 2002), *Land of Six Peoples* [website] (updated 27 September 2003) http://www.landofsixpeoples.com/news02/ns206304.htm, accessed 27 September 2003.

Stabroek News (2002b): Stabroek News, 'Conservation Group Signs Deal with Barama, Forestry Commission: Forest Management Certification Key Issue' (1 November 2002), *Land of Six Peoples* [website] (updated 27 September 2003) http://www.landofsixpeoples.com/news022/ns211016.htm, accessed 27 September 2003.

Stabroek News (2003a): Stabroek News, 'Barama Moves to Fully Certify Forest Concession: Guyana to Earn More from Premium Markets' (27 February 2003), *Land of Six Peoples* [website] (updated 27 September 2003) http://www.landofsixpeoples.com/news301/nc302276.htm, accessed 27 September 2003.

Stabroek News (2003b): Stabroek News, 'Barama Moving Towards Certified "Green" Exports' (3 March 2003), *Land of Six Peoples* [website] (updated 27 September 2003)

http://www.landofsixpeoples.com/news301/ns303035.htm, accessed 27 September 2003.

UNCTAD (2002): United Nations Conference on Trade and Development, *World Investment Report 2002: Transnational Corporations and Export Competitiveness* (Geneva: UNCTAD).

UNDP (2001): United Nations Development Programme, 'Human Development Index', *United Nations Development Programme* [website] (n.d.) http://www.undp.org/hdr2001/indicator/cty_f_GUY.html, accessed 27 September 2003.

Verbeeke, J. (1994) *United Nations Development Programme Country Office: Guyana National Report on Indigenous Peoples and Development* (Geneva: UNDP) [HTML version, SDNP, Guyana] http://www.sdnp.org.gy/undp-docs/nripd/

Whiteman, G. and Mamen, K. (2002) *Meaningful Consultation and Participation in the Mining Sector? A Review of the Consultation and Participation of Indigenous Peoples within the International Mining Sector* [online text] (Ottawa: The North–South Institute) http://www.nsi-ins.ca/download/lit_rev/lit_rev_final.pdf

World Bank (2001a): The World Bank Group, 'Country brief: Guyana', *World Bank* [website] (n.d.) http://lnweb18.worldbank.org/External/lac/lac.nsf/Countries/Guyana/113D6E9973AEDB62852569040050F087?OpenDocument, accessed 27 September 2003.

World Bank (2001b): The World Bank Group, 'GRIS II: Governance Research Indicator Country Snapshot – Comparison within Guyana for All Six Governance Indicators', *World Bank* [website] (n. d.) http://info.worldbank.org/beeps/kkz/sc_chart.asp?Country_ID=29&Country_Name=Guyana, accessed 27 September 2003.

WRM/FM (1998): World Rainforest Movement and Forests Monitor Limited, *High Stakes: The Need to Control Transnational Logging Companies: A Malaysian Case Study.* (Ely: Forests Monitor Limited). *Forests Monitor* [website] (updated 30 July 2003) http://www.forestsmonitor.org/reports/highstakes/title.htm, accessed 27 September 2003.

12
The Raglan Mine and Nunavik Inuit

Frederick Bird and Robert Nixon

Introduction

When mining companies develop their mines in remote lands, they often are criticized and protested against by the indigenous people who live there, and their supporters (Whiteman and Mamen, 2002). These people charge that the mines too often desecrate sacred lands, despoil natural environments, shatter local communities and enrich a few while impoverishing many others – leaving local residents worse rather than better off. The recently opened Raglan Mine in northern Quebec provides a contrasting example, in that it has been developed so far with the full cooperation of the Nunavik Inuit, the local indigenous people – and (so it seems) to their benefit.

The mine was developed at a cost of more than C$550 million by the Raglan mining company – La Société minière Raglan du Québec Ltée (SMRQ), a wholly owned subsidiary of Falconbridge Limited, a multinational base metals mining company. The mine is located at latitude 61 degrees north, on the Ungava peninsula, where the Inuit have lived for about 400 years. The mine itself is expected to operate for 20 years. In 1998, it began extracting nickel and copper from the surface and below ground. The ore is concentrated at Raglan and then trucked to Deception Bay, where it is loaded on ships headed for Quebec City. From Quebec, it is transferred to railcars and transported to Sudbury, Ontario where it is smelted before being shipped on to Norway for refining. The operations at the Raglan Mine are governed by the 'Raglan Agreement,' signed in 1995 jointly by SMRQ, two Inuit communities closest to the mine and the Makivik Corporation, representing Nunavik Inuit generally.

Our aim in this study is to assess the overall value that the Raglan Mine brings to the Inuit people. We will both examine what SMRQ has done and consider future problems that may arise. First, we will analyse the extent of collaboration between the mining company and the indigenous people. In 2000, Inuit made up approximately 18 per cent of the 350 employees at the mine and plant at Raglan. We will explore the factors that made this cooperation possible. We will compare these arrangements to those of other firms, to see what other issues related to the collaboration are likely to emerge. Second, we will review the extensive efforts to train, hire, integrate and retain Inuit into the labour force of this mine and the firms that supply it. We will compare the experiences of SMRQ with other firms seeking to incorporate indigenous people. Third, we will explore how SMRQ has attempted to respect Inuit culture and social life, all the while exploring how SMRQ may disrupt traditional life patterns in ways that may be both welcome as well as unwelcome to the Inuit.

Historical background

Approximately 8500 Inuit live in northern Quebec, above the 52nd parallel. Their economy has connected with Europeans since the seventeenth century, when they began selling furs to European traders in exchange for rifles, ammunition, cloth, tea and flour. These lands were governed as part of the Northwest Territories until transferred into Quebec by the 1912 Quebec Boundary Extension Act. The Indian Act had previously assigned responsibility for the First Nations throughout Canada to the Federal Government. After 1912 the provincial government of Quebec began to provide various social services to the inhabitants of Northern Quebec. The situation there began to deteriorate in the 1930s. The fur trade dropped off as a result of reduced prices and the depression. Inuit moved increasingly to villages along the shores of Hudson and Ungava Bays.

By the 1960s, the Quebec government was becoming interested in the abundant natural resources of Northern Quebec. It began to explore the possibility of damming rivers leading into James Bay, in order to develop hydro-electric power. It began asserting sovereignty over the area, referring to the area generally as 'Nouveau Québec' (New Quebec) and renaming particular localities.[1] In response, the Inuit living along Ungava and Hudson Bay organized the Northern Quebec Inuit Association (NQIA). Together with the Grand Council of James Bay Cree, they launched a court challenge in the early 1970s; development of the proposed James Bay dams was put on hold by a court injunction. The Quebec government then negotiated the James Bay and Northern Quebec Agreement (JBNQA) with the Cree and Inuit of northern Quebec, the federal government and Hydro-Québec, the provincial hydroelectric utility. Signed on 11 November 1975, this comprehensive agreement asserted both the sovereignty of Quebec over this territory and certain collective rights possessed by Inuit and Cree, by distinguishing three different categories of land. The Quebec government claimed mineral rights over the whole territory, but also recognized the exclusive legislative land rights of Cree and Inuit over Category I lands, which constituted about 1 per cent of the total. These lands belonged to the indigenous peoples collectively, but they nonetheless were bound to honour property rights already acquired, and to cede eminent domain to the government for public purposes such as the building of roads or schools. In Category II lands, Cree and Inuit were to enjoy exclusive hunting, fishing and trapping rights, but the title remained with the province and the native groups had no special occupancy rights. In Category III lands, Cree and Inuit retained the right to hunt, fish and trap, but most were designated public lands belonging to the province.

Signatories to the JBNQA included the Government of Quebec, the James Bay Energy Corporation, the James Bay Development Corporation, the Quebec Hydro-Electric Commission (Hydro-Québec), the Grand Council of the Crees (of Quebec), the Northern Quebec Inuit Association and the Government of Canada. Following the Crees' example, the Naskapi Indian Band negotiated the Northeastern Quebec Agreement (NEQA), signed on 31 January 1978, amending the JBNQA (INAC, 1993).

The JBNQA and NEQA enabled Hydro-Québec to build dams and hydro-electric power plants on La Grande River in northern Quebec, but required cooperation with the Inuit and Cree. The two agreements also entitled the Cree, Inuit and Naskapi to a range of services and programmes to which the federal and provincial governments contribute annually (INAC, 2000), and established a number of public and semi-public institutions through which the Inuit could govern aspects of their social, economic and cultural life, and required that any industrial enterprises in the area in Quebec north of the 55th parallel be developed with the cooperation of these public institutions. Through the Kativik Regional Government, they were granted the powers to govern their villages, although this regional government was subordinate to the Quebec Ministry of Municipal Affairs. A Kativik Regional School Board as well as a regional Board of Health and Social services were established. In addition the Makivik Corporation was established to manage public funds, including a Heritage Fund, established for the Inuit by the JBNQA. The executive staff and board of directors of the Makivik Corporation were to be elected by Inuit. These several institutions provided means for distributing funds and services from the federal and provincial governments and Hydro-Québec to the Inuit.

The response of aboriginal groups in Canada to the JBNQA has been mixed. The Cree and Inuit gained wealth, some job opportunities, greater access to Inuit- administered public social and health services and a moderate degree of political influence on developments in the North. However, at the same time, they relinquished claims to vast amounts of land that other aboriginal people think they should have retained. The Quebec government asserted that its approach towards the Cree and Inuit broke with the paternalism practiced by the federal government since the Indian Act. Nonetheless, the Cree and Inuit saw that their Kativik Regional Government, subordinated as it was to the Ministry of Municipal Affairs, was limited to the powers delegated to municipal governments within Quebec.

The James Bay and Northeastern Quebec agreements had even farther-reaching effects for Canada's indigenous peoples. In 1984, pursuant to Section 9 of the JBNQA and Section 7 of the NEQA, the Government of Canada proclaimed the Cree-Naskapi (of Quebec) Act recognizing local Indian government powers and establishing a system of land management. For the first time in Canada, the new act recognized a form of Indian self-government, rendering First Nations peoples citizens capable of exercising local governing powers. The Indian Act, which had hitherto respected First-Nations governance on the lands on which Aboriginal peoples lived, no longer applies to its beneficiaries except concerning Indian status (INAC, 1993; Kymlicka, 1995; Gagnon and Tully, 2001).[2]

The life of the Inuit in Northern Quebec changed significantly after the JBNQA was signed in 1975. Airstrips were developed and upgraded. Contacts with southerners increased. Royalty payments and public investments integrated them into the cash economy. Inuit began spending on consumer goods. They also experienced increasing degrees of social disruption. Levels of family violence increased. Although more children formally attended schools, the drop-out rates remained high. As of 2000 the rates of Inuit teenage pregnancy and suicide ran five times higher than for young people in the rest of the province. Rates for alcoholism increased (Stackhouse, 2001). At the same time, Inuit became more politically vocal; in the late 1980s they joined with James Bay Cree in successfully opposing further hydro development on the Great Whale river system. In 1988 they renamed their territory Nunavik, which is based on their own word for their homeland.

Falconbridge had been exploring the possibilities of mining on the Ungava Peninsula since the 1960s, but was prevented until the 1990s by technical and economic problems. By then, it was able to apply new extractive technologies that were employed successfully at mines in arctic and sub-arctic conditions in Greenland and the Northwest Territories. Also, a new type of ice-breaking vessel was available effectively extending the shipping season for mineral concentrate from arctic regions from four to eight months. Improved modular construction made it possible and cost-effective for Falconbridge to construct housing, mine and mill facilities in the south, transport them to Northern Quebec and assemble them on-site. Meanwhile, further explorations indicated that ore deposits on the Ungava peninsula were much greater than previously thought. Finally, airstrips had been built and upgraded for most Inuit communities, making it easier for Falconbridge to maintain contact with its Ungava operations.[3] By the early 1990s, mining on the Ungava peninsula became economically feasible.

To proceed, Falconbridge needed to find a way of working with Inuit organizations. The land that it wanted to mine clearly was under the joint jurisdiction of the Quebec government on the one side, and the Kativik Regional Government and the Makivik Corporation on the other. But since the James Bay agreement was signed in 1975, the position of the Nunavik Inuit had been strengthened. First, they began to gain leverage over their resources. In 1977 a public inquiry about a proposed gas pipeline through the MacKenzie River Valley made it clear that viable economic projects under federal jurisdiction could be called to halt if the proponents did not gain the support of the indigenous people likely to be affected by their operations (Berger, 1977). Second, since 1975 Inuit had gained experience managing their newly created public institutions. In cooperation with other governmental agencies and private businesses, they established schools and hospitals, an airline service and gained experience with environmental, land-use and resource management. These several newly created institutions retained the confidence and support of Inuit people. Third, they increased their competence to negotiate with governments and businesses about the nature of development in their territory. In 1988 they negotiated the Kuujjuaq Agreement with Hydro-Québec, by which the provincial utility was required to compensate the Inuit for contaminating rivers in Nunavik. In 1993 they successfully opposed Hydro-Québec's proposal to build dams and hydroelectric plants on the Great Whale River. A number of the Inuit leaders feared these projects would cause extensive social dislocation and cultural confusion in their communities. Prompted by the Kuujjuaq Agreement, Hydro-Québec agreed to delay these projects until receiving the explicit consent of the Inuit community.

In the early 1990s Falconbridge's new wholly owned subsidiary, SMRQ, began to conduct explorations and feasibility studies for a mine at Raglan, 65 kilometres south of Deception Bay. SMRQ officials held consultations with the Katavik Regional Government and the Makivik Corporation. They jointly identified a number of sites sacred to the Inuit, which SMRQ promised to respect and protect. They arranged visits for SMRQ executives and Inuit leaders and elders to become acquainted with each other. In 1992 SMRQ conducted an intensive study of the employment and training policies that the firm might put in place. They surveyed the best practices in aboriginal human resource strategy across more than a dozen North American mines, including a successful programme at a recently opened uranium mine in northern Saskatchewan. The Cameco management was required by provincial law to institute a programme to hire and train as many Aboriginal people as possible, especially from the area around the mine. Literacy programmes were organized in local northern communities. Aboriginals were given priority in recruitment, offered regular education leading to high school degrees as well as special training related to their jobs. Cameco allowed Aboriginals to work seven days on and seven days off, so they could continue to live in their own villages. Cameco also worked to educate the non-native employees with respect to the local Athabascan cultures. By 1992, four years after the mine was opened, 12 per cent of the workforce was Aboriginal. Although a number of Aboriginal originally hired had left the Company, the overall size of this native workforce continued to increase. A number had received promotions. Furthermore, several had assumed middle management or semi-professional positions (AEECG, 1992). SMRQ used this experience among others as a point of reference for the human resource policies they sought to develop, especially with respect to employment and training.

During initial discussions with SMRQ, Inuit expressed clear concerns about a mine at the Raglan site. They wanted to be sure the proposed mine would provide good employment prospects for Inuit. They hoped that Inuit employees would still be able to engage in their traditional hunting and fishing. They wanted guarantees that the mine would not cause environmental damage to their lands. Further, they wanted to minimize any possible negative impact caused by the presence of large numbers of non-Inuit. In 1993 SMRQ and the Makivik Corporation signed a memorandum, which set out the main elements of the subsequent Raglan Agreement. The Agreement itself was signed in February, 1995, by SMRQ and five different Inuit associations: namely, the Makivik Corporation, acting on behalf of the Inuit villages not directly involved, the communities of Salluit and Kangiqsujuaq that were the closest communities to the mine site and their respective local land holding corporations.

The aim of the agreement was to foster and guarantee an ongoing working relationship between the mining corporation and the various Inuit communities likely to be affected by its operation. The agreement sought to secure the support of the Inuit groups while ensuring that in turn they benefited from the development and operation of the mine, directly and indirectly, economically and socially. To this end, SMRQ was to guarantee the meaningful participation of the Inuit in all phases and aspects of the mining operation through an oversight committee. This 'Raglan Committee' was to consist of six members: two representing the villages of Salluit and Kangiqsujuaq, one representing the Makivik Corporation and three representing SMRQ. Compensation of the Inuit was to take two forms: an initial payment and then profit sharing. Compensation also was required for damages to the land and wildlife, inconvenience to hunters and communities and the social and cultural disruptions caused by the mine. These payments, which totalled more than C$1 million in 1998, were made to the local villages.

The Raglan Agreement called for continuous monitoring of environmental impacts, and for SMRQ to exceed minimal environmental regulations. The agreement was especially concerned to foster the participation of Inuit in the mine operation. The agreement assigned priority to the awarding of contracts to competitive Inuit enterprises, but this priority was subject to other considerations. Much of construction work was to be conducted off site. Since construction schedules had to be met, SMRQ reserved the right to invite bids from contractors and suppliers of its choice. To carry out the Inuit side of the agreement, the Makivik Corporation agreed to develop and maintain a reliable and up to date list of qualified Inuit enterprises. In 1996 a local Inuit group formed a joint venture with a major Canadian construction company, Les Enterprises Kiewit Ltée, to work the new open-pit mine. This joint venture required initial capital contributions of C$2 million from the Inuit and C$8 million from Kiewit. The Inuit contribution was largely financed by the Makivik Corporation with some assistance from Federal government programmes aimed at helping Aboriginal people in economic development ventures. This joint venture with an experienced and competent firm enabled Inuit to become a supplier for the mine. The venture provided 40 permanent positions for workers to operate graders, tractors, excavators and large trucks.

The Raglan Agreement spelled out a number of provisions with respect to Inuit recruitment, training and work scheduling. The Kativik Regional Government was to advertise and recruit potential mine employees through its local employment officers in each Inuit village. The Inuit parties acknowledged that SMRQ would need to hire a number of non-Inuit to perform highly skilled engineering, technical and managerial positions. However, priority was to be given to hiring Inuit. Educational requirements for jobs were to be waived or reduced for Inuit with relevant on-the-job experience. SMRQ agreed to work with Kativik Regional Government and the Kativik Regional School Board to develop training programmes. The school board was to deliver training programmes for Inuit prior to employment at Raglan, including pre-employment, vocational and technical programmes leading to certification in trades such as the operation of heavy equipment, milling and certain types of lab work, as well as training for supervisory positions. These were funded largely by a contribution agreement from the Kativik Regional Government employment training budgets. SMRQ agreed to provide on-the-job training programmes for employed Inuit, funded with assistance from the federal and provincial governments. There was also to be extensive and individualized training, funded by SMRQ, to enable Inuit staff to gain skills and be promoted at their own pace. SMRQ also was to provide personal and career counselling, by hiring an Inuk specifically to provide support and counselling to Inuit employees. It agreed to provide a scholarship fund for any qualified Inuit youth interested in careers in geology, mining engineering, metallurgical engineering, industrial hygiene and related occupations.

With respect to scheduling, the Raglan Agreement specified that Inuit employees could opt for a work rotation involving two weeks on and two weeks off (non-Inuit alternated four weeks on-site and two weeks off-site). This rotation permitted Inuit employees to spend time in their villages and with their families, and to continue their traditional – and economically valuable – activities such as hunting, trapping and fishing. SMRQ agreed to transport Inuit employees to and from their villages to the work site. It was hoped that such a balance of work with time off would encourage Inuit workers to remain employees of SMRQ. Two years after mine operations began, the rotation schedule was further modified to provide Inuit employees with further options. The Raglan Agreement also spelled out several ways of dealing with the linguistic differences among workers at the site. Recognizing that few Inuit were trilingual in Inuktitut, English and French, the agreement committed SMRQ to identify jobs that could be performed by Inuit who spoke only their native tongue. The SMRQ agreed to provide language-training programmes in French and English, and to guarantee that 'southerners' hired especially as foremen, supervisors and managers could express themselves clearly in French and English. There were to be mandatory orientation programmes in Inuit culture for non-Inuit employees and efforts to encourage and support local Inuit artists.

While the initial consultations were proceeding, SMRQ began to upgrade local roads and the port facilities at Deception Bay. Mine operations began in 1998, and the Raglan Agreement went into effect. The six-member Raglan Committee since then has met regularly to supervise its implementation. Sixty-eight Inuit were hired by SMRQ in 1998, representing 18 per cent of the labour force. These employees received extensive training especially in the operation of heavy equipment. Other Inuit were hired by the joint venture with Kiewit to undertake the open-pit mining.

Analysis and discussion

To what degree has the Raglan Mine benefited Nunavik Inuit?

Overall, the Raglan Mine has benefited the Inuit communities in a number of ways. Inuit have received jobs, skill training and income. Their communities have received compensation payments and profit-sharing payments. The mine has created local employment opportunities. It has provided skilled training, through joint SMRQ–Inuit programmes. At the same time, the mining operation has thus far had minimal environmental and social impact. Non-Inuit workers live in accommodations considerable distance from local Inuit villages. Inuit employees have been able to continue traditional occupations. Falconbridge has hired local contractors and spent modest funds locally. Inuit continue to work collaboratively with the mine on a number of operating committees. Indeed, several different committees meet periodically to foster and maintain a lively collaboration between the mining company and the local community. Thus far many people at Falconbridge and many among the Nunavik Inuit feel satisfied with regard to this particular collaboration between modern industry and an indigenous people. Both will acknowledge weaknesses, such as the high turn over rates among Inuit workers, while pointing to the ways in which the project has gone well.

In order to assess this collaboration in more depth, we analyse operations of the Raglan Mine in relation to four points of reference: its governance; its human-resources practices; its impact on economic development; and its impact on the local culture.

Governance

Often we use 'governance' to view the top of organizational charts. We use the term to analyse the ways 'agents' who manage organizations are directed and held accountable by 'principals' who govern or own or invest in these organizations. In practice, the governance of organizations includes wider concerns. How are basic policy and strategy decisions made? How and to whom are organizations and their members accountable? Who is entitled to what kinds of returns on what kinds of investments? The governance systems of organizations are variously institutionalized in formal authority structures, patterns of accountability and assumptions regarding property entitlements. As we consider governance issues of international businesses in developing areas, we are at once concerned with the extent to which local communities are represented in decision-making bodies and the degree to which local groups and individuals are able to benefit from their investment in these businesses. We are interested as well in the extent to which international firms collaborate with local businesses, voluntary associations and governments to realize common objectives and recognize their varying degrees of accountability to these groups.

Viewing the Raglan Mine from this broader perspective on governance, one is struck by the relatively high degree of collaboration and cooperation. Since the early 1990s, Falconbridge and local Inuit associations and villages have been in engaged in ongoing consultations. The high-profile Raglan Committee addresses concerns through collaborative discussion. The Inuit feel that many of their major concerns have been addressed. They have established a major supplier to the mine, through a joint venture. They were given priority in hiring. Inuit employees were allowed to choose a work rotation that permitted them to live half time in their own villages. They received not only initial compensation benefits but also opportunities for on-going profit sharing. In effect, they have been treated as investors without actually having to make investments. Both Inuit and Falconbridge viewed the Inuit as respected partners in this operation. Moreover, through the Makivik Corporation and the local village land holding corporations, the Inuit have been treated as proprietors of the land. Their traditional rights to hunting, trapping and fishing have been respected. Symbolically, the land was theirs. SMRQ, for its part, has been much like a tenant, in terms of the rights circumscribed by the Raglan Agreement.

Several different factors on each side served to bring about this degree of partnership. The James Bay agreement (JBNQA) extended considerable decisional powers to the Inuit and their institutions. These powers were strengthened by the increased militancy of Aboriginal groups across Canada to seek augmented legal rights and political influence. The recent opposition of the Inuit to the Great Whale project compelled Falconbridge to adopt a consultative and collaborative approach. Increased public concern about the rights and interests of native groups alerted Falconbridge that they would need to formally acknowledge and deal respectfully with the local Inuit authorities. The Quebec Inuit learned that they could bargain effectively. Furthermore, by the 1990s Falconbridge could review and build upon the experiences of a number of Canadian companies like Cameco, Ontario Hydro and the Nova Corporation of Alberta, all of whom had been experimenting with various ways of working with Aboriginal groups. Falconbridge realized that the only politically realistic option was to work collaboratively with the Inuit. The Inuit, for their part, learned from preliminary consultations that they could trust the consultative process to protect their interests; that they would not be forced into arrangements that primarily benefited Falconbridge. The generally optimistic view of the Raglan Agreement contrasts tellingly with a general feeling among Aboriginals of disenchantment with the JBNQA.

It is remarkable that the Raglan venture currently enjoys such genuine support by both parties, even though it is neither a co-managed nor co-owned operation. In law the governing powers of Inuit over the mine are actually quite limited. To be sure, the Inuit co-own the joint venture that serves as a major contractor for the mine. But they do not co-manage it; and the mine itself is fully owned and managed by Falconbridge, headquartered in another province, in which they are not formally represented to any degree. Mineral rights are claimed by the Quebec government, which also treats the surface lands as public properties of the province. The Makivik Corporation has acted more as a renter collecting and dispersing royalties than as a co-proprietor and co-manager of the mining operation. Yet the Inuit retain a modest sense of partnership with those managing the mine. They have been able to influence these operations effectively in a number of ways. They have been able to exercise a controlling influence over land use. They benefit as significant beneficiaries. Their representatives sit on the official committee and sub-committees, authorized to implement the Raglan Agreement. This Agreement establishes basic guidelines on how Falconbridge can operate the mine. If the operations at the mine are in opposition to the terms of the Agreement, the Kativik Regional Government, the Makivik Corporation and the local village authorities can exert significant measures of countervailing power.

Employee relations

How firms like Falconbridge treat their indigenous workers can be assessed in relation to a number of variables. By what means and how successful are these firms in recruiting and employing the indigenous people who live in the area of their operations? What kinds of training programmes do they offer? In what ways do these firms provide opportunities for advancement and career development? How do these businesses treat indigenous employees at work? What kinds of bridges and connections do they attempt to establish between work in their organizations and the community and family lives of these employees? How successful are they in retaining these workers over time?

Fully integrating indigenous workers into modern industrial enterprises is not a simple matter. Prior to their employment, these workers and their employers exist in quite different cultures. They live with different senses of time and timing, different approaches to working collaboratively with others, different ideas about careers and social advancement and different assumptions about the relation of work to family and community life. Indigenous workers often lack the requisite technical and employee skills. For their part, the non-indigenous workers typically neither know nor comprehend clearly local cultures. They may act with unexamined and unacknowledged stereotypes and biases. What often happens is that indigenous employees are segregated to work in selected unskilled positions; they remain only marginally integrated into the labour force of the firms and they are paid less. The relation between indigenous and non-indigenous workers becomes strained. Furthermore, indigenous workers quit or leave their jobs in much higher ratios, frequently without warning.

Falconbridge's employee relations with Inuit at Raglan have thus far been comparatively positive. Falconbridge's efforts to recruit, train, empower and support Inuit compare favourably with what have been regarded as one of the best practices with other Canadian firms like Cameco, Nova and Hydro Ontario (AEECG, 1992). SMRQ has successfully recruited Inuit, providing them with thorough, multi-dimensional training in languages, basic pre-employment skills, and skills for operating various kinds of mining equipment. It has attempted to familiarize non-Inuit employees with Inuit culture. The Inuit way of life has been celebrated through art works, special programmes and ongoing consultations. The firm has adopted a system for rotating work that allows Inuit workers to remain closely connected with their home communities. As a result, many Inuit workers have been fairly well integrated within the firm and have not generally become cut off from their own families and culture.

A number of factors account for the success of these employee relation efforts. Most important are the policies and practices developed jointly through consultations between SMRQ and Inuit representatives on the Raglan Committee, and sub-committees on employment and the environment. SMRQ did not develop employment practices unilaterally, but rather through discussion and consultation with representatives of the Inuit population. Furthermore, these policies were put into practice with the cooperation of other Inuit institutions, including both local Employment officers and the Regional School Board.

Still, the relationship of Inuit workers to the mine have been troubled by a number of difficulties which are focused in the problem of turnover. More than half of the Inuit hired initially to operate the mine left by the end of the first year. Since 1998, turnover has declined steadily, reaching about 15 per cent by December 2001. The 70 or so permanent Inuit employees represent less than 20 per cent of the regular work force and about one-fifth of the total number of Inuit who have worked for the mine (Stackhouse, 2001). The issue of turnover likely will remain an ongoing concern for Falconbridge, the Raglan Committee and its sub-committee on employment and training.

SMRQ is not unique in experiencing high turnover rates among indigenous workers. Many Canadian firms that have sought to employ sizeable numbers of Aboriginal workers have observed comparable turnover ratios. It is instructive in this context to review experiences of other business. One business in Western Canada launched a major campaign to recruit and hire native workers. They actively recruited, offered pre-employment training, placed natives in a wide range of positions, at times adjusted work schedules, provided a range of employee support services and attempted to educate other employees with respect to the culture of indigenous people. However, turnover ratios remained fairly high. The overall proportion of Aboriginal workers dropped slightly from its high of about 15 per cent. Managers and natives at this firm attempted to identify those factors that especially contributed to these high turnover ratios. They thought that some individual workers had probably left because they had been placed in positions where they had little contact with other native workers on a regular basis. As a result, these individuals felt vulnerable; they felt their work was more carefully scrutinized. They also thought they were often looked to as the informal representatives of indigenous workers.

Several other factors, however, seemed to play a greater role at this firm in Western Canada. Many of those concerned about the turnover rates felt that the non-native managers and workers did not fully understand, appreciate and take into account the significant ways in which the culture of the natives differed. They felt that not enough allowance had been made for the different approaches to the timing, craftsmanship, socializing and the claims of community. A number of indigenous workers complained that they were stereotyped from time to time, in small but telling ways. Several native workers complained of subtler and contrasting forms of discrimination. They felt that too much allowance was being made for the ways they were supposedly different from other workers. They experienced some of this treatment as condescension. They felt this special consideration meant in effect that they were not being taken seriously for possible promotion opportunities. In a number of cases, individual indigenous workers had left the firm because they felt called to respond to other challenges, opportunities or commitments. Several left to assume larger roles in local communities. Others left in response to family crises. There was no clear, overall pattern.

The Raglan experience is similar in that the Inuit and non-Inuit workers operate with quite different approaches to time, family life and work. The non-Inuit full-time employees are almost all highly experienced, skilled, middle-aged, French-speaking workers who have lived and worked together for considerable time. They bring to this operation a strong sense of community. In contrast, Inuit employees tend to be much younger workers, not well versed in French, often inexperienced and coming from diverse villages. Such differences may account for the unexamined ways in which non-indigenous managers may stereotype or act condescendingly. But turnover rates also simply reflect structural factors. Some indigenous employees will feel called upon to maintain their multiple roles in their local communities: as providers by means of traditional activities of hunting, trapping and fishing, as local leaders, as household heads and members. Employees will respond to other employment opportunities. Some will take off time because they have been used to changing their typical forms of work with changes in the seasons. Many will consider leaving as an honourable way of dealing with their own sense that they are likely only to remain marginal to these enterprises as largely unskilled, un-promotable employees.

There are a number of ways that Falconbridge might respond to the current situation. Even though Falconbridge has been especially responsive to these concerns so far, the firm might look further into factors that make Inuit employees feel less than comfortable in their employment. SMRQ might explore ways of offering greater services to local villages through Inuit organizations allowing SMRQ employees to stay on the job at times when they might otherwise be called back to their villages. The mine needs to consider more ways to encourage promotion – opportunities for advancement that might persuade some to undertake extra training and other time commitments in which to gain more skills, authority and benefits. With these workers in mind, Falconbridge might also review its work rotation policies. The present rotation allows Inuit workers to remain involved in their local communities while still working regular shifts, but they cannot become as fully integrated as other workers who spend four continuous weeks at the mine. They become identified *de facto* as a distinct grouping in spite of all the other efforts to foster relations between Inuit and non-Inuit employees. Those Inuit employees interested in advancement might be willing to consider rotations corresponding to those of non-Inuits.

Finally, Falconbridge might reconsider whether its view of turnover needs to be adjusted. Certainly, turnover is costly. A firm invests a considerable amount in training programmes; when workers leave shortly after beginning their regular employment, these training costs do not pay off. Such departures make it more difficult for the firm to realize the goal of increasing employment among the local population. But why should Falconbridge suppose that all indigenous workers, once trained and hired, will become committed, career-oriented employees? A critical review of that expectation reveals a purely instrumental notion of training programmes as a means of creating useable and deployable employees. This is credible in settings where the larger North American culture and its school systems socialize people into such expectations, but less credible in an indigenous culture, where workers remain deeply enmeshed in traditional patterns of life – where patterns of work are more episodic and change with seasons, and the work itself is much more closely associated with household and village roles. In such settings, it is probably realistic to expect at least a significant number of trained workers will move in and out of regular employment, to return to traditional work patterns at times, but also seeking other, newer employment alternatives as well. On this view, the firm may simply regard the turnover rates as normal. Training programmes then take on a somewhat different value: as a means for the firm to invest in the social capital of the local community, by ongoing personal involvement with particular individuals over time.

Economic development

The Raglan Mine has enriched Nunavik Inuit in several ways. Royalties have been used for municipal improvements. Workers have received much better wages than they would have earned through other available forms of local employment, and have become less dependent on government transfers. Still, the basic question remains: to what extent is such wealth being invested for the long-term economic development of the area? It will be a serious lost opportunity if the Raglan Mine investment does not also work to strengthen the Nunavik economy in some sustainable ways. The anticipated life of the mine is 20 years – and so it faces closure as early as 15 years from now. Having used up a considerable amount of their natural capital in the form of valued minerals, Nunavik Inuit will want to be positioned so that other resources can provide jobs, profits and revenues for their communities. These resources might assume several forms. The skills that Inuit have acquired through training programmes and employment represent human resources that they may draw upon to foster greater economic expansion. Twenty years from now, will the Inuit have established small-producer cooperatives, fishing businesses, micro-credit associations and other new enterprises? Will they have been able to develop additional physical infrastructures and communication networks? Will they have raised the overall skill levels of Nunavik's residents?[4]

It is not too early to start answering these questions – to determine how effectively the wealth created by the Raglan Mine will be used to foster development of Nunavik. The Makivik Corporation has used its earnings to help start several small joint ventures (Cleghorn, 1999). These represent a beginning, but so far, most of the wealth has been used to increase consumption rather than as a source for further investment. Because the initiative for this project began with Falconbridge, with its considerable economic and social resources, Falconbridge is especially accountable for how these possibilities are explored. Indeed, the responsibility for whether or not such developments take place rests as much with Falconbridge and SMRQ as with the Makivik Corporation and the local Nunavik communities.

Social and cultural contacts

The Raglan Mine is not fully integrated into the Nunavik Inuit society. In a sense, the Inuit have benefited from this non-integration, for the mine has provided wealth and income without displacing a sizeable number of people. On the other hand, the Inuit are becoming economically dependent on what remains an outside institution, one that represents a markedly different way of life and operates according to different cultural values. These differences assume a number of expressions. The emerging cash economy contrasts with traditional patterns of self-sufficiency and barter. The high-tech, capital-intensive work introduced by the mine contrasts with traditional, labour-intensive patterns of work. While the mine operates around the clock on an intensively time-managed schedule, the Inuit are used to leisurely patterns of work guided by the seasons and available daylight. While the Inuit work in a way that centres on homes and families, non-indigenous employees are accustomed to the separation of workplace and household.

A number of Inuit employees have managed these cultural differences in ways that have made them less than reliable as employees. For example, when Inuit feel a need to deal with family matters, they may miss planes transporting them to the mine or temporarily absent themselves from work. Such differences generally help account for tension between Inuit and non-Inuit workers on the work site. The Western Canadian firm described earlier experienced such tension. Informal studies indicated that the relations between Aboriginal workers and others were often strained, even when they appeared to not to be. Aboriginals privately talked of being treated with either suspicion or paternalistically; many felt less than fully integrated into the workforce. At Raglan the hints of such strain assume several forms. Many Inuit, already estranged in a work environment that is so different from what they are used to, feel marginal also because non-Inuit have more experience, different work schedules and different languages. The old-time workers are unilingual Francophones, while most Inuit speak Inkutitut or English. Back in the village, evidence of such strains is visible in somewhat elevated rates of alcohol and drug abuse and family tensions (Cleghorn, 1999).

How well have the mine and the Raglan Committee addressed the strains represented by these cultural differences? The mine has not been operating long enough to provide an adequate answer. SMRQ might step up its initiatives for enabling workers from different backgrounds to get to know and respect each other. For example, it might increase the numbers of workers who are developing linguistic skills in one or more of the three languages used at the mine. SMRQ has been working slowly at a number of initiatives at the work site that are likely to make a difference over time. But the Inuit need to take initiatives as well. Economic development likely will help. Inuit might also work to facilitate community development in their villages, perhaps assisted by the Makivik Corporation and/or Falconbridge.

Conclusion: what can we learn from the Raglan Mine?

In order to extract the copper and nickel found on the Ungava peninsula, Falconbridge, as an international mining firm, has had to find ways of working cooperatively with Nunavik Inuit, the people who live in this area. Beginning in the early 1990s, Falconbridge sought to develop this mine collaboratively, with considerable success. After six years of operation, the mine has helped reduce the threat of poverty by enriching the Inuit in three ways. First and most obviously, the standard of living has improved modestly for Nunavik Inuit. As long as the mine operates, the wages and royalties they receive make them less dependent on government aid and grants. Second, because of the Raglan Mine, Nunavik Inuit workers have learned a number of marketable skills. They have also begun to learn broader sets of social skills – not only learning how to function as employees and undertake tasks with people from different cultures but also how to engage politically to represent their views and negotiate cross-culturally. Third, the mine has provided an occasion for Nunavik Inuit to work collaboratively, both in their own organizations and with strangers in newly formed institutions. The Raglan Agreement and subsequent arrangements have strengthened the networks of communication, trust and informal exchange among Nunavik Inuit and between Inuit and other employees and representatives of the mine.

These three achievements need to be qualified. Wealth from the mine has also led to increased consumer spending and instances of social unrest. The mining company has not succeeded in hiring as many Inuit as it had originally expected or in retaining them as regular employees for as long as initially anticipated. The mine has not acted as effectively as hoped to catalyse the development of other business enterprises. There is some tension between non-Inuit personnel and the local indigenous population. The three language communities working at the mine often work in social isolation from each other. Both sides point regularly both to examples of what seems to be inappropriate stereotyping and exaggerated resentment. The mine also has given rise to social animosities and unrest among Inuit, but these should not be exaggerated. The people most affected by the mine's operations are often distracted by whatever current difficulties, misunderstandings and disappointments focus their attention. However, the initial commitment by Falconbridge to work in ways that were genuinely collaborative has enabled all sides to talk with each other about their concerns. In so doing, the company is helping to reinforce and construct larger interweaving patterns of communication. In modest ways, therefore, the mine has fostered the growth of social capital.

A number of important challenges remain. Can SMRQ find ways to increase the percentage of its employees that are Inuit? Can it discover ways that enable Inuit rise to positions of greater skill and authority? What are the realistic prospects for reducing the social tensions between the different language and cultural communities? What steps might be taken so that greater proportions of the wealth produced by the mine are invested broadly in fostering on a sustainable basis the overall economic development of Nunavik? Can they protect the fragile environment of Nunavik from unintended accidents? These challenges are difficult and perplexing. They do not admit of ready solutions. It is probably the case, that Falconbridge and its partners in the Makivik Corporation, the local municipalities and land holding groups will not successfully address all these challenges equally well. It is too early in the history of this enterprise to predict how things will eventually turn out. Expectations have been high. Nonetheless, they have constructed and continued to support a framework through the Raglan Agreement that allows them both to address these challenges and acknowledge forthrightly what still has to be done.

Notes

1. This historical background draws upon Cleghorn (1999), Drummond (1997), Jensen and Papillon (2000), Pelly (1995), Stackhouse (2001) and JBNQA (1988). Rob Nixon has participated on the employment committee established by the Raglan Agreement. We are grateful to Chris Mount and Fred Louder for carefully reading this chapter and suggesting extremely helpful additions.
2. For non-Canadian readers, it may helpful to explain that there is no universal agreement in Canada as to whether 'native', 'Indian', 'first nation', 'aboriginal people' or 'indigenous people' is the appropriate expression in any given context. In this study, none of these expressions has been used exclusively. Some speakers or communities preferences are strongly held; but many Canadians simply take it as linguistic fact of life that the Canadian Aboriginal News Services will report the activities of the federal department of Indian Affairs or the Assembly of First Nations. That the word 'Inuit', meaning 'people' in the Inuktitut language, came into currency in Canada during the 1970s is another significant (if indirect) consequence of the JBNQA negotiations; today it has entirely replaced 'Eskimo', except in historical contexts.
3. Much of the basic information about these mining operations comes from the study prepared by International Council on Metals and the Environment (1998).
4. Compare the findings from the Harvard Project on American Indian Economic Development (Cornell and Kalt, 2002).

References

AEECG (1992): Aboriginal Employment Equity Consultation Group *Aboriginal Employment and Community Relations: Best Practices in Canada* (Ottawa: Treasury Board of Canada Secretariat).

Berger, T. R. (1977) *Northern Frontier Northern Homeland: The Report of the McKenzie Valley Pipeline Inquiry* (Toronto: James Lorimer and Company).

Cleghorn, C. (1999) 'Aboriginal Peoples and Mining in Canada: Six Case Studies' [online text], MiningWatch Canada (Ottawa) (updated 13 September 2003) http://www.miningwatch.ca/issues/aboriginal_gathering/Case_Studies.html

Cornell, S. and Kalt, J. P. (eds) (2002) *What Can Tribes Do? Strategies and Institutions in American Indian Economic Development* (Los Angeles: American Indian Studies Center).

Drummond, S. G. (1997) *Incorporating the Familiar: An investigation into Legal Sensibilities in Nunavik* (Montreal and Kingston: McGill-Queens University Press).

Gagnon, A. -G. and Tully, J. (eds) (2001) *Multinational Democracies* (Cambridge University Press).

INAC (1993): Indian and Northern Affairs Canada, 'The James Bay and Northern Québec Agreement and the Northeastern Quebec Agreement: History' [website] (updated July 1993) http://www.ainc-inac.gc.ca/pr/info/info14_e.html

INAC (2000): Indian and Northern Affairs Canada, 'Principal Provisions of JBNQA and NEQA' at *James Bay and Northern Quebec Agreement and The Northeastern Quebec Agreement, 1998–1999 Annual Report, 1999–2000 Annual Report*, [website] (n.d.) http://www.ainc-inac.gc.ca/pr/agr/que/cin005_e.pdf

International Council on Metals and the Environment (1998) 'The Raglan Project', Case Study C (photocopy).

James Bay and Northern Québec Agreement and Complementary Agreements, 1988 edn (Quebec City: Publications Québec), *Indian and Northern Affairs Canada* [website] (n.d.) http://www.ainc-inac.gc.ca/pr/agr/que/jbnq_e.PDF

Jensen, J. and Papillon, M. (2000) 'Challenging Citizenship Regimes: The James Bay Crees and Transnational Action', *Politics and Society*, vol. 28(2), pp. 245–64.

Kymlicka, W. (1995) *Multicultural Citizenship: A Liberal Theory of Minority Rights* (Oxford: Clarendon Press).

Pelly, D. F. (1995) 'The Faces of Nunavik', *Canadian Geographic*, vol. 115 (January), p. 14ff.

Stackhouse, J. (2001) 'Everyone Thought We Were Stupid: Canadian Apartheid, Part 15', *Globe and Mail*, 14 December.

Whiteman, G. and Mamen, K. (2002) *Meaningful Consultation and Participation in the Mining Sector? A Review of the Consultation and Participation of Indigenous Peoples within the International Mining Sector* [online text] (Ottawa: The North–South Institute) http://www.nsi-ins.ca/download/lit_rev/lit_rev_final.pdf

13

International Trade as a Vehicle for Reducing Poverty: The Body Shop's Community Trade Programme

Frederick Bird

Introduction

In the late 1980s The Body Shop International (BSI) became interested in global poverty. Anita Roddick, BSI's founder, sought ways to involve her company directly in efforts to ameliorate the poverty faced by people in developing countries. She explored how BSI might source from these areas some of the ingredients and products sold in their shops. These initial efforts, undertaken with the Kayapo Indians in Brazil and a Boys Town in India, occasioned mixed responses. While BSI established trading relations that brought new wealth to these communities and considerable publicity for BSI, the company ran into unexpected difficulties. It was sharply criticized by some journalists and NGOs, who felt these projects served more to enhance the Body Shop's image than to help the affected peoples. BSI expanded and refined its Community Trade programme over the next 14 years. Beginning in early 1990s, it linked its efforts to well-established Alternative Trade organizations (ATOs) and the Fair Trade movement. From its own Community Trade programmes, BSI learned a number of lessons about how to manage relations with their suppliers and foster the organizational capacities of the groups with which it worked. BSI demonstrated that regular commercial enterprises can source from developing areas in ways that are not only beneficial for their own businesses but directly help trading partners strengthen their own capacities and reduce poverty in their communities. By 2002 BSI was purchasing more than £5 million (US$8 million) in products and ingredients from more than three dozen producer groups in 25 developing countries.

History of The Body Shop

Anita Roddick opened the first Body Shop store in 1976 in Brighton, England. Her idea was to sell cosmetics made from natural ingredients.

In contrast to others in the cosmetic business, BSI attempted to market its products without advertising. The first franchise opened a year later. In 1984 BSI began selling shares publicly. In 1988 it opened its first stores in the United States. Since then, its expansion has been extraordinary. By 1999 BSI had over 1200 stores in 46 countries. It was marketing over 600 skin and hair products and 500 accessory items. In 1996–97 its retail sales exceeded £625 million (US$1 billion) and its pre-tax profits were more than £38 million (US$61 million). It developed an exceptionally well-known brand image that was associated with distinctive packaging, natural ingredients and exotic fragrances. The brand image also was associated with social values championing women, the environment and human rights (London Greenpeace, 1998; Hartman and Beck-Dudley, 1999; Klein, 2000).

The Body Shop has been involved with a number of social causes. In 1986 it worked with Friends of the Earth to promote a 'Think Globally, Act Locally' campaign. It widely voiced its concern for animal rights and its opposition to animal testing. It joined with Greenpeace to gain public support to help save whales. In 1988 Anita Roddick began contributing to save tropical rain forests, which she saw as an environmental concern, an issue of social justice and object for social welfare contributions. She explored ways in which BSI could help those affected through social protests, through charitable contributions and through trade. In the 1990s BSI offered both financial and volunteer support to refugees from Eastern Europe. In 1995 BSI Foundation contributed more than £1 million to a variety of charities and voluntary agencies including a major healthcare project in Brazil, various humans rights initiatives, the Fair Trade movement, as well environmental groups (BSI, 1995, pp. 123–4). BSI vigorously protested against the human rights abuses afflicted on the Ogoni people in Nigeria. In 1991 the firm began monitoring its social and environmental practices. Still, in the mid-1990s, BSI was subjected to public scolding. Critics argued that the BSI fell short of its own high standards and rhetoric (Entine, 1994, 1996). BSI responded to these criticisms by instituting more comprehensive environmental and social audits (Hanson, 1995).

Early projects

The Body Shop's involvement with the Kayapo Indians of Brazil began in the late 1980s when Anita Roddick attended a rally in Altamira, Brazil, to protest a proposed dam. The rally also protested against the Brazilian government for permitting farmers to burn forests in order to clear the lands for cattle grazing. At the request of the rally organizers, BSI provided funds to transport Brazilian Indians to this event; there Anita Roddick met an articulate Kayapo named Paiaken, who had already set forth the plight and concerns of his people before various foreign governments. As a result of this chance encounter, BSI decided to launch a major anti-burning campaign, which included distributing posters and selling campaign T-shirts. Roddick met with the heads of franchise stores in England and raised approximately half a million dollars to help save the rain forests. BSI leaders then discussed how to spend these funds with non-governmental organizations (NGOs) such as Friends of the Earth, Greenpeace and Survival. The funds were used both for political protest and to help indigenous peoples directly. BSI supported organizations such as the Union of Indian Nations and the Nucleus for Indigenous Rights, working with indigenous people in the Amazon area. BSI enabled representatives of the Yonomani people to meet with government officials in Brasilia, the capital, to protest the invasion of gold miners. In a different vein, BSI offered funds to buy, maintain and fly a light airplane to enable Kayapo villages to have better access to urban centres for health care and other purposes. In the early 1990s, the Body Shop Foundation joined with UNICEF and the World Bank to fund health clinics (Roddick, 1992, 188–92; STP, 1994; Petean, 1999).

With the backing of BSI franchise heads, Roddick and BSI representatives then met with local leaders in the Kayapo area to explore how BSI might help these people in a sustainable way by purchasing goods that they might produce for market. Two initiatives were launched. First, women from four Kayapo villages drew upon their skills in traditional beadwork to make glass bracelets, belts and necklaces for sale by BSI, which flew in 100 kilos of glass beads and paid US$20000 for their work. The project was eventually discontinued. The second and far more important initiative was to purchase oil pressed by the Kayapo from Brazil nuts, for use in hair conditioners. This operation was begun by Paiaken but managed by Saulo Petean, another Brazilian hired by BSI. More than 70 villagers gathered the Brazil nuts and extracted the oil in Aukre village, using a press donated by The Body Shop. They were paid at a rate determined both by the hours worked and the needs of the community, a rate much higher than relevant market prices. According to Petean, they received about US$850 each per year for their labours.

The Brazil nut project ran into unanticipated difficulties and as a result was scaled back. There were initial difficulties managing the labour of people who had little experience with organized shop work. The workers were paid much more money than they had previously received and many times consumed these wages in purchases rather than investing in household or communal resources. Some villagers benefited from this project while others did not, occasioning social tensions. The villagers became what some critics regarded as overly dependent upon a single customer. BSI was criticized by an NGO, Survival for Tribal People (STP), for using marketing schemes to address the threat to tropical forests. Trade programmes were rendering the forest peoples more vulnerable to and dependent upon distant economic forces. STP argued that the forest peoples would benefit more from lobbying to bolster their land claims (Corry, 1993; STP, 1994; Petean,

1999). In response The Body Shop reduced its involvement, but did not withdraw. The health clinic service continued, and in the later 1990s indigenous people involved with this service formed the Amazon Cooperative, encompassing eight tribes. Since then, this cooperative has established an Internet café and an Eco Lodge for environmentally concerned tourists and has marketed various green pharmaceutical products. It continues to sell to BSI batches of Brazil-nut oil pressed by Aukre villagers.

In the late 1980s Roddick also learned about a Boys Town in Tamil Nadu, India. Operated by a Christian religious order, it enabled boys and girls to study trades while working to earn money to support and educate themselves. BSI ordered several products, beginning with handcrafted Christmas cards, a baggy trouser-suit to be worn by BSI sales personnel and miniature wooden foot-rollers. This project ran into difficulties: Body Shop staff did not like the uniforms; worse yet, BSI learned of alleged abuses of children by the staff of the Boys Town Trust. A Boys Town employee named Amanda Murphy volunteered to establish a parallel business working with young people in the same area; called Teddy Exports, her venture has been selling foot-rollers, cotton bags and other products to BSI since 1993. By 2001 Teddy Exports was employing 300 workers; it also was functioning as a community centre, providing various social services. Twenty per cent of the profits on sales are used for community programmes (BSI, 1998g).

The Kayapo and Teddy Exports projects shared four features that limited their success. First, the projects seemed as much oriented to aiding these communities through charitable donations or social protests as through establishing sound business relations. Second, the projects were personally initiated in response to Roddick's interests and were personally overseen by her. Third, although BSI attempted to develop trading relations with third-world producers by assuming much of the initiative to identify possible products and/or organize actual production, in its initial enthusiasm the company sometimes ordered more products than it could actually sell. Fourth, BSI did not fully anticipate the unsettling ways in which the money it paid for labour and products might affect the communities involved.

The next two Community Trade projects BSI initiated bore similar traits. In both Ghana and Nepal, BSI became involved because of Roddick's interest, and efforts to establish viable business relations were mixed with a charitable intent to make donations and foster social services. If these projects were more successful, it was probably because BSI contracted to source from existing organizations.

While travelling through northern Ghana in 1992 with a television crew making a documentary about alternative technologies, Roddick learned about women who made butter from Shea nuts. These women, from a number of villages near Tamale, had been gathering the nuts and hand-grinding them for years. During the colonial era, the British administration had created an agency to buy and market this product. After independence the

Ghanaian government continued this operation through its Produce Buying Company and over the years various foreign donors and NGOs had contributed as well. When Roddick learned about this operation, she had BSI order 5700 kilograms (12 800 pounds) of Shea-nut butter for use in cosmetics. BSI bought the butter through an international NGO specializing in alternative technologies, at a price 50 per cent higher than the market. One-third of the proceeds were invested in local community projects; BSI helped villagers to build a local school, in part with direct company contributions. BSI also donated a machine that greatly speeded up the grinding of the nuts. For a time, the local women produced far more nut butter than BSI could purchase, effectively reducing the price that villagers could obtain. This oversupply occasioned some passing conflict (Roddick, 1992; BSI, 1998c; Stackhouse, 2000, ch. 8). BSI hired a Ghanaian to help the villagers regularize their production and so manage supply. BSI then worked with the village women to recruit a licensed export agent in southern Ghana who could market their product locally and internationally. In due course, BSI's relationship with the village women settled from a personal campaign into more regular business relations.

BSI evolved a similar relationship with a small company in Nepal – another relationship that evolved from personal enthusiasm to professional business processes. Roddick learned from a BBC special about a Nepali named Milan Bhattaria, who in the mid-1980s started a local firm named Get Paper Industries (GPI) near the capital of Kathmandu. GPI was making paper by hand from the bark of the Lotka, a local shrub. Bhattaria's business was threatened when the Nepalese government placed severe limits on the use of this endangered shrub because its survival as a species in the area was threatened by over-use. Mara Amats, an expert in handcrafted paper made from non-wood fibres, suggested to Bhattaria that GPI turn to fibres from banana palms and water hyacinths. GPI learned how to make paper from these more plentiful plants. BSI jumped in with enthusiasm, and once again its involvement changed over time. At first, BSI blurred trade with aid; the GPI relationship was presented to BSI as a case for charitable assistance rather than a potentially smart business relationship. A special appeal was made to franchise heads, in response to which a number raised funds for GPI's social welfare services. BSI helped GPI develop its own community agency to provide health care services, establish a credit fund and initiate an AIDS awareness campaign. BSI placed an initial order for 25 000 pounds of paper products. This order was so large that it kept the factory operating full-time for four months (Roddick, 1992; BSI, 1998k). However, BSI had in fact ordered more paper than Body Shop stores could sell; forced to cut back its large orders, it temporarily destabilized GPI. Afterward, the relationship became more businesslike as BSI helped GPI to electrify and expand its operations, clean the waste-water produced from dyeing the paper, develop effective quality controls, cultivate new customers, build relationships with local suppliers, set up retail shops in Kathmandu and expand its line of products.

BSI moves into Community Trade

In the same period, The Body Shop was moving to make the principle of Community Trade integral to its sourcing practices. To make this goal a reality BSI needed to do more than take on one well-publicized project after another. BSI trade contacts with third-world producers needed to be integrated into the BSI business plan, with clearly thought-out plans for developing community organizations instead of episodic crusades in corporate social responsibility. BSI therefore set out to locate a much larger number of third-world suppliers upon which it could reliably depend. These new contacts allowed BSI to expand the proportion of its suppliers from underdeveloped areas. By establishing these contacts, BSI was able to make its practices more closely correspond to the rhetoric of its 'Trade not Aid' campaign (BSI, 1998n, 1999a). For example, in 1992 BSI developed a contact with established producer cooperatives in Mexico and the south-western United States; it arranged to buy hand-crocheted scrubs made by Indian women in several remote Mexican villages and blue-corn powder produced by the Santa Ana Pueblo in New Mexico. Both these Indian communities, though small and remote, were already selling their products locally and shipping them to more distant markets. BSI became simply one more customer for each group. Unlike its relationships with the producer groups in Ghana and Nepal, these contacts resulted less from Roddick's personal sense of mission than from business strategy.

To make Community Trade central to its business strategy, BSI took three significant steps, beginning in 1993. First, a new manager was hired who had experience in the Fair Trade (alternative trade) movement – the former director of Oxfam's Fair Trade company in Canada. The result was a much more professional and businesslike attitude, though still based on principles of international development. Second, BSI began working with southern Fair Trade organizations (FTOs) like Safrudi in Philippines and NGOs like the Christian Organization for Relief and Rehabilitation (now Caritas) in Bangladesh – rather than simply following their example. The new relations stemmed from contacts and initiatives by a number of other northern FTOs and ATOs such as Traidcraft and Max Havelaar, which were already very involved in supporting third-world producers through trade relationships. BSI was simply acknowledging that it was not inventing a new wheel. From now on, BSI's projects would be developed far more collaboratively with Fair Traders, NGOs and federations of producer cooperatives. Not coincidentally, the name of The Body Shop's programme was changed in 1995 from 'Trade not Aid' to 'Community Trade'.

Third, in 1994 BSI developed formal 'Fair Trade Guidelines': a coherent set of policies for targeting appropriate third-world suppliers and monitoring the conduct of those suppliers. These policies were framed as benchmarking standards, in five key areas (BSI, 1996b):

1. Community. Suppliers should be established community organizations that represent their people's interests (primary producers must have a say in how the group is governed).
2. Community in need. Supplier communities should be economically disadvantaged or limited in their opportunities.
3. Benefits. Producers and their communities should benefit from the trade socially as well as economically.
4. Commercial viability. The trade arrangement with BSI has to make sense in terms of price, quality, capacity and availability.
5. Environmental sustainability. The trade must meet BSI standards for environmental and animal protection.

In return, The Body Shop promised to pay these producer groups a fair price for their goods – a price defined by the producers' actual needs and contributions rather than by current markets and the practices of other purchasers. BSI agreed to consult with other FTOs to determine these prices, where appropriate.

Several aspects of these guidelines are noteworthy. First, the guidelines are in the form of a practical handbook rather than an industry-wide code and therefore can be used by BSI both to select its suppliers and to suggest practical reforms for those suppliers, once selected. Second, in addition to defining the conduct expected of its producer groups, BSI presents its guidelines as actual objectives that it can help Community Trade suppliers to realize – not merely reference points for monitoring others, but goals that producer communities can attain. Accordingly BSI has helped Community Trade groups develop their capacities to standardize products, manage labour relations professionally, make effective use of new technologies and manage their budgets. Third, although in practice BSI has worked with identifiable enterprises – specific groups organized at least in part to market specific products – still, the language of community remains paramount, a reflection of BSI's producer groups as self-organized community enterprises.

BSI greatly expands its Community Trade operations

By early 1994 BSI was sourcing supplies from six third-world community producers. Despite considerable publicity, these efforts amounted to only a very tiny portion of BSI ingredients and products (Entine, 1994). This volume soon expanded rapidly and BSI's commitment to Community Trade solidified. By the end of 1995 BSI was purchasing 2.2 per cent of raw ingredients and 17.8 per cent of accessories from community producer groups, at a cost of roughly £2.3 million (US$3.6 million). By the end of 1996, BSI had established ongoing business relations with more than two dozen third-world community producer groups. Two projects in particular illustrate how BSI's Community Trade programme has evolved over time.

In 1994 BSI arranged to buy Babassu-nut oil from a Brazilian group, Cooperative of Agricultural Extractionist Producers of Lago de Junco (COPPALJ). By 1998 BSI was buying huge quantities, approximately 38 tonnes per year, for use in lotions, sunscreens and lipsticks. COPPALJ was formed in the late 1980s with assistance from rural Brazilian trade unions, cooperatives and technical assistance from a Brazilian NGO. By 1994 it had more than a hundred members located in 12 villages in north-eastern Brazil. The Babassu nuts are harvested largely by village women, who bring the nuts to small retail stores established by COPPALJ and receive either cash or merchandise in payment. COPPALJ extracts oil from the nuts and sells it to BSI, among a number of other customers. The business strength of the relationship lies in the fact that neither party is particularly dependent upon the other; in fact, the most decisive events in the history of the cooperative took place before The Body Shop became involved. In the mid-1980s, intense lobbying by diverse groups gained villagers in the area the legal right to harvest nuts from the Babassu trees, which were growing on large tracts of land that legally belonged to others. BSI arranged its purchases through ASSEMA (a federation of cooperatives founded at the same time as COPPALJ) and reinforced this local self-reliance by providing a large, guaranteed market for the oil produced (BSI, 1998a).

In 1994 BSI also began buying sesame-seed oil from the Juan Francisco Paz Silva Cooperative in Nicaragua. This cooperative was formed by farmers in the 1980s to serve as a vehicle for marketing grains, corn and animal products as well as sesame seeds. For the most part these products are sold locally. They began selling sesame-seed oil in 1992 after a slump in the price for seeds. An Anglican charity, Christian Aid, helped the farmers to organize the cooperative and donated the presses for squeezing the oil. The cooperative, which possessed 150 members and 200 affiliates in 1998, is a participatory democracy. It functions as a self-governing benevolent association as well as a business (BSI, 1998b). Members of this co-op have led the way in developing a larger organized association of cooperatives in Nicaragua, called the Del Campo Federation of Cooperatives. Del Campo actively seeks out, develops and maintains markets for goods produced by local associations like the Juan Francisco Paz Silva Cooperative. BSI purchases sesame-seed oil from this cooperative though Del Campo; in 1997 it purchased 10 tons of oil, which it uses in a variety of products.

The two cooperatives in Brazil and Nicaragua are similar in a number of ways. Indigenous farmers and harvesters organized both these producer groups in the 1980s. The founders had been influenced deeply by the base-church community development movements of the 1980s. This shared religious grounding included a political commitment to bring about improved social conditions through collaborative social action at the grass roots. Both cooperatives were committed to mutual self-help as well as to growing their respective business; both were well organized, with help from local or international NGOs. For both, The Body Shop represented a new kind of customer to be added to their existing customer base – foreign instead of local. Furthermore, by the end of the 1990s BSI was dealing with these producer cooperatives primarily through newly developed federations designed especially to market the products of these groups at home and abroad. Because these federations were established by and answerable to local cooperatives, they did not demand excessive rents for the service they performed.

By 2002 the number of producer cooperatives from which BSI was purchasing had grown to three dozen; but the relationship was becoming less direct. The producer cooperatives were established to empower their local communities, but they were involved with much more than developing products for sale; they variously operated schools for children, day care programmes and classes teaching particular trades or skills. Many operated local stores where people could buy merchandise not found locally, as well as seeds or tools used for their production. Several had established micro-credit systems or emergency health care funds. Many, like the Bahi cooperative in the Philippines, required their members to make regular contributions into these funds (BSI, 1998r). Increasingly, BSI worked through associations like Del Campo and Assema, which were established by local cooperatives to do business with retailers and to strengthen their own advantage in the marketplace. Examples outside Brazil and Nicaragua include Tropical Forest Products, which bought honey and beeswax from Zambian farmers (BSI, 1998o), or the Safrudi organization, which marketed craft works made by producer cooperatives in the Philippines (BSI, 1998f). BSI also negotiated purchases through established Community Trade organizations like Twin Trading (BSI, 1998f, 1998i).

By the end of the 1990s BSI Community Trading programmes had become more significant and less dramatic. The company was no longer making special appeals to owners of local Body Shop franchises – appeals that often resulted in widespread publicity. Nor was it initiating new projects or groups on its own. Rather, BSI developed Community Trade by connecting with existing programmes. Some of the groups who supplied BSI were very small, like the 18 women in the Hemming Group in Manila, from whom BSI has purchased hair accessories and brightly coloured pouches filled with fragrant potpourri (BSI, 1998p). Others were very large, such as Kuapa Kokoo Limited, which represented 35 000 cocoa bean farmers in Ghana (BSI, 1998i) or Minka, which consisted of 62 allied cooperatives, representing almost 10 000 local producers in Peru (BSI, 1998l). In most cases, BSI is only one of a number of ATOs and other customers to whom these producer groups are marketing their products. But even where BSI makes its purchases through a larger organization, these supply chains are typically organized so that the product comes from a particular village; for example, the clay bowls BSI purchases through Enfants du Monde Handicraft come from a group of 55 families in rural Bangladesh (BSI, 1998e).

By 2002 BSI was purchasing over £5 million (US$8 million) worth of products through its Community Trade programme. These included basic ingredients like jute, sesame-seed oil, Shea-nut butter, cocoa beans, Babassu-nut oil, honey, beeswax, blue-corn powder and Brazil-nut oil. They also included diverse products and craft items, such as paper goods, foot-rollers, hair accessories, scrubs, gift boxes, clay bowls, knitted goods, jewellery, potpourri and bath mitts. This growth in volume was possible because BSI was building upon well-established efforts initiated by many different non-commercial groups. Local and international NGOs and even governments have played a major role in initiating, encouraging and assisting the producer cooperatives with which BSI works. For example, the Evangelical Church in Luzon helped to establish the Barcelona Multi-Purpose Cooperative in the Philippines, from which BSI bought Buri boxes (BSI, 1998f). Locally organized Christian groups helped to develop the COPPALJ cooperative in Brazil and the Juan Francisco Paz Silva Cooperative in Nicaragua. The Christian Organization for Relief and Rehabilitation (Caritas) helped to develop CORR, a jute works cooperative in Bangladesh (BSI, 1998d). International FTOs such as Max Havelaar and Twin Trading have played a major role helping third-world producers like the Kuapa Kokoo co-op in Ghana and the Barcelona co-op in the Philippines (a self-help group aided by Saffy) to organize. In 1976 the Swiss government helped to establish Enfants du Monde to work with third-world cooperatives. German and Zambian governments contributed funds to establish the Northwestern Bee Products cooperative in Zambia. These groups were looking not simply for inexpensive suppliers of products to market, but to facilitate changes in these third-world communities. In broad terms, they sought to make communities become more self-sufficient economically through internal cooperation and externally developed trade.

Still, although BSI still purchases only a small portion of its total products and supplies through their Community Trade contacts, this programme had become integral to BSI's sourcing practices. What has been especially noteworthy about that The Body Shop's interactions with its third-world suppliers has been the way BSI has worked to help these organizations develop their competences so as to meet expected standards; perhaps the most significant feature of the Community Trade programme has been its implicit commitment to building the capacities of BSI trading partners.

Discussion: lessons learned

When BSI took its first step of helping Kayapo Indians in the Brazilian rainforest, it hoped that ways could be found to benefit these people materially.

Initially, BSI seemed to think it could aid such groups as much by publicizing their problems and raising contributions for them as by providing expanding markets for the goods they produced. Over time, BSI has shifted its orientation, emphasizing even more the importance of developing viable trading relations. In so doing, BSI has pursued a vision that a number of groups in the Fair Trade movement already had been working at for more than two decades (Brown, 1993, ch. 11; Fair Trade Yearbook, 2001, ch. 2; Traidcraft, 2001). That vision remains important and perhaps even more important for regular commercial businesses (Watkins and Fowler, 2002). Developing viable trading relationships with developing countries can serve to help these countries reduce their poverty (UNCTAD, 2002).

Nonetheless, as this chapter has demonstrated, developing effective and mutually beneficial trading relations with third-world producers is not a simple matter. The Body Shop's initial efforts had mixed results: at first it tried to do too much; its early aid projects were perhaps more expressions of protest than calculated business initiatives. But BSI learned from its mistakes, and the character of its projects shifted from being Anita Roddick's personal crusades to promoting well-thought-out Fair Trade practices. BSI also recognized that it was important to work with existing businesses; it encouraged its trading partners to find other customers so as not to become too dependent on BSI as a single, distant buyer (Gibbon, 2001, p. 351). Despite its shift from prime mover to reliable trading partner, BSI helped these communities reduce their poverty in small but significant ways by paying fair prices, providing a guaranteed source for some of their products and – most decisively – assisting them in building a range of organizational skills and competences for producing quality goods for local and distant markets.

Still, it is reasonable to ask whether the exchange between these producer groups and BSI have constituted genuinely fair exchanges (STP, 1994; Petean, 1999). Certainly, BSI has benefited greatly from its Community Trade initiatives. For more than a decade customers at Body Shop stores have assumed that many of the products on sale (and ingredients in other products) were sourced from producer groups in developing countries. In the early 1990s, considered in terms of providing a model for Fair Trade initiatives in the third world, BSI's reputation probably exceeded its actual performance. Over time, however, it has done genuinely important work in organizing direct, transparent and economically efficient supply chains. As well, the ongoing public relations benefits and consumer brand loyalty generated for the Body Shop have been very considerable, and in that regard alone its Community Trade programme can be seen to have made good business sense.

BSI has been able to attract customers who assumed that by purchasing cosmetics and accessories at Body Shop retail outlets they were in some way making a small difference on behalf of poor people in developing countries.

Several commentators have criticized this belief as illusory, far-fetched and/or misguided (Corry, 1993; Entine, 1994, 1996). It might be argued that because of its quite significant gains, BSI should explore other ways to help the needy communities in which its producer groups are located. There may be other significant ways by which retail firms like BSI and their customers can act on behalf of impoverished groups in developing countries. BSI might, as some critics urge, join protests in support of the property rights of indigenous people. The company has certainly engaged in a number of these kinds of campaigns to support human rights and environmental concerns in conjunction with groups such as Amnesty International, Friends of the Earth and Greenpeace. Perhaps they should explore other ways of working with these producer groups and local NGOs to invest in local infrastructures (Bedford *et al.*, 2001). This seems to be a legitimate possibility even if it is not yet clear how these collaborations might be undertaken.

Still, BSI has intentionally shifted away from an approach governed by political, philanthropic and social-welfare considerations to a perspective that is more professional and businesslike – for a good reason. Its own distinctive competence lies in business. And its smart-business approach to Community Trade focuses attention on the basic question of whether such a form of trade is indeed fair.

The fairness of Fair Trade should not be taken for granted. Current studies of supply chains reveal that initial producers in developing areas typically receive an unfairly low share of the eventual retail prices of their products. The retailers or agents who control particular nodes in the chain often have been able to gain disproportionate shares of the wealth created by retail sales (Bedford *et al.*, 2001; Ponte, 2002). Rarely do small producers have much influence. Gereffi (1994) has contrasted buyer commodity chains controlled by large and powerful retailers and producer chains controlled either by producers or other agents in the chain. If supply chains are not dominated by buyers, they are decisively influenced by agents who control particular transactions or processes in these chains (Gibbon, 2001; Kaplinsky and Morris, 2001). Viewed in relation to overall supply chains, primary producers receive less than a fair price for their products because other agents in the supply chain are able to charge excessive rents for particular services they perform.

Primary producers suffer in several ways. They often receive small and uncertain prices, which they often feel constrained to keep low in order to be sure they can sell their products. In turn, they place excessive pressure on their own labourers to produce as much as possible for wages that are as low as possible. Many retailers see few alternatives to working within this system. Periodically they may demand that their suppliers treat workers fairly. However, given the highly competitive character of retail markets, they may well feel that they cannot expend measurably more to purchase their supplies. For example, one popular clothing brand retailer in Montreal gives its agents enormous leeway. This company contracts with agents from east Asia either in Montreal or Hong Kong and provides detailed specification for the products it wishes to order; the agents are required to manage the supply chain, and are not paid until clothes shipments arrive and meets the Montreal retailer's quality expectations. Under such an arrangement, an agent has very considerable power to oversee relations with producers, pressure them to meet production expectations and deadlines – and pay them as low a price as the agent can manage to secure.

BSI has addressed this problem by establishing direct links with particular producers and the associations that represent them. This strategy is probably more effective than policing suppliers using particular Fair Trade standards. To be sure, efforts to improve working conditions through monitoring can make a difference; such monitoring, however, is more likely to be undertaken effectively when it is either conducted collaboratively or by the producers group itself. Here BSI's strategy has evolved in a helpful direction. BSI first developed direct relations with a number of producer groups, and helped them to meet its guidelines. But over time BSI has moved from working with direct producers to working with agencies or federations representing these producers – groups like Safrudi in the Philippines, Del Campo in Nicaragua, Kuapa Kokoo Ltd in Ghana, Tropical Forest Products in Zambia or Assema in Brazil. These agencies differ from typical exporters or processors in most commercial commodity chains; for the most part they are organized to represent the interests of local producer groups, much like coffee growers' federations in Columbia (Thorp, 1991). They specialize both in developing commercial links to eventual retailers and in helping producer groups develop their capacities to meet of these buyers' expectations.

In sum, The Body Shop has made a significant difference in the way it purchases goods from suppliers. It has demonstrated that commercial firms as well as not-for-profit organizations and ATOs can choose to develop mutually beneficial trading relations, dealing directly with third-world producer groups and offering fair prices for their goods. Building upon the precedents developed by the Fair Trade movement, BSI emphasizes equally the importance of developing its host communities, working with the primary producers to create jobs, empower workers and help them operate their enterprises through participatory councils. In many respects, this collaborative transfer of organizational, productive and commercial know-how has been The Body Shop's most important contribution. It is this larger flow of empowerment – not merely the exchange of product for cash – that suggests that BSI's Community Trade programme indeed has been fair.

Note

Much of the information about The Body Shop came from interviewing those most involved in developing Community Trade programmes. The author would like to thank Jacqui MacDonald, former head of Fair Trade for BSI and currently an Associate Director of The Prince of Wales International Business Leaders Forum and Elaine Jones, whom I interviewed in 1999 and who currently manages Ethical Trading for BSI, for their assistance in conducting this research.

References

Bedford, A., Blowfield, M., Burnett, D. and Greenhalgh, P. (2001) 'Value Chains: Lessons from the Kenya Tea and Indonesian Cocoa Sectors' (London: Resource Centre for the Social Dimensions of Business Practice).

Brown, M. B. (1993) *Fair Trade: Reforms and Realities in the International Trading System* (London: Zed Books).

Corry, S. (1993) 'Harvest Moonshine Taking You for a Ride: A Critique of Rainforest Harvest – Its Theory and Practice' (London: Survival for Tribal People).

Entine, J. (1994) 'Shattered Image', *Business Ethics*, September/October, pp. 23–8.

Entine, J. (1996) 'The Queen of Bubblebath. Exploiting the "Integrity Premium": An Evaluation of the Body Shop's Use of Cause-Related Marketing', Unpublished essay.

Fair Trade Yearbook 2001 (Brussels: European Fair Trade Association).

Gereffi, G. (1994) 'Capitalism, Development and Global Commodity Chains', in L. Sklair (ed.), *Capitalism and Development* (London: Routledge). ch. 11, 211–31.

Gibbon, P. (2001) 'Upgrading Primary Production: A Global Commodity Chain Approach', *World Development*, vol. 29(2), pp. 345–63.

Hartman, C. L. and Beck-Dudley, C. L. (1999) 'Marketing Strategies and the Search for Virtue: A Case Analysis of the Body Shop, International', *Journal of Business Ethics* vol. 20, pp. 244–63.

Kaplinsky, R. and Morris, M. (2001) A *Handbook for Value Chain Research* (IDRC), *Institute of Development Studies* [website] http://www.ids.ac.uk/ids/global/pdfs/VchNov01.pdf

Klein, N. (2000) *No Logo* (London: Flamingo).

London Greenpeace (1998) 'What's Wrong with The Body Shop? A criticism of "green" consumerism', *Beyond McDonald's* [website] (updated 24 April 1998) http://www.mcspotlight.org/beyond/companies/bs_ref.html

Petean, S. (1999) 'Broken Promises', unpublished essay.

Ponte, S. (2002) 'Are Standards Good for Development? Lessons from the Specialty Coffee Industry', Unpublished essay.

Roddick, A. (1992) *Body and Soul* (with Russell Miller) (London: Vermillion).

Stackhouse, J. (2000) *Out of Poverty and into Something More Comfortable* (Mississauga, Ontario: Random House Canada).

STP (1994): Survival for Tribal People, 'Survival International's Contacts with the Body Shop: Paper Prepared at the Request of the Ethical Investment Research Service' (London).

Thorp, R. (1991) *Economic Management and Economic Development in Peru and Columbia* (University of Pittsburgh Press).

Traidcraft (2001) 'Traidcraft: What is it?' and 'A Brief History of Traidcraft' *Fact Sheets* http://www.traidcraft.co.uk

UNCTAD (2002): United Nations Conference on Trade and Development *The Least Developed Countries Report: Escaping the Poverty Trap*. The United Nations.

Watkins, K. and Fowler, P. (2002) *Rigged Trade and Double Standards: Trade, Globalization and the Fight Against Poverty* (London: Oxfam).